BACKYARD
Battle Plan

BACKYARD
Battle Plan

The Ultimate Guide to
Controlling Wildlife Damage
in Your Garden

Cooper Rutledge

PENGUIN BOOKS
Published by the Penguin Group
Penguin Putnam Inc., 375 Hudson Street, New York, New York 10014, U.S.A.
Penguin Books Ltd, 27 Wrights Lane, London W8 5TZ, England
Penguin Books Australia Ltd, Ringwood,Victoria, Australia
Penguin Books Canada Ltd, 10 Alcorn Avenue,
Toronto, Ontario, Canada M4V 3B2
Penguin Books (N.Z.) Ltd, 182-190 Wairau Road,
Auckland 10, New Zealand

Penguin Books Ltd, Registered Offices:
Harmondsworth, Middlesex, England

First published by Penguin Studio 1998

1 3 5 7 9 10 8 6 4 2
Copyright © Cooper Rutledge, 1998
All rights reserved

Technical line iIllustrations by Mark Stein Studios

CIP data available

ISBN 0-14-027208-9

Printed in the United States of America
Set in Egypt Heavy, Futura, and Goudy
Designed by Kathryn Parise

v

Contents

Foreword

All one wants is to garden in peace, but the garden is constantly attacked and destroyed by different animals. Though the pests change from year to year, the battle remains the same. When a woodchuck mows down the beans, when birds eat all the blueberries, when deer nibble the buds off everything, it is war.

To garden, one needs a backyard battle plan.

Let's turn to some writers on war and battles for help. Baron von Clausewitz (1780–1831), in his lately fashionable and oft-quoted book, *On War*, wrote for the Imperial Army of the kaiser; however, his ideas still apply. To begin, he says, analyze the problem. What are the desired results? What are the short- and long-term consequences? For a battle is only a means to an end. Von Clausewitz continues: To win, one has to know the enemy, to understand his ways, his weaknesses, and his strengths. Then tailor a battle plan to accommodate each skirmish. Also, one must not let the enemy impose his will.

His ideas apply equally well to the backyard battle with problem animals of today. Old von Clausewitz is probably turning over in his grave to find his classic work on war applied to chipmunks, but such is the price of fame, particularly if what you said is two centuries old.

Our modern problem is that good honest information on animal control is accessible but fragmented and hard to find. It's almost as though there is a movement to discredit science and rely on sentiment and old wives' tales instead, which is compounded by the intense fervor of some animal groups.

A much earlier battle strategist, Sun Tzu, in about 400 B.C., espoused the same principles as von Clausewitz in his classic battle treatise, *The Art of War*. Divide and conquer, he said. Always attack weakness. Don't let the enemy dictate anything. Right knowledge and strategy is important. "Good applications of these principles will insure victory before you begin."

Let's hope so.

So out with the traps and the wire and the fences and the repellents and poison plants to do battle in the backyard for a rose, a blueberry, a bean, a green, a tree, a vista. There are 100 million gardeners in the United States who just want a little peace and a verdant retreat to nourish the human soul, but who must fight for such a space.

To make a garden is a task sublime. To give it permanence requires a battle plan.

Ad Usum Delfini

AUTHOR'S NOTE

Before taking any specific action for the removal or disposal of wildlife, be sure to consult your local, state, and federal authorities, such as any fish and wildlife service, or local game warden, for information on all appropriate guidelines, regulations, and laws, including laws regarding the use of firearms.

LEGEND:

  means use caution.

  points to control methods that usually are not particularly effective. The author reports them rather than recommends them.

Introduction:
Whose Backyard Is It Anyway?

This planet, Earth, is our home, but exactly who does the housekeeping? Left alone, Mother Nature is a cruel, nonreligious, nonthinking force. She has no compassion or pity. Nor love. Things sprout and grow, decay and die. In natural systems birth and death are as one.

Animals in the wild are a treasure to be cherished. But sometimes, in search of food or shelter, they come into conflict with humans and cause problems in the space that humans inhabit. Thus they become designated "Problem Animals."

Outdoors, problem animals ruin crops and gardens. They may pollute streams and wells. They damage buildings and chew on electric wires. Indoors, they contaminate food, ruin clothes, despoil furniture, and damage building systems. The most serious problems are the diseases they spread.

It is said that nature abhors a vacuum and so every space gets filled up. Where a favorable habitat exists, a wild creature will find it. Problems arise when there are too many mouths to feed. As animal populations grow unchecked, protected by new "politically correct" laws, they cause problems in city and country. While it's true that in many places, suburbia has spread into rural areas where animals find themselves surrounded by unwelcome humans, most current animal problems are directly linked to increases in animal populations in the last century. Inevitably conflicts over space occur, especially if humans want to grow things. For a garden is just one big supermarket to animals. So whose area is it to be? In the backyard, a war ensues.

It's not a new war. Farmers and herdsmen have been fighting it since long before Sun Tzu in ancient China. He says that to battle, one must know the numbers of the enemy as well as their strengths and weaknesses. A millennium and a half later, war strategist von Clausewitz repeats these sentiments. So to win the backyard battles, one must try to understand the enemy and learn his ways.

The Conspiracy of Silence

Unfortunately, useful accurate information about animals, and how to deal with the problems they cause, is not easy to find. Newspapers and magazines rarely print objective, scientifically correct articles about animals. It seems to be part of a wider antiscience fashion, which glorifies feelings rather than facts.

Despite the explosive increase in animal articles, it almost seems that animal rights groups determine the choice of stories. Media coverage, by and large, consists of romanticized portrayals of animals. Anything that paints wild animals as other than fuzzy friends of the nursery or pussycats in the wilderness is essentially censored and ignored.

The coverage of the rabies epidemic in animals that began near Washington, D.C., is a case in point. It started in 1977 but was largely unreported. This terrifying scourge of old, which had been essentially eliminated by the 1950s, was allowed to spread anew, unchecked. Even after en-

gulfing many states as well as our nation's capital, it was still not widely covered in the national media.

When Ebola virus felled a few folks in Zaire, the whole world was quickly informed and mobilized. However, as the heavily populated East Coast of the United States was allowed to turn into a reservoir of rabies, the only major public health efforts, all local, were to immunize dogs and cats. In the first year, it cost over $1 million just to immunize the pets in a few counties in one Maryland area. Meanwhile in 1977, the *Washington Post* carried an article urging suburbanites to make their yards into wildlife refuges.

Vaccinating the wild animal population against rabies only began in the mid-1990s, almost two decades later. Today the Canadians hoping to keep rabies from crossing their border are immunizing wild animals with baited vaccine. Perhaps vaccination will work. If it doesn't, raccoon rabies could spread north into Canada and west down the Ohio River valley into the Midwest.

Instead of covering these kinds of animal problems honestly, what instead appears is these media animal soap operas. Poor animals, sick animals, noble animals, helpful animals, romantically portraying how they live, what they supposedly think, and what they feel. They are turned into little animal-humans, endowed with human characteristics.

Face Appeal

Some wild animals seem more lovable than others. Much of the perception depends on something called "face appeal." Sophisticated cartoonists and artists clearly understand its importance. Because of the facial proportions and expression of some animals, they seem more human-looking and so we relate to them better. When animals are portrayed in cartoons (Mickey Mouse, Pooh Bear, Peter Rabbit's mother, animal birthday cards, baby clothes, books, etc.), the proportions of their faces are altered to make them look appealing. They are almost always smiling. When was the last time you saw a teddy bear with a threatening expression?

Let's Face It— Animals Sell

By treating animals as humanoid, the advertising and entertainment industries augment the conspiracy of silence. This overexposure is not by accident. Neither is it by chance that news broadcasts frequently end with a sentimental animal story. Animals sell. Everyone likes them, especially the babies. Baby wild animals are a stock item of the film entertainment industry. They are adorable, and television shows every single species of clumsy, helpless little creatures. They arouse a paternal instinct in humans. Baby animals sell like crazy.

Wilderness programs about wild animals, with incredibly beautiful nature photography, crowd the airwaves. We save the whales, the seals, the bears, the wolves with the same concern we would save our own lost kitten. Yet in reality, it's a cold, cruel world for animals in the wild. Honesty is necessary if one is to understand wild animals, their real nature, their allegiance to food and procreation. Also their value to society.

How we garden must be decided by us humans. Wild animals should not dictate the terms of the backyard battle. Nor should Mother Nature be in charge of the housekeeping.

Animal Population Cycles—Understanding Habitats

Animal populations are habitat driven. That is a basic truth. Without an understanding of habitats, one can't understand animal populations or problem animals. The population growth of any species is controlled by the available food supply and the predators that attack it. These are the main elements of a habitat. In the wild, animals are on a constant quest for food, either fighting one another for possession of a territory or eating one another.

Population expansions and contractions occur with cyclical repetition. Because weather influences food supply, it affects population cycles. When it rains, plants grow and animals eat well. As their food supply increases, they reproduce more and their population growth travels down the whole food chain.

However, when one animal population becomes too large, it becomes vulnerable. Naturally occurring catastrophes, such as starvation, diseases, predation, or loss of habitat will cause the population to collapse, often very quickly. Then a small number of survivors, at a sustainable level, quietly carry on the species until the right set of circumstances permit it to grow again.

For example, the dense population of raccoons along the populated East Coast, which can reach 500 animals per square mile in cities, provided a perfect highway for infection, allowing rabies to spread. As the disease attacked them, many of the animals died, and the raccoon population crashed. For a short time there were few raccoons, then the population began to build again.

Only the fittest survive in the constant struggle for food. Some weak animals become extinct; other tough ones flourish. The process is an ongoing, dynamic one. It is interesting that in the man-made, self-contained habitat of Biosphere in Arizona in the 1990s, the species that survived were cockroaches and ants. The hummingbirds died.

Enter Man

Humans are now the most dense species on Earth. As the number of people increase, they need food and habitat, and so they come into conflict with animals that want to use the same space. The problem is not new. Early man grappled with all kinds of animals and hunted for food, which reduced the numbers of certain species. As animals were domesticated and fields planted, wild animals killed the flocks and ruined the harvest. They were the problem animals of those days. The solution was hunting.

Humans have always been a significant factor in controlling wild animal populations. And that's about where we still stand today. For example, habitat loss contributed to a previous low population of deer. When the eastern forests were cut for timber, and the land plowed for farming, the deer's preferred habitat, the forest/shrub edge, was lost. And since they also made good stew, their population fell.

However, with abandoned farms now reverting back to forest, deer populations have increased. There are more deer in Massachusetts now than there were a hundred years ago, and perhaps more than when the Pilgrims landed. Nationwide, the total number of white-tailed deer was about 500,000 in 1900. By the 1980s, it had grown to 12 million. By 1995, it had doubled to 25 million.

Population Dynamics

The dynamics of population cycles are complex but hardly mysterious, when one understands that populations are habitat driven. In nature, the populations of any species, insect, plant, animal, even human, rise and fall in relation to their food supply, and in relation to whose food they in turn are. Humans fight wars for possession of land. Animals, too, fight for their territories, though in other ways. Biology and weather can explain some of the cyclical variations in nature. While controlling the weather is beyond man's ken, we do understand, albeit imperfectly, how to control wildlife cycles. When we don't, Mother Nature makes decisions for us. If man wants a habitable planet, he has to determine what should be the balance of animal, vegetable, even insect populations, to allow him and them to best survive. When some of these populations grow out of control, the balance is upset and problems arise.

Certain animals and insects often are implicated in the spread of disease. For example, as the deer population has been allowed to explode, Lyme disease, spread by deer ticks, has become endemic. In some places, mountain lions have followed their favorite food, which is deer, into the populated suburbs, thus creating a different kind of public health danger. Recently, in the West, mouse droppings caused an unusual outbreak of contagious hantavirus, which was tragically fatal to a number of people. The theory accounting for the hantavirus chain of events is intriguing. The previous year was very wet and rainy, which fostered a huge crop of pine seeds, a main food of the mice. The abundance of food caused a mouse population explosion the following year, which is thought to have triggered the unusual virus outbreak. Interestingly, in Hopi Indian tradition mice were feared, perhaps because in the past the Indians had noticed a rise in sickness and death associated with large populations of mice.

Dealing with Problem Animals

The sensible way to deal with problem animals is to keep their populations in line with what a habitat can comfortably support. Where man and animal come into conflict over the same space, suitable measures should be taken to remove animals that cause problems. One can then cherish the appropriate numbers of remaining animals. Not all wild animals are problem animals. Most are not. But when they are, the decision has to be made as to whose planet this is, and whose claim to the land is more important.

Most advanced countries have laws that protect wildlife and yet keep their numbers down. This is particularly true in Europe, where people and animals have coexisted in a limited space for centuries. In Africa, large areas are set aside as game parks to protect wild animals, and the remaining land is given to the people to farm. Otherwise, in hungry countries, wild animals are quickly eliminated as they conflict with the people's needs.

In the United States, historically farmers and ranchers simply cleared problem animals from their land because there was always lots more wilderness left. As the country continues to become more crowded, sensible land use policies have to be devised to protect the land, the farmers, the animals, and people's rights to be safe outdoors, as well as to garden in their own backyards. However, some valuable animal habitats need to be preserved to protect the creatures that live there, free from the pressures of development. In some places, the building of new houses, shopping centers, and industries may have to be done elsewhere to protect valuable wilderness habitats.

Animals as Humanoids

An issue that complicates sensible land use policies is thinking of animals as though they were human. It's called anthropomorphizing. There is little real understanding of the natural world as it exists.

Most people today have grown up in urban areas, where wild and farm animals are scarce or nonexistent. Other than domestic pets, many folks have had little real interaction with animals. Most have never farmed. When a cow escaped in the Bronx in New York City, someone reported that a large dog was running loose. People who have lost contact with the land may romanticize and personalize wildlife. And why not? They get that perspective from television. Their knowledge of the wild comes from shows where nature is a superficial celluloid tour de force. Beautiful photography sells very well. Some people may have had a short camp experience or an ecology course given by a sensitive teacher who offered some nuggets of wisdom. However, few folks now have the opportunity to closely observe nature unfold and reveal its mysteries over time.

Children's primary impression of animals is formed in the nursery, from sweet books. Typical is the very humanlike Winnie the Pooh, depressed Eeyore, and little Piglet. The other overwhelming source of animal imagery has been cartoons. Most famous is Mickey Mouse, around whose sanitized persona a huge entertainment industry has grown. And we can't forget his group of friends like Minnie Mouse, Donald Duck, Bambi, Simba, who becomes the lion king, Nola, his mate, and even a Pink Panther. Though animals, they're more like you and me. Consider, too, the millions and millions of teddy bears, for they are the most common, most beloved childhood animal of all. Even the United States Forest Service has its Smoky the Bear, an overall-clad darling, who, shovel in hand, begs you to save his forest home from fires.

The media, including cartoons and books, endow sentient creatures with human characteristics they certainly don't have. Peter Rabbit and family was the creation of a refined English lady, a fantasy of her mind. The hare in the backyard knows nothing of her tales, nor does he read them to his children.

Animals as Animals

Mythical imaginary creatures have become the emotional reality of our times, far removed from the honest truth of where and how animals actually live. This unreality makes it difficult to deal with animals as animals. So it's hard for some to accept nature as it exists. Wild animals grow up to be wild animals, not pets. Wild animals are not like dogs and cats, which, eons ago, adapted to people and have always been important partners in human domesticity.

Some wild animals can be tamed for, true to their nature, they will follow the hand that feeds them. Since their primary instinct is finding food, they quickly learn what produces that commodity. Domesticated rabbits are charming and can be housebroken. Pet hamsters are endlessly amusing. Even pet mice and rats are interesting. The list of animals that have been turned into pets is myriad. Someone from Egypt brought his pet crocodile to the United States as baggage on an airplane. He explained to customs that he had to bring it with him because it wasn't the kind of pet one can easily leave for a neighbor to feed.

For too long, the conspiracy of silence has anthropomorphized the likes of Peter Rabbit—part of the original single-parent dysfunctional family, whose father was a thief—and Mickey Mouse. In real life both carry diseases. Also there's Bucky Beaver, who is doing to streams and wetlands what humans are disallowed to do by law. In Massachusetts, the fine is $25,000 for opening a beaver dam, which is larger than for most criminal offenses against people. In California, a farmer was told to donate many, many acres to the government before he was permitted to repair the beaver damage to his water supply. Don't forget sweet Bambi, whose doe-eyed mother abandons him before he's a year old, to forage for himself or starve. So he shambles off carrying his Lyme disease ticks with him. Meanwhile, ordinary humans struggle with problem animals and predation in their gardens. Many have given up growing certain vegetables or any vegetables at all. Others give up particular flowers, trees, or shrubs because of animal damage. In the backyard, the friends of the forest are just more mouths to feed.

Animal Protection Groups

The view of wild animals as the fuzzy companions of the nursery who grow up to be something like furry folks next door has received much publicity because many Hollywood types have taken up animal protection. Some attractive actors, singers, and models have become drawn to this cause. Since their every utterance, no matter how vapid, pulls in the media, the animal rights movement receives lots of free publicity. The movement is sophisticated, uses the media effectively, trains political operatives, and attacks one issue at a time with intense efficiency and concentration. As animal protectionist policies have flourished, problem animal populations have skyrocketed.

The aim of many animal rightists, though not all, is to outlaw any use of animals for any purpose. People should be vegetarians. Leather should not be used, but replaced with plastic or other materials. Testing medicines or techniques to cure disease should be limited to test tubes and tried on people, never animals. Research labs have been blown up and vandalized. One group tried to dump a truckload of manure outside a federal building to protest federal approval of a drug made from horse urine. Research to save human lives using animal transplant organs has been attacked. Laboratory animal research has been curtailed and in some instances stopped altogether. Some promising investigations have been abandoned. The use of a circus elephant to advertise a new perfume was picketed by animal rightists. Wearers of fur coats have been sprayed with paint, naked models paraded against the use of fur, and mink farms have been vandalized repeatedly. Yet none of this has ended the demand for fashion furs.

There is also a small subgroup that believes animals are entitled to fundamental legal rights, including the right to sue. In one case, when two St. Bernard dogs were sentenced to death for mauling a passerby, their owner hired an animal rights lawyer who successfully defended the animals' rights. They were "having a difficult day" when they broke their chains, testified a dog psychiatrist. The town spent $50,000 in legal costs, and the dogs' owners spent $20,000, including the cost of the dog psychiatrist.

Although the media eagerly cover the passion as well as the virulence of animal rightists, it has become politically incorrect to say anything against animals, except in very gentle ways. Not long ago, a group of AIDS sufferers staged a sit-in to force the testing of an AIDS drug on mice before trying it on them.

The Real Problem

The humanization of animals causes us to avoid the real issue: how to achieve sensible, sustainable populations of all creatures, as well as keep their numbers large enough to protect biodiversity within species. All animals need to be represented on Earth, and if necessary protected in wildlife preserves. If the animals we have are to be kept alive, much more money needs to be funded into cost-effective birth control techniques to prevent them from reproducing with abandon. This is where humane funds and efforts should be directed.

WITHER THIS WORLD

Animals are causing more problems in the United States not so much because humans are moving into their territory, as is routinely charged, but because there are so many more of them than existed before. The following table illustrates the growth of six species in this country during the twentieth century.

QUANTITY IN THE UNITED STATES

Species	pre-1950	1980	1995
White-tailed deer	500,000 (1900)	12,000,000	25,000,000
Canada geese	1,110,000 (1940)	2,320,000	
Trumpeter swan	73 (1935)	900	
Rocky Mountain elk	41,000 (1907)	1,000,000	
Wild turkey	650,000 (1900)	2,000,000	4,200,000
Pronghorn antelope	12,000 (1940)	500,000	

MORE FACTS

- In New Hampshire, despite yearly hunting and extensive building, the moose herd almost tripled in a decade, from 1,600 in 1983 to 4,500 in 1995.

- In Massachusetts, there were virtually no beavers in the 1930s, but by the mid-1990s, there were about 30,000. As for Massachusetts bears, in 1930 there were just a few, by 1980 there were 300 to 600, and by the mid-1990s there were 1,300 to 1,600.

- Since the 1980s, bear growth elsewhere has been very rapid too. In New Jersey, between 1982 and 1995, bears went from 30 animals to 400. In 1995, Maine had 21,000 bears; Vermont, 2,500; and Colorado, 12,000.

- The main reason for the rise in problem animals is the increase in safe habitat where they can procreate undeterred. While development does invade some wildlife territory and causes conflicts with man, ending such developments will not solve the problem.

Animal Damage

Animal damage to agriculture is significant enough that there is a special program in the United States Department of Agriculture called Animal Damage Control, a part of the Animal and Plant Health Inspection Service. Its purpose is to help solve problems caused by wildlife. The government is involved with this effort because professional biologists are more likely to protect wildlife than irate folks frustrated by problem animals and economic loss.

Some examples of animal damage are:
- predators attacking livestock
- beavers flooding roads and timber
- deer damaging orchards, farms, and plant nurseries
- bears damaging beehives
- ungulates from deer to moose causing automobile accidents and deaths
- mountain lions attacking pets and humans
- coyotes, foxes, and wolves preying on pets
- wild animals spreading rabies
- Canada geese fouling golf courses and sports fields with their slimy droppings
- birds presenting hazards to aircraft
- starlings fouling feedlots
- birds damaging agriculture and aquaculture
- starlings and pigeons building roosts in urban areas.

The cost of animal damage is significant. Auto accident statistics are shocking. In 1996 alone there were 269,000 accidents involving animals resulting in 19,000 human injuries and 153 deaths. In 1990, birds caused about $100 million in damage to agriculture. In seventeen western states, animals caused a $60 million loss in sheep and goats, and a $20 million loss in calves. In the Southeast, beavers caused $100 million damage to roads and timber.

The Not So Peaceable Animals of the City

Wild animals are even calling cities home, and they are not always benign. Deer have become the main problem animal in orchards, nurseries, and backyards. They are everywhere, eating gardens, carrying tickborne Lyme disease, and attracting mountain lions, which come into human settlements to stalk the deer.

Actually, deer are the most dangerous wild animal we have, responsible for killing more people each year than any other. Auto accidents are the reason. In 1995, there were 12,000 auto-deer accidents in Maryland alone. Michigan had 68,000 with 6 human fatalities. Occasionally bizarre incidents occur too. In Baltimore, a buck charged a playground filled with children. And a pregnant deer ran through the plate-glass window of a Boston insurance agency.

Bears too, attracted to landfills and garbage cans, are seen almost everywhere, often near many large cities including Los Angeles. Mountain lions exist in Los Angeles, as well as much of the West, while their kin, wildcats of various sorts, abound

in many parts of the country. Large felines can pose a danger, and they have killed several people.

Beaver also are spreading, moving closer and closer into cities. They've been seen in Denver, Houston, and Dallas, among others. In Massachusetts, their dams cause backups that flood septic systems and pollute wells.

Moose, which were remote and hard to find, now are widespread. Not so peaceable are these large, fascinating, but unpredictable creatures. Though their major danger is to autos and motorists, in Anchorage a moose killed an elderly man on the campus of the University of Alaska.

From the Bronx to San Francisco, coyotes live in cities and suburbs. Useful hunting predators, they help keep some problem animals under control, but unfortunately, they also like garbage cans and unhesitatingly eat chickens and pets.

Canada geese cause problems at parks and golf courses, since they will take up residency on any large area of grass. Although they carry diseases, the main nuisance is their droppings, which slime playing fields and pollute ponds and lakes. Sea gull populations are a problem too—as a hazard to aircraft, a messy pest, and by crowding out important wild shorebirds. In cities as well as the countryside, vultures and wild turkey populations are on the rise as well.

Raccoons are the most troublesome

city animal. Only rats are more numerous. Raccoons are in every single city and county. One was even captured by police after a chase through a Bronx subway station. Smart, dextrous, adaptable garbage eaters, they have carried rabies to all the previously safe wild animals in the eastern United States.

Although dog rabies was virtually wiped out by a concerted public health effort, wild animal rabies has emerged as the new public health threat. The cost for control exceeds $300 million a year, most of it for vaccinating pets plus more than another $15 million for postexposure treatments for people.

The Problem Animals of Summer

No one needs to tell gardeners that problem animals are on the increase. It's especially bad in midsummer when the current year's offspring are kicked out of the nest and encouraged to get their own territories to feed themselves. If they find your flowers and vegetables, you will notice.

Woodchucks eat most everything and do the most damage, leaving bare stalks and foliage that looks like a weed wacker went over it. Chipmunks and squirrels eat delicate plants and flowers. Rabbits eat tender greens, vegetable tops, and grass. Raccoons always abound, so watch the raspberries, corn, and other vegetables. Skunks mainly

eat birds' eggs and bugs so don't bother gardeners too much, except for their unmistakable perfume and their spring and fall holes in the lawn, which they dig to hunt for grubs. Deer eat most everything and are becoming the most troublesome problem animal in the country.

Not only plants but trees are often ravaged by many animals, too. Twigs and branches may be chewed off or broken. Chewed or scraped bark, with distinctive animal tooth marks, identifies the culprits as rabbits, mice, or deer. Birds make multiple holes in trees looking for insects and peck away at the fruit. When the ground under a tree is covered with cut litter, it means squirrels are having a banquet above.

The Bottom Line— What to Do

What to do about problem animals that are destroying your garden? It's one of those simple questions to which there is no simple answer. But here are some suggestions:

- Trap or shoot (usually necessary to repeat yearly)
- Fence (keep fences mended)
- Plant poisonous plants (many are quite attractive)
- Try smelly or bitter deterrents (use often and repetitively)

- Wait for better animal birth control
- And sometimes throw up your hands and rail at the sky!

Stores and catalogs offer many items that are purported to solve the problems. They rarely do for long. New animals will come each summer to stake out territory in your backyard. As the wild animal numbers continue to increase, so will the problems. Inevitably there must be more honesty about the clash between animal rights and traditional human activities.

In the meantime, until man becomes a perfect manager, the backyard battle will continue as each gardener tries to keep a small part of his or her world safe, productive, and satisfying. Von Clausewitz advises that there are diverse ways to victory in battle, and it does not always imply the total conquest of the enemy's country.

SECTION ONE
The Enemy

ALLIGATORS

See you later, alligator.
In a while, crocodile.

Alligators are American crocodiles, the remaining representative of these large ancient reptiles. Alligators were hunted almost to extinction for their fine leather, but under current wildlife protection policies, their population in the wild is mushrooming. In addition, they're raised on animal farms for meat and for tourists to see. Lake Okeechobee in Florida, which once had only a few alligators left, now has about 12,000. Florida's Everglades Preserve, with its swamps and waterways, is a veritable alligator nursery.

There are state programs that buy eggs for alligator farmers, the theory being that if alligators generate income, it helps encourage people to preserve the swamps.

Problem Alligators

Most people don't have problems with alligators, not only because they're still not very numerous, but because they aren't as aggressive as crocodiles, except, of course, when they're hungry. Although attacks are extremely rare, accidents do happen. There have been 225 attacks and nine deaths since the Florida Fresh Water Fish Commission started to keep records in 1943. And in 1997, tragically, a three-year-old boy was snatched from knee-deep water as his mother watched. A trapper found the body floating a mile away with an eleven-foot gator nearby protecting his quarry.

As protected animals, the rising alligator population increases the opportunity for human contact. They could end up near many people's backyards in the South, and they might even become a backyard problem to folks whose backyards border swampy waterways. Recently, a boy fell off his bicycle into an alligator-infested drainage creek in Florida and had to be pulled out. Each year the state of Florida kills an average of 5,000 nuisance alligators.

Scientific Information

Alligators are large creatures. Males can reach fourteen feet in length and weigh 750 pounds; females can be seven to eight feet. They can live in all the southern states where adequate swamplands exist. Fat and lazy, they spend most of their time in the sun, appearing dead, except when they're eating. On farms, they're fed once a week, usually chicken and grain. Alligator meat, which sells for about the same price as steak, is white and has a mild taste.

Alligator farms have to be completely fenced not only to keep the alligators in but to keep alligator predators out, especially out of the baby pens. Florida's main predator animals are bobcats, foxes, raccoons, wild boar, and chicken hawks. Buzzards as well as alligators are protected species.

Control Methods

Six-foot-high chain-link fences are used around alligator farms. And as the old boys of the Everglades say, "Beware red eyes at night." If you see two bright, reflective orbs with a reddish cast slowly approaching, "you've gone too far from camp."

BEARS

A True Story

Once upon a time in a suburb of Los Angeles, there was a bear who liked to raid garbage cans and then digest his food while lolling in a particular hot tub in the neighborhood. He became a regular visitor, was discovered by the press, and became a TV celebrity. They named him Sampson.

Unfortunately, bears who lose their fear of people become a public safety risk. What if he jumped in when the family was in the hot tub? What if he was angered by someone while on his regular garbage runs? And because he was so habituated to humans, it was feared he would just return to the nearest garbage cans if he were set free in the wild. So a decision was made to trap and destroy him.

But wait . . . he was not an animal . . . he was LA's pet hot tub bear. Scores of people called the governor, who, being a politician, stayed the execution. But no one wanted "Sampson," nor did anyone volunteer to assume the costly responsibility for his permanent keep. After a year at an unsatisfactory wildlife farm, a local zoo got stuck with him because no one else would take the bear.

Problem Bears

The problem in southern California, as in most urban areas, is the romanticizing and personalizing of wildlife. To many in cities, bears are pets or children's toys.

TEDDY BEARS

Despite the realities of bears in the wild, the teddy bear has become the universal soft, cuddly toy for children. Bear cubs are pudgy and clumsy, traits humans consider charming. And they have face appeal as well. Sweet eyes and smiles have been sewn on millions of teddy bears and drawn onto their multiple cartoon likenesses. The only stern-looking bear is Smoky, the overall-clad mascot of the United States Forest Service, who, with shovel in hand, warns you not to start forest fires.

People who grow up in rural areas deal with wild animals more realistically.

Bears are omnivorous opportunists. They eat everything, and if their habitat has too little food, they go in search of it and will travel many miles. When they find a suitable and reliable food source, they settle in. Often that source is garbage.

Now that the bear is a protected animal, its populations are rising, and bears are returning to most parts of the country. In Massachusetts, for instance, after decades without any, the bear population reached 1,300 by the mid-1990s. Vermont's was 2,500, Maine's 21,000. According to one Maine biologist, about every four or five years the animals become an unusual nuisance, though it's not clear why.

Colorado's 12,000 bears are becoming accustomed to people, particularly as more houses have been built in wilderness areas. Bears raid garbage cans, bird feeders, even climb onto second-story decks (so the stories go) to lick barbecue grills. One was videotaped sauntering through downtown Aspen late one night, stopping to look in the window of a lingerie shop, then rolling in some flower beds. Snowmass Village, near Aspen, passed the country's first ordinance to store trash in bear-resistant sheds. Once bears discover garbage, they will return again and again for the tasty pickings. This may be their undoing, because as they become urbanized they become a public health risk and often have to be killed.

Being omnivorous, bears sometimes get a hankering for red meat. In 1982, there were fewer than 30 bears in New Jersey. By 1995, there were over 400, and they weren't just eating berries:

- In 1993, a lamb was killed.
- In 1994, sixteen rabbits, four chickens, and two goats were reported killed.
- In 1995, the number was thirty rabbits, twenty-one chickens, one goat, and eight pheasants.
- In 1996, bears killed twenty-nine rabbits, twenty-four chickens, two goats, one lamb, and one poodle in just the first four months of the year.

The poodle brings the reality of problem bears close to home.

How to Tell If You Have Bears

Usually you can see them. Rifled garbage cans can be the work of many animals; however, bears are big and make a lot of noise, banging things around. Also, they will break through screens and doors to get to food. Claw marks and tooth marks may be on vehicles or buildings, or trees.

If You Have Bears

When bears become habituated to humans, whether in the backyard, in garbage landfills, or in campgrounds, they become a public safety risk because they are big, strong, dangerous, and very unpredictable. If a bear is sighted, a mental note should be made of when and where it frequents. It may be just passing through, in which case it should be allowed to mosey on, but given a wide berth. Repeated sightings could mean it may be settling in near your backyard. If it seems to be unduly bold or friendly, it should be reported to the local wildlife service. The service will decide if that particular animal has habits that might make it a potential danger. In the wild, left alone and not threatened, bears are not a problem. Unless you encounter them on a trail. Never approach a bear, particularly one with cubs. They may look like the teddy in the nursery, but they are not.

Scientific Information

Bears are big animals. The largest is the notoriously fierce grizzly bear of Alaska, which can be up to nine feet long and weigh three-quarters of a ton. To early Native American Indians, to kill a grizzly was a mark of manhood, and they proudly wore bear teeth necklaces. Because of their size, grizzlies once were the masters of the land, but they were largely eliminated from most the United States except for a few parks and the state of Alaska. (See the next section for current proposals to increase the grizzly population.)

Smaller American black and brown bears are the most common. The males may be six and a half feet in length, the females four and a half feet. They can weigh 300 pounds and live for twenty-five years. Most American bears are normally shy and retiring, as is their European relative the Eurasian brown bear. They prefer life in the forest, and if left alone in such habitats, rarely attack people. However, in national parks and similar protected areas, where a bear has constant contact with humans, it loses its timidity and becomes a nuisance. Though a bear may appear tame, even cute, it remains a potentially dangerous wild animal.

Bears in the wild eat berries, fish, small and large animals including occasional domestic livestock, and have been known to even stalk buffalo. In the spring, they graze like cattle, also eating roots and insects. They're especially partial to cured meats and sweets, much to the dismay of campers, and because of their liking for sweets, bears are one of the few wild animals that get tooth cavities.

They hunt larger prey by stalking and then making a quick charge. Smaller animals are caught by digging out their bur-

rows, overturning protective rocks, and tearing apart rotten logs. Bears can run up to twenty-five miles an hour, climb trees, and swim. They have a keen sense of hearing and pretty good sense of smell, but see less well.

Solitary animals, bears live singly and apart, except during the month-long mating season, which often includes affectionate courtship in which mates caress each other. The female breeds every second year. One to four young are usually born during the winter dormant season and stay with the mother until they are half grown at about two years. During this time, she defends them fiercely, even against their father because males are known to cannibalize cubs.

Bringing Back the Grizzly Bear

As of 1996, there were two main populations of grizzlies in the mainland United States: about 300 in Yellowstone Park and about 200 in western Montana. Recently there has been a push to reintroduce the grizzly bear to Montana and Idaho to connect the two populations in a wildlife corridor of sorts. This would help provide the genetic diversity needed for healthy animals. Among the proposals is one to bring in five bears a year for five years, another to bring ten bears for five years, and another to allow the bears to come back on their own. Although usually opposed to environmentalists, the timber industry supports the reintroduction of grizzly bears, fearing it will come with or without its support. The governor of one of the affected states, Governor Marc Racicot of Montana, has endorsed it; the other, Governor Phil Baff of Idaho, is opposed. The following quote from Montana State Senator Steve Benedict appeared in an April 27, 1997, article in *The New York Times*: "Those bears were eradicated for a reason. It's like saying there's a nice big park in the middle of New York City: let's put bears there. Bears kill people."

Control Methods

Exclusion (Which Means Not Attracting Them)

You can't really exclude a big, determined bear. However you can limit the attractiveness of your area by not having food available. Bear-resistant garbage sheds are one deterrent, but they have to be strong. In bear country, don't put household food on the mulch pile. Store the barbecue indoors. Site fruit and berry patches far away from the house.

Noise

Get a boombox. Supposedly, bears don't like loud noises, so turn up the radio to loud static when they're around. And stay indoors! Perhaps they will go elsewhere.

Trapping

Bear trapping is not a battle for the backyard gardener. Call your local wildlife service. In many places there are laws that protect bears, so you could get fined heavily for trapping them. Outright robbery carries less governmental risk and punishment. Recently, certain states passed regulations outlawing leghold traps, baiting, and hunting with dogs, but special waivers are usually available for problem animals. Research projects that are judged to be "humane" are often exempted from these restrictions too.

Bears are territorial. When bears are trapped and relocated, even 60 or 80 miles, they frequently find their way back within weeks.

Hunting

The hunting of bears as sport is strictly controlled by wildlife laws. Hunting seasons, where allowed, are limited, and a license is usually necessary. Killing a bear in self-protection is another matter, but not as simple as you might think. Although bears are dangerous, wildlife advocates often question whether a person really was in danger and had no other option than to harm the bear. The question is usually brought up, well after the fact, in a safe and secure courtroom. There was a big fuss in a medical magazine, of all places, about whether a doctor who had killed a threatening bear acted in self-defense or committed murder.

Even Boy Scouts are not blameless these days. Another case, dutifully reported in a New York City newspaper, concerned a hapless Los Angeles scoutmaster. One night, while he was camping with his troop in Yosemite National Park, they saw some bears approaching. To scare the bears away, they made lots of noise and threw sticks and stones. One hit a bear in the head. It died. The scoutmaster was charged with "blunt force trauma" to the bear, and blamed for improperly storing food and thus causing the unfortunate animal's demise. The young scouts and two leaders were threatened with destruction-of-wildlife charges as well. Park rangers said the investigation did not indicate it was self-defense. Perhaps they would have liked to see a few scouts clawed and chewed up first?

Our delightful nursery friend, Winnie the Pooh, was supposedly inspired by a black bear cub from White River, Ontario, where townsfolk erected a statue in his honor. Originally Disney, which holds the copyright to Pooh Bear, refused to allow the statue, but bad publicity made them relent. Pooh's author, A.A. Milne, lived in England where there are no bears.

BEAVERS

"To beavers, all the world's a dam waiting to be made," says an old Maine farmer. "They tip a tree and carry it to wherever they hear running water." Because they can't look up or figure out which trees will fall where they want them, many of the trees don't fall down. Instead they catch and lean on other trees. Experienced foresters call these leaners "widow makers" because they are tons of wood ready to spring and fall at the slightest movement. It takes a very knowledgeable woodsman to take down a leaning tree without killing himself. "Priorities are all wrong," says the old Maine farmer. It cost him $500 to hire a forester to clean up the widow makers for just one year.

Beavers make an unsightly and dangerous mess of the water's edge, be it a pond or a stream. Their dams are not neat. They stuff the spaces between the trees with logs, twigs, clay, and organic material, from which plants sprout. The whole mess decays, uses up oxygen, kills fish, and increases eutrophication. And it smells. Beavers smell like musk, you know.

The trees whose roots are submerged by the beaver pond suffocate and die. With time, the area behind beaver dams becomes a wetland and finally a wet grassy meadow good for grazing cows. In neighboring Massachusetts, under certain conditions the fine for breaching a beaver dam is $25,000 per day.

The history of the beaver population in Massachusetts is interesting. Because of hunting and deforestation, beavers were probably eradicated in the state by the time of the American Revolution. However, a few of these rodents reappeared in the 1930s. Under well-intentioned wildlife policies, they were relocated all over the state, except in the southern part and on Cape Cod, because they would have damaged the cranberry farms there. By the mid-1990s about 30,000 beavers were in residence.

Not only do beavers gnaw down trees and dam running water. Their activities also cause damage to water supplies, septic systems, roads, and bridges. They flood private property and create unwelcome wetlands in inappropriate places. Because their dams can't be touched, water backs up farther and farther and not infrequently inundates homes built originally on dry land. Annual complaint calls to the Massachusetts Division of Fisheries and Wildlife about beaver damage more than doubled in six years: from 154 in 1989, to 388 in 1994.

After the town of Chelmsford, Massachusetts, outlawed leghold traps at a town meeting in 1988, beavers and problems multiplied until beaver pond water backed up and contaminated a town well. (Beaver-contaminated water has a musty old-leaf smell.) In 1992, the town rescinded its trapping ban, caught over 100 beavers, and the flooding abated. The alternative was a $1.2 million water filtration plant.

Massachusetts is a state with well-organized, well-financed, and very politically active animal protectionists. A citizen referendum article was passed in 1996 outlawing leghold traps, which are the only dependable way to trap the animals that cause problems. Smart beavers are not easily fooled into entering Havahart box traps, which are also very expensive.

From November 15 to February 28, a licensed Massachusetts trapper can take beaver; however, since men don't wear tall beaver top hats anymore, the pelts aren't that valuable. Currently, with reliable leghold traps outlawed, trappers don't have much incentive to keep down the state beaver population. Because beavers have a low annual mortality rate of only 10 percent, without trapping, a beaver population can double in three years.

In 1997, the first year outlawing leghold traps, 623 beavers were trapped, all before the law took effect. This number was 45 percent less than the 1,135 of the year before. However, complaints of beaver problems tripled. Trappers say there won't be much trapping using box traps, even to help homeowners who obtain the special state permits needed to remove a problem animal.

New England is not alone. In the southeastern United States beavers annually cause $100 million worth of damage, mostly by flooding roadways and timber.

How to Recognize Beaver Damage

Trees will be chewed off rather cleanly about a foot off the ground. The stubs are pointed, with chisel-like teeth marks all around. When areas that were dry become boggy, follow brooks and streams looking for the telltale dams, stumps, or leaning widow-maker trees. Streams can also become clogged with silt, so sometimes this is the cause of flooding.

Scientific Information

Though famed as a builder of dams and valuable for its luxurious fur, the beaver also has the distinction of being the largest rodent in North America. A beaver can weigh 80 pounds and continues to grow throughout its life, which may be up to twenty years. It reaches three to four feet, of which one-third is a large flat tail. Beavers whack the water surface with their tails, perhaps for amusement.

Beavers eat mainly bark, twigs, and some vegetation. To get to their favorite tender twigs and bark at the treetops, they chop down the trees. They also fell trees across water or drag them into place to create the ponds in which they build their homes.

A prodigious woodsman, a beaver can cut down a tree with a trunk diameter of four inches in fifteen minutes using its powerful, yellow chisel-like teeth, which also continue to grow throughout its life. Beavers usually work in pairs; one chisels, one keeps watch. When the tree begins to crack, they wait to see if it will fall. If not, they continue to work. When it starts to fall, they run off, usually diving into a nearby pond to wait.

Also skilled swimmers, beavers have been known to cover a quarter of a mile in fifteen minutes under water, or two miles an hour at the surface. The flat tail serves as a rudder, particularly when the beaver hauls logs to construct its dams. To help transport logs, they also dig remarkable transport canals, filled with water.

For an animal, it has remarkable engineering skills. To make a dam, it lays down branches side by side, with the thick ends facing the current. Then it packs them down with mud and rocks. Layer upon layer is piled up high enough to create a suitable pond. The final coat is of mud. Beaver dams stand for many years. The dams can be large, up to twelve feet high and fifteen to twenty feet wide at the base. One giant dam in Montana was measured at 2,140 feet in length. Early farmers in western states often relied on beaver ponds for irrigation water.

Beavers mate yearly, producing two to six young, to whom they teach these skills. At two years, young beavers leave to find their own territory. Home is a dome-shaped wood and mud lodge, built in the shallow ponds they create. The entrance is under water, and winter food (cut branches and twigs) is also stored under water, anchored in mud and just a quick swim from home.

Diseases

Beavers carry several diseases, particularly tularemia, which can contaminate water in their pond as well as downstream. If their ponds drain into wells or reservoirs, the possibility of diseases exists from drinking or swimming in the water.

Control Methods

Because beavers are generally protected animals, one needs a hunting or trappers' license to deal with them. Excluding them is virtually impossible.

Trapping

Difficult animals to trap, it's best to get help from a professional. Removing all the beavers from an area is the only permanent solution.

Because it is against the law to break a beaver dam in many states, and because beavers will repair dams as fast as one can break them, trapping is one of the few solutions that solves the immediate problem. Sometimes wildlife officers will not give trapping permits if they believe that beavers are necessary to that particular ecosystem even when they flood backyards and kill forestland by drowning the trees. They generally issue permits when streams and water supplies are contaminated. Beavers are hard to catch, so leghold traps are the usual method. Often they are set under water. Although there are Havahart box-type traps for beavers, they are expensive and professional trappers don't think they work well.

Other Methods

Dams can be broken open and destroyed, particularly when they are first begun. However, wildlife control laws may preclude humans from exercising this option. And besides, since the beaver will repair any break as fast as you can cause it, it's a question of who hangs in the battle longer.

One method under consideration is to install a pipe at the bottom of the dam, as a permanent spillway, which allows the water to continue to flow, yet keeps it from backing up and flooding too much, but still provides enough of a pond for the beaver to call home. The pipe may fill with silt or the beaver may plug it, so repetitive maintenance and cleaning is necessary to keep it open.

This last stratagem exemplifies a main von Clausewitz dictum, of finding a "simple scheme that conquers the object while avoiding war." In this case, a pipe to keep the water flowing prevents destructive backflooding and avoids killing the beavers. The problem is that when the beavers hear running water, they immediately work to dam it up again. This means that the pipes have to be checked and cleaned frequently, and since no one likes wading in muck to clean a pipe, the beavers often win by sheer perseverance. Then it's back to trapping.

BIRDS

One for the rook,
One for the crow,
One to die,
And one to grow.

So goes the old English proverb that advised planting four times as much as one expects to harvest. Notice that half of the loss is from birds. Such thieves of the harvest were birds of old that the word *rook* also means a swindler or a cheat at cards. The only species that can catch a crow are man and the great horned owl. Birds are the most destructive agricultural predator and cause more crop damage than any animal. Because they fly, often in huge flocks, they can't be fenced out, so control is very difficult.

Around the end of the nineteenth century, some theater fanatics wanted to bring into the United States every bird mentioned by Shakespeare. They imported 200 starlings, a bad bird, into New York's Central Park. Today these pests number 140 million. The poor bard is just one more historic icon unwittingly used for purposes he never envisioned.

Humans have always been fascinated by birds, especially the raptors, or birds of prey. In days of yore, no self-respecting nobleman would go hunting without a trained falcon on his arm. The Chinese believe a pet bird in a cage indoors brings good luck. Nightingales, which are actually several species of small Old World thrushes, have always been famous for the melodious song of the male during breeding season, its liquid silvery song enchanting the evening air.

There are good birds and bad birds. Birds live by a pecking order. There are leaders and followers. The bigger ones threaten and scare the smaller ones, which wait patiently for their turn at a bush or a bird feeder until the larger ones are bored and leave. If you watch them at the bird feeder, you'll see that they are not polite and don't wait their turn in line.

Good Birds

Most birds are good birds, inflicting little damage and providing pleasure, and gardens should include plants that attract them. Such plants provide fruit, nesting sites, and shelter from weather and predators. Obviously birds like fruit, particularly when it's somewhat sour. Some good bird-attracting trees are apple, red cedar, birch, dogwood, elm, hawthorns, mountain ash, sour gum, pine, sassafras, hackberry, holly, sweet bay, serviceberry, bitter cherry, juniper, and madrone. Some useful shrubs are barberry, bayberry, chokeberry, elder, snowberry, spicebush, viburnum, winterberry, coral bead, inkberry, and beautyberry.

Some of the choice birds that may come to these plants are song sparrows, catbirds, thrushes, warblers, brown thrashers, cedar waxwings, robins, vireos, mockingbirds, and the beautiful but threatened bluebirds. Bluebirds have been the object of a recent movement to bring them back by putting nesting boxes in open fields to attract them, with some success. The design of the boxes is quite particular, with a very small hole. However, for the bluebirds to thrive, the murderous male English sparrows, which kill the bluebirds and appropriate the boxes in breeding season, must be physically removed at frequent intervals.

Unfortunately, many animals and birds also eat the eggs and chicks of our cherished songbirds and so decimate their numbers. Also loss of habitat, both their winter resting grounds in Central and South America, as well as fragmentation of forested areas farther north, has led to a sharp decrease in their numbers. Every ef-

A humane way to capture birds that need help or that you want to relocate but which won't enter a trap, is to soak corn kernels or seeds in whiskey. They get drunk and can be caught. Just don't give them too much.

fort should be made to encourage these birds and to provide food, habitat, protection, as well as nesting boxes.

Bird feeders are a time-honored way to attract good birds to the garden. Birds feel more protected if feeders are placed near bushes or sheltering evergreens. Different birds prefer different kinds of feeding sites. Chickadees, titmice, finches, pine siskins, woodpeckers, nuthatches, and wrens prefer hanging feeders. However, all birds, even the larger ones, will eat from a hanging feeder if there's a large enough, secure place for their feet. Low platform or ground feeders are preferred by cardinals, towhees, song sparrows, juncos, mourning doves, jays, and grosbeaks. However, in areas where wild animals like raccoons carry rabies, it's best not to attract them to the yard with food on the ground.

Although each bird has its own food preferences, sunflower hearts is a universal bird food that almost all will eat. With regular sunflower seeds, the dark husks are not eaten so they make a mess on the ground. Also, sunflower husks contain a natural herbicide, and plants won't grow where they fall. Other typical bird foods are shelled peanuts, peanut hearts, suet, niger seeds, and white millet. Some birds insist on thistle seed, which can sprout into a noxious weed. Hummingbirds need hanging nectar feeders filled with red-colored sugar water. In the wild, birds aren't picky eaters and will get by on most anything: grain, berries, nuts, grass seed, fruit, sprouting seedlings, bread crumbs, insects, animals, and other birds.

What to Do When Good Birds Cause Problems in the Garden

Birds love berries and fruit. Though our feathered friends make the garden come alive with their fluttering wings and cheery songs, and though they consume pounds and pounds of insects, harvesting a fruit crop is difficult when little beaks peck away. Birds will eat every single sour cherry or blueberry if left to their own devices. One of the problems is that they prefer the fruit sour, while humans like it sweet. Blueberries are a particular problem because they have to remain on the bush for five or six days to fully ripen, but birds will grab them the moment they color. It's the same with apricots, grapes, plums, and raspberries, although usually they don't eat every one. So what's a person to do that doesn't hurt the birds but protects the harvest?

OLD WIVES' TALES

- Try stringing black sewing thread or nylon sewing thread around a bush or tree. The birds usually can't see it but may get tangled in it and become frightened. Pray they will stay away.
- Plant so many bushes so densely packed that there will be enough for everyone. Of course, this may just attract more animals and birds. It's hard to figure out the long-term consequences of seemingly simple remedies.

Control Methods for Good Birds—Exclusion

Exclusion is the main backyard deterrent. Birds are usually kept away by covering trees and shrubs with netting or building berry cages that are totally enclosed (top and sides). For berry cages, it's best to use wire netting because nylon or light plastic eventually will have holes chewed into it by squirrels, who love fruit as much as birds. (See the chapter "Understanding Control Methods" in Part II.)

However, for temporary netting to protect a ripening crop, plastic or nylon is

best because each is pliable and also easy to put on and take off, but even cheesecloth will do. Most nurseries carry appropriate bird netting. Buy the biggest piece available. If it isn't tightly tied around the trunk or the bottom of the bush, the birds will fly up underneath and inside and it will look as if you're keeping an aviary. Another option is to hold the netting up with sticks and anchor it on the ground with rocks.

It's a nuisance to harvest under the nets. Though openings should be small enough so little birds can't get through, sometimes one can use a net with openings wide enough for getting fingers through. It depends on which birds are the culprits. Another help is to put a cloth or clean sheet on the ground beneath the tree or shrub and pick up fruit every morning and evening. Lots of fruit falls. Some will be in perfect condition, some only good enough for cooking or jam.

Raptors—Birds of Prey

These hunting birds are much cherished and are also very useful because they help control both problem birds and animals. They are still a status symbol in some

parts of the world and
are valuable enough
to be kidnapped
and exported. En-
dowed with keen
eyesight, they cap-
ture their prey by dive-bombing straight
down and flawlessly grabbing the intended
beast or bird with their talons. The rest of
the time they swoop and slowly circle, riding the thermal air masses much like a
surfer rides the waves. Thermal updrafts
allow them to change altitude without ex-
pending much energy flapping their
wings.

Our national bird, the American bald
eagle, is a raptor. Benjamin Franklin, ever
the utilitarian, proposed the wild turkey as
our national bird, calling the eagle a bird
of "bad moral character." More recently,
an old Connecticut Yankee is reputed to
have said, "Should have been the chicken.
At least they lay eggs."

Wild Turkeys

When the colonists arrived in America,
they found these delicious birds a welcome
addition to the table. It is thought that
there were about 40,000 of them in southern New England in the seventeenth century. The Indians not only ate turkeys with
relish but used the feathers for their arrows
and also wove them into a soft cloth. So
plentiful were these big birds that they
were hunted indiscriminately and often
only the white meat was eaten; the rest was
just discarded. By 1840, they had become
scarce in New England, and by 1940, they

were essentially gone from the land of the Pilgrims.

Because of breeding programs started in the 1970s, turkeys have made a remarkable comeback. In 1972, a flock of 37 birds was introduced in Massachusetts, which has since grown to an estimated 15,000 statewide. The 25 that were released in New Hampshire in 1977 have multiplied to more than 7,000. The National Wild Turkey Federation estimates that there were only about 30,000 birds left nationwide in the 1930s, but because of aggres-

sive breeding programs, there are about 4.2 million today.

You may hear their gobble-gobble noise in the woods long before you see any turkeys. They put on fat during the winter and weigh in at about twenty pounds by April when they begin their interesting mating display. The males strut, drop their wings, raise and fan out their tail feathers, and puff themselves up with air to become a big, round, red-necked ball. The females just keep eating.

The females lay about a dozen eggs but don't start incubating them until the clutch is all laid. The reason is to ensure that all the eggs will hatch at once. Turkey chicks have to stay with their mother and

Turkey hunting is an old national sport. When it was recently reintroduced into Massachusetts (to be done before noon only), it incurred the wrath of bird watchers for harming sentient beings and destroying the serenity of the woodlands for kinder, gentler folk.

can't be left alone unprotected in the nest. Any eggs that don't hatch by the second day are abandoned. The mother protects her poults ferociously, and few predators think a battle with an angry turkey is worth such a small meal. The young can fly after about ten days. Wild turkeys live on acorns, beechnuts, berries and fruit, grasses, frogs, slugs, and insects and may visit manure piles in search of seeds in winter.

If you are lucky enough to have wild turkeys, just enjoy them. Fence the yard if they become a problem.

Bad Birds

Some of the worst, pigeons, starlings and English sparrows, have been imported, but we have numerous troublesome native ones as well. Among them are sea gulls, cowbirds, blackbirds, Canada geese, woodpeckers, and cliff swallows. These birds cause many serious problems, particularly the roosting birds , which fly in huge flocks, sometimes with as many as one million members. Bad birds eat crops, spread disease, cause airplane accidents, and are a general, untidy nuisance worldwide. Many methods and myths have been used to try to control their crop damage. On rural farms scarecrows were put up to reinforce the bird's fear of man and his musket when buckshot still ruled

the roost. In India, swarming flocks of grain-eating birds were blown up by dynamiting the roost tree where they'd all settle after sunset.

In Uganda, where women are responsible for the food crops, grandmothers of old taught their daughters to randomly scatter the seeds or "the monkeys would eat them." It turned out, after some research at the local agricultural station, that the Ugandan national bird, the crested crane, was actually the culprit. When seeds were planted in a straight row, the birds methodically pecked along the rows, eating every single sprouting seed. However, with random seeding, they missed quite a few, so there could be cornmeal mush on the family table.

Not all problems are agricultural. Large flocks of birds can be especially dangerous. On October 4, 1960, at Boston's Logan Airport, a flock of starlings was sucked into a plane's engines at takeoff. Without enough power, the plane crashed, killing sixty-two of the seventy-three people on board. Since that time there has been a dawn-to-dusk airfield patrol by a shotgun-toting employee who disperses gulls, crows, geese, and blackbirds. In addition, pilots are warned to beware of birds and deer when taking off.

How to Recognize Bird Damage in the Garden

Birds in the backyard cause less serious problems. Usually you will see them during the day eating seedlings or fruit. Generally they only come when a particular crop is ripe, such as their favorite blueberries, or when they're migrating through. Because of this, most people have problem birds for only a few weeks at a time. Controls are generally not needed on a year-round basis.

Diseases

Birds are a main carrier of about forty diseases—among them salmonella, histoplasmosis, toxoplasmosis, transmittable gastroenteritis, thrush, encephalitis, aspergillosis, psittacosis—and insect pests such as bedbugs, chiggers, foul ticks, mites, and fleas as well as parasites. Infections can be very serious and may be transmitted through the skin or eating, but more often by inhalation of infected dust or insects. For this reason, wild birds should be handled with proper infectious precautions, especially when sweeping up the mess they make. Professionals use a face mask or disposable breathing apparatus and protective clothing, including gloves, caps, and rubber boots. If you clean up bird mess,

take off contaminated clothes, put them in a plastic bag, and wash them separately as soon as possible. Boots should be hosed off before entering buildings or vehicles where spores or fungus fragments can get blown around in the heating system.

Control Methods for Bad Birds

Many birds are protected species, and a permit is needed from the state wildlife service to trap or hunt them. So find out which species are protected in your state. Scaring problem birds, however, is generally allowed. Let's start with the bottom line: no one method works quickly or alone. However, when several methods are used together and repeated as long as necessary to discourage birds, they may change their habits. Then peace can be achieved, at least for a little while.

Birds are smart and adaptive. They know when something is a bluff, just as they know when a gun has real bullets. One way they know is from distress calls made by injured birds, but each species or subspecies responds only to the distress calls of its own kind. Because each kind of bird has different habits, one should modify the control strategy to suit the species. Sun Tzu says that to win, one has to know the numbers of the enemy, their strengths and weaknesses, and the terrain, for battles are won by good planning before they're actually fought. Therefore, some of the most common problem birds will be discussed individually. The control methods are similar for all birds, but the timing, repetition, and combinations vary depending on the species and the problem.

Each state wildlife agency as well as the United States Department of Agriculture, Animal and Plant Health Inspection Service, Animal Damage Control–Wildlife Services Division has good handouts for the birds in your area. They are the best local information you can get.

Roosting Birds and Large Flocks

When large flocks fly, they roost in certain places or certain trees at night. They make a lot of noise and drop a lot of disease-carrying debris underneath. Once they've habituated to a spot, they're very hard to get rid of, so start trying to scare them off as soon as they arrive.

When harvest time comes to the vineyards in California, it's a time of peril. Massive flocks of grape-eating birds peck at the fruit while it's ripening and can ruin the crop. The birds, mostly European starlings, less often finches or robins, start eating the grapes when the sugar content reaches 15 percent. The grapes aren't ready to harvest until it reaches 21 per-

cent, so for three weeks the farmers battle the birds to limit the damage.

Attracting Raptors

Lately, a new technique has been tried. Some farmers are building nests to attract raptors, particularly kestrels and other hawks. These are natural predators of grape-eating birds and rodents as well. When the starlings see them, supposedly, they won't stick around. It remains to be seen if enough birds of prey will take up residency to be the only control method needed, but this is certainly a good idea that's worth a try.

Distress Calls

The use of distress calls has been successful when combined with other scare devices. Calls should be played in the roost for ten to fifteen seconds each minute as the birds attempt to enter a roost, or continuously when most birds have settled in.

Propane Exploders

These produce loud explosions, which should be fired at about thirty-second intervals. Move them frequently because birds easily get used to exploders, which should be combined with other scare devices.

Pyrotechnics ☠

Shellcrackers and whistle bombs can be used. Shellcrackers are 12-gauge shotgun shells containing a firecracker that explodes high in the air. Whistle bombs are fired from flare pistols and travel about seventy-five feet before exploding. Each shooter should be given fifty or more shells and cautioned to conserve ammunition for the last few minutes the birds are moving, which is when the most firepower is needed.

Live ammunition may be used as reinforcement because taking a few birds in the roost will reestablish their fear. One person shooting shellcrackers or with a distress speaker can cover about one or two acres.

Frightening Devices

Flashing owls, owl decoys, helium-filled balloons are often used in conjunction with recorded distress calls and noise, but they have little effectiveness when used alone.

Poisons ☠

There are certain avicides, one is called Avitrol, ☠ which can only be used by a licensed pesticide applicator. The public is not allowed to buy or handle these avicides, for they are quite dangerous.

To Disperse a Roost

Begin scaring as soon as possible after a roost begins, ideally the first evening. It takes several days, and there won't seem to be any results the first or second night. Use a combination of the above, especially in early evening and again for about a half hour before the morning departure. Once settled at night, the birds won't move, and may get habituated to the control measures if they're continued after dark. So go home to bed.

Large flocks are not just a farm problem. One day 10,000 migrating crows camped out in the trees around a venerable insurance company in Hartford, Connecticut. The exterminator tried firecrackers, but the birds came right back. Then a crow distress call was played over a loudspeaker, and they moved on. Which was lucky because if they hadn't, the exterminator was going to start shooting next. When enough of a flock are shot and killed (some say 10 percent), the others eventually get the idea that it's not a good place to stay.

Canada Geese

We know what *doesn't* work for this most common and most troublesome of pests: swans, barking dogs, guns, Mylar balloons, large flapping flags, shrubs, fences near the water, nonlethal noise-makers, a string or fishing line "fence" around the water's edge, and letting the grass grow tall around the pond. One golf magazine asked for ideas, but no good solution materialized. Trained, sheep-herding border collies have been tried with some success.

These large geese used to migrate north to Canada; however, many now remain year round when food and water are available. Their favorite food is close-cropped grass, and if there's a small pond nearby, they're happy. Many athletic fields, industrial parks, golf courses, and swimming holes have been unpleasantly overrun. The birds eat a lot, and they poop a lot. It is estimated that an adult Canada goose produces a half pound of slimy manure per day, which messes up the grass and contaminates any water body it washes into.

In 1940, their population nationwide was 1.11 million. With few natural population controls, by 1980 it had reached 2.32 million. On the Eastern Flyway alone, their numbers soared from about 50,000 in 1950 to 1 million by the early 1980s. (The Eastern Flyway, which runs from Canada to Florida, is the route that migrating birds follow as they go south to Florida, the Caribbean islands, and South America during winter.)

Control Strategies for Geese — Hopeful Pest Management

Using specially trained border collies—a natural sheep-herding dog—has been tried. A few golf courses report some success, reducing the populations by perhaps 80 percent. The dogs must be specially trained to harass the geese and are run every day, both morning and evening, and sometimes in between. Dogs should not go after the birds in the water because the more facile birds would have the advantage in a fight. An even better idea is a "dog patrol." This can be started by inviting people (through a notice in a local newspaper) to run their dogs, unleashed, where geese are a problem. If enough come with their dogs twice a day, it may cause the geese to go elsewhere.

You can try the same techniques as for roosting birds, but they usually don't work well. Harassment has to be started as soon as the geese arrive, and not one goose can remain to act as a decoy. Dawn, dusk, and rainy weather have to be covered. For a year-round bird, this is a big order.

Other Ideas

You can also try a few of the following methods suggested by some government wildlife handouts. Though not as unscientific as old wives' tales, they haven't solved most people's geese problems. If you're really lucky, something might work, but don't hold your breath.

- Don't let people feed the geese, particularly in parks.
- Allow the grass to grow tall to remove the tender green browse they prefer. Also, they can't see predators in tall grass and brush.
- Install permanent barriers all around a pond, like stone riprap or a twenty-four-inch concrete ledge.
- Create a buffer of hedges or fences between their feeding areas and their protection—the water.
- Keep a three-foot-high fence around an area to enclose the geese, in May and June. At that time, the goslings can't fly, and the parents won't leave them. Once the little ones can fly in June, forget it.
- Use the repellent ReJex-it AG-36, which irritates their noses. Geese won't eat treated grass, although they will sit on it. Broadcasting pellets of grape-flavored methyl anthranilate, which they

don't like, has been suggested, though these pellets are not currently approved for this purpose.
- Addle the eggs, by shaking them and killing the embryo. The mother will sit on them, but they won't hatch. If you destroy or remove the eggs, she will lay another batch. Of course, you have to find the nest (often on an island), shake the eggs when the aggressive parents aren't looking, and put them back. A wildlife permit is required.

Hunting and Population Control

When nothing works but killing, frustrated people turn to it. There is a hunting season in most states, and it does help to keep the population down. The statement that when 10 percent of the flock is shot, the rest will leave, applies to Canada geese.

Feral Pigeons

Pigeons were first brought to the United States from Europe. Some escaped into the wild and have adapted well to the shelter and easy food in urban areas. Their numbers have grown so large that they've become a nuisance. Flocks foul parks, buildings, statues, damage cars and plants with their droppings, which also carry many diseases.

Recently there was a big to-do in London's Trafalgar Square, where pigeons are the main attraction for tourists and little old English bird lovers. It seems there were just too many, about 200,000. With usual English wit and scorn, the pros (for killing some) and the cons (save'em all) battled it

out in the world press. There was even a mysterious snatcher who caught about 1,500 and sold them to restaurants. It is estimated that about 10 percent of the Trafalgar pigeons are diseased.

Pigeons usually aren't a problem in rural areas, where other birds and animals crowd the habitat. In cities, however, they just reproduce and reproduce to fill urban spaces that won't support many other species. Fortunately skyscrapers do support raptors, such as peregrine falcons, those graceful birds of prey who feed on pigeons. New York City has brought in a number of

them, who have happily taken up residence on tall buildings that remind them of their ancestral cliff homes. While this hasn't yet solved the Big Apple's pigeon population problem, it's another good idea.

Roost Elimination

Eliminating roosts is a lot of work because pigeons roost and nest in many places: on eaves, dormers, window ledges, and decorative areas on buildings. Sticky stuff doesn't last more than a few months but might be worth trying when a bird first appears. Sharp "porcupine wire" made of pointed metal prongs is costly but effective and permanent.

Frightening Devices

Urban birds are used to noise, so owls, balloons, snakes, streamers, et cetera, have little lasting effect. It has been suggested that spraying roosting pigeons with streams of water will make them relocate, but it has to be done consistently for several days until every single bird is gone.

Trapping

Most traps catch pigeons alive. The usual types are funnel traps and Bob-type traps, which can be purchased from commercial manufacturers. Set the traps, baited with whole corn or grain in a feeding or roosting area, and put a light-colored pigeon inside as a decoy. When live birds are inside, supply water. (See the chapter "Understanding Control Methods.") Many people raise pigeons as pets. Treat them as you would your puppy or kitten and immediately free any banded pigeons or return them to their owners.

Chemical Control

There are some avicides and some birth control products. Poison bait is available only to licensed pesticide applicators. However, there is a birth control chemical called Ornitrol that causes sterility for about six months. To use, feed the pigeons for several days with whole corn, then put out corn treated with the Ornitrol; repeat every six months.

Shooting

In rural areas this is often effective, but in cities it is neither allowed nor safe.

Woodpeckers

Surprisingly, these charming birds, which eat quantities of insects and liven up the woods as they whiz by with their red head patches flashing, can become problem birds. It happens mostly when their nesting area and roost cavities are destroyed, or when a building is constructed in their home area.

Tough little birds, they won't leave their territory. They just start pecking away at the next available piece of wood, which may be a building or a cherished tree. Normally they peck holes in trees to get insects that are under the bark, or to hollow out cavities for nesting or overwintering. But they also drum on resonant dead woods to establish their territories and to attract a mate. When they take a shine to a particular tree or building, they will cover it with holes, although the trees they choose usually are infested with insects and are already weak.

Sapsuckers peck parallel rows of small holes in thin bark, providing an entry hole for decay organisms. Woodpeckers make larger holes. The pileated woodpecker may excavate a cavity two inches wide, six to eight inches long, and as deep. Not a tiny nick, indeed. You would think they'd turn their brain to squash with all that pounding away, but a hinged beak absorbs some of the shock. That, plus very strong head bones and neck muscles allow them to tolerate the repeated jackhammer pecks.

Exclusion

One way of preventing damage to wood siding under a building's eaves is to cover the area with nylon or plastic netting, hung about three inches away from the wall. For a favored tree, wrap loose cylinders of hardware cloth around the trunk and main branches. Where woodpecker damage is common, build in brick, aluminum, stone, or steel. If leaf-cutting bees are nesting in wood siding, woodpeckers will go after them. Also, suet should be removed from bird feeders.

Frightening Devices

Some success has been reported with Mylar tape attached to the side of a building with vertical strips mounted every two or three feet. Magnifying mirrors and hawk silhouettes may be tried, as can wind chimes, strips of aluminum foil or colored cloth, aluminum pie pans that will flash and rattle. Noises made by clapping hands, firing cap pistols, playing a radio on a talk station, and spinning windmills have all been suggested, as well as the more effective propane exploders and firecracker shells. There is a sticky repellent that may be applied to trees. As with all birds, these techniques may or may not work, although each one will probably frighten the birds for a period of time. Woodpeckers are generally not city birds, so they aren't used to the intrusions. If all are used promptly and persistently, they might leave for another area.

Shooting

On occasion, woodpecker damage becomes serious, and if nonlethal methods don't work, a permit may be obtained from the federal wildlife service to shoot or trap. Set a bait of suet or nut meats.

Common House Sparrows

This small English sparrow has adapted here very well and is a common resident in urban and suburban areas. Although primarily a grain eater, it will happily gorge at garbage cans, dumps, bird feeders, home gardens, and outdoor tables in restaurants. Most problems are caused by its nesting and feeding habits; its droppings are messy and carry diseases, insects, fleas, and mites.

An aggressive little thing that travels in small flocks, it will drive away more desirable songbirds and move into nesting boxes for martins and bluebirds. In the spring, the male sparrow will go inside a bluebird box and kill the more valuable male bluebird, which is setting up housekeeping for a mate. People who are trying to reestablish bluebirds by installing boxes for them will trap and kill competing English sparrows weekly during the mating season.

Exclusion

To exclude sparrows from nesting sites, all openings larger than three-quarters of an inch should be screened or blocked off, and all crevices should be covered with hardware cloth or netting.

To keep them from taking over bird feeders, don't scatter seed on the ground, where they like to scavenge, and use large seeds such as sunflower. Suet blocks and hummingbird feeders don't usually attract them.

Repellents

Porcupine wire is best for keeping sparrows off ledges, sills, rooflines, and other bird-roosting areas. Sticky repellents last about six months.

Noise and Visual Scare Tactics

These methods are essentially useless for any extended period.

Poisons ☠

Several chemicals are available to control these birds, but are very poisonous and have to be used by a licensed pesticide applicator.

Trapping

Funnel traps are useful, and during nesting season sparrows are easily attracted to nest box traps. Place the traps near low shrubs or hedges, and bait with seeds or bread. Bait around the outside as well as inside the trap. One or two birds may be left in the trap to act as decoys. The law requires food and water be in the trap, or they will die. (See the chapter on control methods.)

Nest Destruction

Populations can be lowered to some extent if the nests and eggs are destroyed at two-week intervals during the spring and summer. A long pole with a hook is an effective tool. Use appropriate health measures to protect yourself against their diseases, and throw out the nest in a sealed plastic bag.

Cliff Swallows

Most swallows are a treasure as they swoop and skim, eating their weight in insects. Swallows are delightful, and nest anywhere they can find a space. Barn swallows usually come in small groups so don't cause problems. However, cliff swallows may gather in large colonies and do become problem birds when great numbers of them attach their mud nests to buildings. Their droppings are dirty and unsanitary, particularly near agricultural establishments.

Troublesome cliff swallows usually make their solid nests outside, under eaves and overhangs. Barn swallows make open nests, usually on the inside of barns or other sheltered spaces rather than outside.

Cliff swallow nesting habits stem from their ancestral homes in canyons and on cliffs, but they are equally happy to plaster their gourdlike mud nests on buildings and bridges. The swallows return after migrating from South America and quickly claim old nests, repairing them with mud pellets. They make new nests as well, sometimes building two or three a year, though they don't use them all.

Nest Removal and Exclusion

As with other protected birds, a permit is needed for nest removal, which should be applied for early, before the birds arrive. Nesting sites can be eliminated by knocking down the old nests and filling the overhang with porcupine wire or netting. (See the chapter "Understanding Control Methods" in Part II.)

Sea Gulls

Sea gulls have become a bad bird just in the twentieth century. Landfills and fishing fleets have provided the food to allow their population to expand to problem numbers. They are responsible for one-half of all bird-aircraft incidents worldwide. In addition, they nest and roost on roofs, in marinas, pollute reservoirs, feed on duck farms and fish hatcheries, and push other less aggressive shorebirds out of nesting areas. As with other problem birds, using a combination of methods works best.

Exclusion

Grid wires may be used to keep sea gulls from landing on rooftops, reservoirs, and marinas.

Noise and Scare Tactics

Frightening devices are useless alone but may reinforce other techniques. Firecracker shells or whistle bombs combined with gull distress calls may help. The distress calls have to be those of the exact subspecies of gull, however.

Poisons ☠

Avitrol is a poisonous ☠ avicide that can only be bought and used by a registered pesticide applicator.

Shooting

Although shooting is sometimes resorted to, it is only useful in combination with other methods to scare them away. There are just too many sea gulls for shooting to make a dent in the population.

Jonathan Sea Gull Lives On

An interesting flap has been going on for a long time about the 2,750 acre Monomoy National Wildlife Refuge off Cape Cod. Because about 25,000 sea gulls nest there, there's not enough room for more desirable terns, piping plovers, and other shorebirds, whose populations are threatened. There were only fourteen plover nests on the islands in 1995.

In 1980, poisoning was tried to lower the gull population, but some of the birds flew off and died on the main streets of nearby towns. Because of the public outcry this engendered, the poisoning effort was stopped. The wildlife service then tried to control the population by nonlethal means but without success. In 1996, poisoning was tried again on over 5,000 gulls, and again dead birds dropped in people's yards. Bowing to public pressure, poisoning was again abandoned.

However, to enforce a 175-acre gull-free nesting zone (after the poisoning), about 500 additional gulls were shot in 1996. That year, roseate terns, laughing gulls, and black skimmers returned to Monomoy for the first time in years. Least tern nests increased from 28 to 103, while common tern nests went from 63 to 1,219. Of course, there were protests.

Finally, in 1997, after working all year with eighteen different activist organizations, the United States Fish and Wildlife Service came up with a plan to shoot gulls in order to make room for and protect other bird species. Even so, not everyone was happy.

That spring, fish and wildlife agents shot, trapped, or broke the necks of 148 gulls who tried to nest on 89 acres of the refuge. That summer U.S. Senator Edward M. Kennedy, a longtime Cape Cod resident, asked U.S. Interior Secretary Bruce Babbitt to halt the shooting, ensuring that the battle of the gulls versus the terns will be fought in the august halls of our nation's capital.

Efforts at preservation of nesting sites for desired bird species is costly. On Nantucket Island, near Monomoy Wildlife Refuge, a favorite local beach was restricted in 1995 to protect plover nests. In 1994, before restrictions, eight plover eggs were laid, and eight chicks hatched on the beach. In 1995, twenty-four plover eggs were laid. Fifteen employees were hired to monitor the birds and protect them by restricting human access to the beach. Yet despite their efforts, out of the twenty-four eggs, only two chicks survived. Gulls, crows, and other predators killed the others. The management program cost the town $100,000, enough to send the two chicks to an Ivy League college for two years.

BISON OR AMERICAN BUFFALO AND ANIMAL GRAZING HABITS

There still are folks who long for a home where the buffalo roam and the skies are not cloudy all day. There is a smaller group of folks who believe that the Midwest should be given back to the buffalo and farming should be exterminated. Sounds silly, but they are serious. Pieces of the Midwest, some around Chicago, are being returned to the flora and fauna of the original prairie as it was before white men destroyed its pure "virgin" state. These events, sometimes announced with great fanfare, are often connected to the restoration of buildings designed by the midwestern architect Frank Lloyd Wright. Poor gentleman is probably turning over in his grave, as another famous person who has been made a champion for causes he never envisioned. Reestablishing and preserving the original prairie is admirable and desirable. How much should be returned to buffalo is another question.

Buffalo meat is much appreciated as a healthier alternative to beef because it has much less fat yet tastes the same. There are buffalo farms where the animals are grown for meat, as well as beefalo farms where an animal that's part buffalo and part steer also produces leaner meat. For many years, buffalo steak, though somewhat chewy, was a regular menu item at the Harvard Faculty Club, reputedly introduced by Theodore Roosevelt.

Buffalo are not a problem in most people's backyards. However, in some areas, near wildlife preserves, they roam outside when the population density increases too much or when winter forage is poor.

How to Tell If You Have a Buffalo Problem

It won't be hard. They're very big! If you don't have buffalo, but want to watch these wonderful lumbering animals, consider a winter trip to Yellowstone National Park, where they'll come close to the road, and the snow and lack of leaf cover provide superb visibility. Be warned, though, they're dangerous wild animals. If you notice that they smell and you have flies, you're much, much too close.

Scientific Information

These bison, which is their correct name, are very unpredictable. Sometimes they're passive and can be approached without alarming them, while at other times, they stampede at the least provocation. It is never safe to approach them. Even buffalo farmers are careful. Despite their lumbering gait and huge girth, they're agile and fast, having been clocked at up to forty miles per hour. Huge herds, estimated at 60 million, roamed this continent until they were almost exterminated in the late nineteenth century. The government had its reasons then. Today's popular press thinks there were hidden agendas, and this may well be true. Reinventing history in terms of our current

sensibilities and political correctness is a fascinating exercise, which we will not attempt here. Today, thanks to government efforts, wild buffalo are not endangered, and the species is also preserved on buffalo farms.

The mating period, called the bison rut, occurs in the summer and autumn. The males fight, using up much energy and depleting their strength. They don't eat much during this time, being totally consumed with procreation and doing battle over the cows. The females, on the other hand, munch along merrily to put on weight and a good coat, which will carry them through the sparse winter and pregnancy. By late fall, as a result of their obsessive fighting, the males are in poor shape—weak and thin—making them

vulnerable to wolf packs and other predators, as well as winter's cold and sparse food. Many males die in winter while the fatted cows make little buffalos.

Understanding Grazing Animals' Habits

Buffalo graze in the morning and at dusk, and rest during midday and at night. Because buffalo eat in one area for a while, then move to another, buffalo buffs say they conserve the grasslands better than domestic cattle. Also, buffalo eat different heights and tougher grasses than do cows. At low population densities, this grazing pattern leaves more vegetation intact, which is why some environmental groups think the West would be better suited to buffalo than livestock. However, buffalo

can deplete an area as do other herbivores. When there is lots of land and fewer animals, the range is conserved and protected. When there are too many for the land to support, they eat every blade of grass and denude the land, as in parts of Yellowstone Park.

Different animals all have different habits and graze land differently. Sheep and goats are not fussy eaters and chew all plants down to nubbins. This leaves pastureland agriculturally exhausted, bare, treeless, and subject to drought and erosion. Such overgrazed barren hillsides are common in countries that have depended on livestock for food, particularly those in the Middle East.

In biblical times, sheep played an important role in the civil and spiritual life of the ancient Hebrews, although sheep were kept for their milk rather than as a meat source. The flocks were carefully tended. Obtaining water was uppermost in the

shepherd's mind, and he faithfully watered them, always at noon, at hidden wells and oases, even in desert areas. The shepherd's solicitous care is metaphorically chronicled in the Twenty-third Psalm, "The Lord is my shepherd, I shall not want. He maketh me to lie down in green pastures. He leadeth me beside the still waters." The lifestyle of nomadic Arabic tribes today still revolves around the convenience and food supply of their animals. Overgrazed land is today the scourge of the Middle East and parts of Africa, as well as other places where animals are domesticated and rainfall is sparse.

Once denuded of vegetation, particularly by sheep and goats, the topsoil blows away, few plants can take hold, and heavy rains cause erosion. Without the climate-ameliorating effect of sheltering trees, the land becomes windswept, too cold in winter, and too hot in summer. Such hardscrabble land remains bare and poor for centuries, and the forests rarely return. It requires the conscious effort of humans to restore such land. In Israel, reforestation and reclamation have been ongoing efforts for a century.

Where domesticated animals are important, custom and lifestyle are often determined by the needs of the animals. Cattle need fresh grazing in green fields because they require better forage than sheep and goats. Primitive societies burn off the land, just before the rainy season, to get fresh green grass to sprout, which is higher in nitrogen than old, dry, brown grass. Sometimes in southern Sudan, Ethiopia, northern Uganda, and Kenya, the entire horizon may be a circle of flame at night as the herding tribes burn the range to renew their forage.

More advanced animal husbandry dictates field rotation as each area is grazed down, to give it time to recover and regrow new grass. This rotation preserves the fields and allows for long-term grazing without burning or exhausting the land. In Switzerland, domesticated animals start grazing the lower slopes in spring and then move up the mountains following the new grass, which appears as the snow melts farther and farther up the mountainsides. And their droppings fertilize these meadows.

More modern and sophisticated is the practice of growing fodder in fields as a sustainable crop. The grass is harvested and brought to the animals, which saves their wasting energy walking from field to field. Also, sanitation and climate control can be better managed under cover, both in summer's heat and winter's bitter cold. The animal waste is returned to the fields as manure and straw fertilizer.

Wild animal herds such as buffalo are not so lucky. Their grazing is totally dependent on the weather. The supply of food determines their population, their health, and in turn the population of the predator species that feed on them. When the rains are good, the grass is green and the females produce healthy babies who have enough to eat. During times of drought, starvation limits both the population survival as well as the fertility of the females.

There is an interesting natural birth control coincidence in the Serengeti National Park, a game preserve in East Africa. When the rains are good, the grass is high and the wildebeest population swells. During times of drought, the grass is sparse and eaten much lower. Creeping on the ground, there is a plant with a white morning glory flower that looks like bindweed, which causes the females to abort. When the grass is high, these plants are shaded out to some degree and the animals don't eat as close to the ground, so they aren't as likely to eat it. But during times of drought, as they graze closer and eat the weed, their birthrate goes down.

When Wild Grazing Herds Are Likely to Walk Through Fences

Worldwide, animal migrations follow the rainfall and fresh grass. Closer to home, understanding this fact allows residents in areas with wild grazing herds (particularly antelope, elk, and buffalo) to know when they will likely be crossing an area in search of food. Then gates and fences can be opened to let animals pass through. Saves on mending fences.

Diseases

Brucellosis is carried by buffalo and elk. First identified in 1887, it can be a serious human disease characterized by low-grade fever, chills, aches and pains, nervousness and depression, which generally subside in three to six months, but the disease can become chronic. It also causes spontaneous abortions. Treatment is with antibiotics, and vaccines are available. However, the main danger is to cattle, which also get the disease. Milk production is lowered, and spontaneous abortion is common, resulting in severe economic losses. Animals can be tested for infection, which is not always externally apparent.

The causative microbe is spread by aborted material, vaginal discharges, infected urine, and milk. Infection can be by ingestion, through eye membranes and skin abrasions, or by handling buffalo droppings. Pasteurizing and cooking kill the microbe.

Public health control measures have lowered the incidence of the disease in cattle and humans. However, as the population of buffalo and elk in public parks grows, more and more animals will seek new grazing areas on cattle ranches. The concern is that they may reintroduce the disease to clean cattle.

Buffalo migrations are usually repetitive journeys over the same routes. So far, these routes are inside parks and preserves. But when animals stray outside, there can be problems, especially with brucellosis if one keeps livestock. If infected buffalo are allowed to run free, ranchers would have to pay for expensive brucellosis tests for their animals.

Control Methods

In Yellowstone National Park, the buffalo herd had grown to 3,500 by the winter of 1997, and animals moved out of the park in various places in Montana. Several horses were gored by buffalo, and ranchers were worried about the spread of disease. Despite criticism from animal rights groups in large cities far away, government wildlife services removed or shot buffalo that threatened domesticated animals or ran into conflicts with private landowners. The meat was donated to Indian tribes.

In 1928, a study concluded that Yellowstone could not sustain a bison population larger than 1,000. Later, even that number was considered too high, and the rangers began to shoot bison to reduce, or cull the herd, and protect the park. However, beginning in 1967, park officials adopted a policy of "natural regulation" in which starvation would limit their numbers. Unfortunately, it hasn't. The land is overgrazed by both the buffalo and elk herds. And the hungry animals move outside the park to find forage because they can't read the boundary signs too well.

During the winter of 1997, about 1,000 buffalo from the Yellowstone Park herd were shot as they crossed park boundaries in search of food. Another 1,000 or more died of starvation in the winter. This left about 1,200 in the park, which is near the number suggested in the 1928 study. Nevertheless, animal protection groups protested, in the press, the shooting of strays, which prompted the Interior Department of the United States to question whether the shooting should be halted.

Over the years, the cattle ranchers in Montana have spent more than $30 million to receive a brucellosis-free status from the Animal and Plant Health Inspection Service (APHIS). Now they are afraid that buffalo will carry the disease to their cattle. And so the battle in the large backyards of Montana rages on until a political decision will determine the size of buffalo herds and how they should be controlled. It's the new tug of the old battle between ecology and Wild West mythology.

In 1997, the United States Secretary of Agriculture and two senators had rotting bison entrails dumped on them by a member of the Bison Action Group protesting the shooting of buffalo.

CATS AND DOGS

Cats and dogs are not problem animals, although sometimes they cause problems. They live with us and share our lives, giving comfort and companionship. Perhaps their greatest virtue is that they can't talk. They can only empathize, sit with us, nestle and purr, respond to our every mood and feeling. They are the perfect companion! As such, they should be cared for like members of the family, particularly in matters of health, for they are subject to many diseases and can transmit them to humans.

There is a widespread problem with stray dogs and cats. These strays suffer from hunger, cold, and fear. Stray dogs often band together and become threats as their ancient wolf survival genes rise to the surface. In the Bronx, the problem with abandoned dogs became so bad a while ago that the police had to round them up and kill them. Even worse, with rabies in wild animals on the rise now, stray dogs are once again the potential reservoir of the disease, as they were in the past, before rabies control was seriously pursued and stray dogs were killed.

Some stray dogs and cats get lost, and a few run away, but the vast majority are just abandoned by people who don't want to care for them anymore. The numbers of strays are staggering. There are 300,000 to 400,000 feral (wild) cats in the state of Massachusetts alone. About 13 million unwanted dogs and cats are euthanized, or "put to sleep," each year. For Valentine's Day 1997, one humane society offered free neutering operations for pets. Universal free neutering should be made available by all groups who care about pets. It's certainly the best way to prevent so much killing of unplanned for and unwanted animals.

Protecting Your Pet from Problem Animals and Disease

Be sure to give pets all the recommended vaccines and shots to prevent illness and, more important, to protect your own family. Cats can suffer from about forty diseases, dogs close to sixty. Over twenty of these may be transmitted to people, including rabies, leptospirosis, tetanus, cat scratch fever, worms, diarrheal diseases, and some viruses, one of which may cause cancer. Because pets often interact with wild animals when they run outside, they are exposed to the numerous maladies carried by wildlife. Transmission can be from tangling directly with live animals or from animal droppings.

Dogs should be trained to bark a lot and loudly, but to not approach or attack large wildlife like raccoons, woodchucks, foxes, deer, or carnivores. The dogs can be hurt or infected with disease and will certainly get fleas. Cats usually have sense enough to run away.

Dogs

Dogs have been man's most useful friend for a long time. As shepherds'

helpers, watchdogs, hunters, beasts of transport, these smart, trainable, and loyal animals have been a well-loved part of the human family for hundreds of years. In most parts of the world today, big watchdogs are still the most reliable burglar alarm and family protectors. Surely there is no pleasure that can match a well-trained dog that relates to its owner with precision and understanding. A good dog can read its master's moods and needs, and respond with amazing insight. Seeing eye dogs, police dogs, hunting dogs, herding dogs, and lap dogs are remarkable. A person who has never had a dog has missed one of the joys of life.

Dogs probably separated from wolves about 100,000 years ago and have evolved into a myriad of dissimilar breeds. Consider the big husky Newfoundland, which is calm, gentle, and responsible. Such dogs were used in previous ages to save people from shipwrecks on rocky shores during storms. Newfoundlands are very different from the smaller border collie, whose herding instincts make it jumpy, acute, and very expert at controlling sheep. These two were recently interbred to see how genetic traits are inherited. The first generation (F-1) had a combination of both parents' traits. However, the traits segregated out again, in odd permutations, in the second generation. Unfortunately, not all dogs are perfect. Some are so highly inbred that bad traits are concentrated in their genes. Some breeds, like pit bulls, are bred and trained to be vicious, to fight and bite. Some dogs are just badly trained, so they don't know what is and is not appropriate behavior.

The Centers for Disease Control and Prevention report that in 1994, there were 52 million dogs in the United States, and there were 4.5 million dog bites. Over 800,000 of these bites required medical care, and 15 were fatal. The insurance industry paid $1 billion in claims for dog bites, which amounted to about 30 percent of its total bodily injury claims. The average claim was more than $12,000.

Garden Problems with Dogs

In the garden, dogs occasionally dig things up, but they can be easily trained to stop, particularly if they are given some other place to play and, ideally, a roomy fenced dog run. With training, dogs will respect garden fences, so using green plastic-coated dog fencing will keep them out of choice areas.

Bonemeal, organic fertilizers with fish or chicken feathers, and anything that smells of food will entice them to dig, so spare the poor dog and use chemical fertilizers. There are repellent dog sprays and also rope twine impregnated with a strong odor that's supposed to repel them. Another repellent uses methyl nonyl ketone, which has a strong, persistent industrial-type odor but isn't unpleasant. The downside is that it's poisonous, can't be used on food crops, and is irritating to the skin, so hands should be thoroughly washed with soap and water after using.

If the whole yard is fenced, dogs have a habit of running around the inside edge of the fence and wearing down all the plants. If your dog does this, give the animal a run, which is a wide swath of about two feet around the inside of the perimeter. Then put low, green, unobtrusive dog fencing between the run and the garden area. Wood chips make a good base for dog runs and keep their feet from being muddy. It's also possible to train dogs to use one area in the yard as their private bathroom, which keeps the rest of the yard cleaner.

One nice thing about a dog, particularly males who run and mark the yard as their territory (with urine), is that most pesty animals will stay out. Coyotes and wolves will be attracted, however, and may mate with domestic animals. In areas where these wild animals are common, keep a dog in heat confined, or better still, have pets neutered unless they are breeding-stock show dogs.

The best way to prevent problems with

dogs in the garden is to train them properly, as all dogs should be. They are happiest when they understand what's expected of them and praised when they do it.

Cats

According to the television show *Wall Street Week*, in 1995 for the first time in history, cats outnumbered dogs as pets. Although pussycats sometimes dig in the garden, they are not problem animals. They are our friends and pets, our helpers and mousers.

It is not by chance that Egyptians worshiped cats and even had a cat goddess named Bastet who represented love and joy. Being careful observers, they probably noticed, over the course of 1,000 years or so, that people who had cats had less disease. That is just common sense, we know now, because cats keep rodent populations under control and so prevent the many diseases rodents carry. Also, cats surely were important in keeping rodents out of the stored harvests of grain on which the stability of Egyptian civilization depended.

Garden Problems with Cats

Cats like to scratch in newly dug soil and occasionally will dig because they think they smell something good to eat. Organic fertilizers, particularly those with fish or chicken feathers, will be a magnet, so use chemical fertilizer if your cat likes to hang around in the garden.

To minimize digging, spray cat repellent or put out a cat repellent rope. Another trick is to plant a little catnip far away, which cats surely prefer to dirt. Also

place some kitty litter in a convenient place outside for them to use instead of newly dug soil.

Cats also like to sometimes eat and roll around in certain plants, especially catnip, which may be mood enhancing. Nonedible plants can be protected with repellents, the others just have to be dealt with on a plant-by-plant basis. It's very difficult to train a cat to do exactly what you want.

Cats will keep the squirrels, mice, rats, chipmunks, and rabbits out of the garden; that's why they hang around it. Sometimes they chase birds, but a small bell on the cat's collar will stop that problem. Make sure you pick a tinkly bell whose sound you can stand, because you will hear it often.

In Australia, cats were brought in 200 years ago by the European settlers. Now there are 18 million cats, and about one third of the households have pet cats. However, cats are decimating many endangered native birds and animals, plus they have been blamed for the extinction of at least nine native species. One lawmaker proposed killing all the cats on the continent with a fatal virus. The Royal Society for the Prevention of Cruelty to Animals and the Cat Protection Society called the proposal outrageous and laughable. It's unlikely to happen, but cats reproduce rapidly and should be neutered so these kinds of problems don't arise.

In nature, members of the cat family are the greatest hunters. Domestic cats are carnivorous because of a genetic inability to synthesize at least three biochemical compounds necessary for their health. To supply these nutrients, cats must eat meat or fish. They hunt because their genes say they must. This is fortunate for us because it makes domesticated cats the most useful of animals as well as wonderful pets. Anyone who has ever had pet cats (and doesn't have asthma from them) always craves their cozy company.

CATS (WILD)

Many species of cats, large and small, exist around the world, and some of them are just hanging on the threatened precipice of extinction. Certain wild cats are tolerated, some are hunted, others are protected. All deserve our cautious respect.

Hunting by predatory cats reduces the populations of herbivores. In Africa, for instance, lions, leopards, and cheetahs hunt wildebeests, zebras, giraffes, and gazelles. Without these carnivorous hunters, populations of herbivores would expand exponentially, overwhelm their food supply, and eventually starve to death. Although this kind of "animal population control" is acceptable to animal humane societies because it is "natural," it certainly is neither gentle nor humane.

Most large cats of prey such as lions, leopards, and tigers are protected on game preserves because otherwise villagers in underdeveloped countries would kill them out of fear or for money from poaching. But protection of cat habitats and preserves has to be cost effective for the natives, which means infusions of money from people in the West who care about preserving these fascinating animals.

Some natives believe that once a large cat develops a taste for human flesh, man becomes the preferred prey, so once an animal kills, that animal has to be hunted down and destroyed. In India, there still are instances of humans killed by tigers in some rural regions. Certain international groups are very concerned about tigers' shrinking habitat and possible extinction, although the frightened local families feel otherwise. However, money is usually the balm that soothes.

Large Wild Cat Problems in the United States

There are many large wild cats in the United States, variously called bobcats, pumas, panthers, cougars, and mountain lions depending on their size and where they are.

The number of large wild cats depends on two factors: the numbers of available prey and the amount of protection humans provide. Game preserves are a solution. They must be large enough to provide ample food as well as the necessary genetic diversity to sustain the species. However, the population numbers should be determined and controlled by wildlife biologists who can also keep them from threatening inhabited areas.

The problem is that public attitudes restrict the best judgements of wildlife management experts, particularly when it comes to population control strategies. So as the numbers of edible wildlife—particularly deer—expand, wild cat populations are expanding too. In parts of the West, mountain lions are relentless in following their favorite food, the deer, down from the hills into towns, suburbs, and sometimes even cities. Unfortunately, it puts pets and children, and even gardeners who are bending over at risk.

In the United States and Canada, in the century between 1890 to 1991, there were ten deaths from 53 recorded lion attacks. Half of the attacks were in the first 80 years, and half in the twenty years from 1970 to 1991. From 1991 to 1997 there were five more fatalities.

In 1997, a ten-year-old boy was attacked and killed by a mountain lion in Colorado's Mountain National Park. Hiking a bit in front of his parents, they came upon him with his head in the animal's jaws. Two other people had been attacked in that park in the two previous years. Colorado's other fatality was a jogger near Idaho Springs.

Part of the problem stems from the explosion of the lions' food supply, namely elk and deer. In 1906 there were an estimated 2,000 elk and 7,000 deer in Colorado. By 1997, the state had the largest elk population on the continent, 200,000 animals, plus 600,000 mule deer. In addition, the animals are protected, and since 1965 the $50 bounty on lions was eliminated.

California has had an increasing problem with mountain lions too. Although in the past they rarely attacked people, since 1986 there have been nine human injuries and two deaths. The injuries were mostly to children visiting parks, but two adult women were killed and partly consumed in 1994.

Between 1907 and 1963, when hunting of mountain lions was allowed in California, about 220 were killed each year. They feared man and kept their distance, eating mostly cattle and sheep. However, after 1972, one had to get a special permit to kill them, which was issued only if a particular animal was doing damage. Without the yearly hunting, cat populations grew quickly from about 2,400 in the 1970s to around 6,000 now. Problems grew as well. Permits for killing problem animals rose from 4 in 1972 to 322 in 1994.

The human killings raised public awareness and prompted the California Wildlife Agency to publish an excellent guide to these animals. It says that the best rule of thumb is to assume lions are around whenever there is a large deer population. The agency's safety tips are worth printing.

Summarized, they suggest that, "If one lives in mountain lion country (about half the state) one should:

1. Not feed wildlife
2. Deer-proof the landscape
3. Install outdoor lighting
4. Keep pets and livestock secure
5. Keep children safe"

Their "If You Encounter a Mountain Lion" is information worth knowing if one goes hiking or camping into lion country. It reads, "The following suggestions are based on studies of mountain behavior and analysis of attacks by mountain lions, tigers and leopards:

1. *Do not hike alone.* Go in groups with adults supervising children.
2. *Keep children close to you.* Observations of captured mountain lions reveal that the animals seem especially drawn to children. Keep children within your sight at all times.
3. *Do not approach a lion.* Most lions will try to avoid a confrontation. Give them a way to escape.
4. *Do not run from a lion.* Running may stimulate a mountain lion's instinct to chase. Instead stand and face the animal. Make eye contact. If you have small children with you, pick them up if possible so that they do not panic and run. Although it may be awkward, pick them up without bending over or turning away from the lion.
5. *Do not crouch or bend over.* A person squatting or bending over looks a lot like a four-legged prey animal.
6. *Do all you can to appear larger.* Raise your arms. Open your jacket if you are wearing one. Throw stones, branches

or whatever you can reach without crouching or turning your back. Wave your arms slowly and speak firmly in a loud voice.

7. *Fight back if attacked.* Some hikers have fought back successfully with sticks, caps, jackets, garden tools and their bare hands. Since a mountain lion usually tries to bite the head or neck, try to remain standing and face the animal."

According to the California Wildlife Agency, "It has been estimated that removal of 25–50 percent of the lions' population would be necessary to sufficiently reduce competition for food among lions in order to reduce the potential for threats to public safety and lower the probability of attacks."

One of the recent human victims was a jogger, whose running may have precipitated the attack. The other woman was walking her dog. California voters recently defeated a referendum that would have allowed preemptive killing of problem lions.

Cougars are a problem in many parts of the West as well. Though officially absent in the eastern United States for over half a century, there have been reports of sightings in Vermont and Maine. Recently, in

> A newspaper in Massachusetts reported as newsworthy that a wild bobcat was hit by a car, received six months of free medical care in a veterinary hospital, and was then released again into the wild.

Vancouver, Canada, a woman was mauled to death while riding horseback with three of her children. The cougar jumped on the six-year-old child's horse and pulled the child to the ground. The mother freed the child and told her two other children to get the injured child, with severe head and back puncture wounds, to safety. When they returned with help, their mother was dying.

In Yosemite National Park, a $232,000 study has been funded by the nonprofit Yosemite Fund because mountain lions have been exhibiting behavior that isn't normal, such as going into campgrounds and walking around the parking lot in broad daylight. Since they have been protected from sport hunting, their population has risen and the worry is they may have lost their fear of humans as well.

CHIPMUNKS

These adorable little creatures skip and skitter across the garden and the landscape to give it life and charm. As long as that's all they do, they are to be cherished. However, sometimes their population gets so large that they eat the tender flowers and sprouting bulbs usually in spring, and their days become numbered. Sadly so.

How to Recognize Chipmunk Damage

Unless you actually see a chipmunk in the act of eating a plant, it is not a problem animal. Their usual food is seeds, grains, nuts, and berries, which they store in their burrows for winter sustenance. Mainly you'll see them under the bird feeder eating spilled seed, or chewing fruit that has fallen on the ground. However, they eat soft green shoots and leaves, plus they dig holes all over the place looking for food or eating roots and tubers. This is most infuriating, because it not only ruins valuable plants, but also the appearance of the garden. Most plant damage is actually done by squirrels and voles, even though chipmunks may be poking around in the same places.

Scientific Information

This pert little creature has bright brown fur with a central dark stripe on its back bordered by two white stripes. Additional white stripes are on its cheeks. Its shrill call brings answering responses from other chipmunks in open fields and sunlit woods. Chipmunks are really ground-dwelling squirrels. Their nests are underground or in stone walls or fallen logs. A long entrance tunnel connects a number of chambers, some for storing food,

others for sleeping. Several families will share one burrow. There are usually two breeding seasons, spring and summer, when four or five young are born. They are able to care for themselves at about three months of age.

Diseases

Chipmunks normally aren't a health threat, although they have fleas, which can carry diseases.

Control Methods

You can exclude chipmunks from buildings by closing up their holes and entrances, though they can squeeze through tiny openings.

Trapping

To trap these creatures, watch where they run. They follow regular trails in search of food. You may think you have only one because they all look the same, but usually there are several, even a dozen or more. They are so small that they can squeeze through the holes in the wire mesh in squirrel traps; so chipmunk traps with smaller wire must be used instead. Indoors, rat traps may be used, but outdoors birds might be caught in them.

Bait

Seeds will attract chipmunks, as will peanut butter, oats, bacon, and apple slices.

Poisons ☠

Poisons should not be used for chipmunks. Because they carry food back to their nests, the poisons could appear anywhere and become a hazard to desirable birds, animals, even children.

The Bottom Line

Chipmunks should be cherished in the garden, enjoyed, and trapped only if they are truly a problem.

COYOTES AND FOXES

Foxes First

Throughout history, proverbs and myths portray foxes as wise and wily. One Chinese saying goes, "The woodchuck knows many small things, but the fox knows one big thing." However who knows what this inscrutable proverb means. In reality, foxes are just good hunters. Their main food is small mammals, especially mice, also birds, grasses, and summer insects. They stalk smaller animals with great skill and patience, usually ending with a sudden, lightning-quick pounce. While they rarely attack larger animals, they will wait patiently to scavenge leftover kill from wolves or coyotes. They also feed on carrion.

As quarry, foxes are evasive. When chased, they outwit horses, hunters, and hounds with maneuvers that would make an army general proud. Foxes have been known to retrace their steps, then take off at a right angle to confuse the dogs. They will travel across or up streams for the same reason. Also across the tops of stone walls. While being pursued, they hide in all kinds of unlikely places. One story claims a refrigerator sheltered a fox during a hunt, while another found refuge in church during the Sunday service, jumping into the arms of a praying parishioner. Seldom seen, these shy hunters rarely cause problems for humans except for their occasional forays into henhouses and an occasional mass.

How to Tell If You Have Foxes

Usually one sees them or their footprints in the snow. Sometimes you may catch their distinctive, strong scent. Fox scent can be purchased. Its main use is to drag over a course for hunters on horseback, so they don't have to chase a real animal. Fox scent is reputed to repel small animals like rabbits and such. While it may work, it usually does not. The scent dissipates in a short time and it does rather repel people.

Scientific Information

The name fox is applied to several species of small carnivorous mammals, all of the dog family, though it usually refers to the midwestern gray fox or the common red fox, a reddish brown animal the size of a slim dog with a white-tipped bushy tail. Foxes are charming animals to watch. Their usual walk is a mincing tiptoe with tail down, though sometimes up. When they are pursued, however, their gait becomes a graceful bounding and leaping. Foxes can run up to forty-five miles an hour but can't keep up that pace for more than a mile.

Their preferred habitat is brushy fields and hedgerows, but they will happily inhabit woods, marshes, and urban areas as well. They breed in winter. In spring, one to ten helpless babies are born; by midsummer they will be ready to be taught hunting. Foxes are lone hunters and go

out several times a day for small game, mainly mice and rabbits (for which gardeners should be grateful). They have very sharp ears, eyes, and scent, which probably accounts for their supposed wisdom. Man is their only predator, and they've become very adept at avoiding detection, traps, and capture.

Diseases

Rabies is the main problem. Use careful preventative measures when handling foxes or their traps, or when touching any of their bodily fluids. If a dead animal is found, assume it may be diseased. In Europe rabies vaccine has been used widely and successfully to control the disease in local wild fox populations. See "Animal Diseases (Zoonoses)" and "Raccoons" for more on rabies.

Control Methods

Except for fencing the henhouse, locking the garbage, and watching small pets, foxes should just be enjoyed. There aren't that many around.

Coyotes

Called the singing dog of the prairies, after sundown the coyote finds a knoll and serenades in the still night air. A whole gamut of cries (yaps, barks, whines, howling) is a regular ritual evening performance. Sometimes, it's a little off-putting to hear the call of the wild so close to the backyard.

The flip side for gardeners is that these predators help keep the populations of rabbits, rats, mice, woodchucks, raccoons, and opossums under control. These are the animals that cause the most grief for gardeners. So when you hear the coyotes howl at the moon, be glad, it may be they've just eaten the woodchuck that ate all your beans yesterday. Coyotes are the gardener's friend!

Coyote populations are on the comeback trail today, after being heavily hunted for killing farm animals. The secret of why this predator has made a comeback is that it has learned to live with man as the wolf never could. But even though coyotes are around, they keep so low a profile that you don't see them often. They're well reestablished in the wild now. In addition, they've naturalized in many suburbs, even heavily populated ones in New York, New Jersey, and Massachusetts. They exist downtown in core cities as well, having been seen in the Bronx, the ultimate urban wildlife challenge.

Coyotes' fast spread into suburbia is

surely due to the favorable habitat, coupled with their extreme adaptability. They eke out a living by eating a wide variety of foods and can survive in habitats from the deep forest to the backyard. For the moment, because of their stealthy ways and low population, coyotes are not a problem in the garden but help us get rid of many other animals that do cause problems.

Currently, there is a debate in New York State about whether to reintroduce the timber wolf into the Adirondack Mountains. Locals claim they already have their "brush wolf," which is the coyote. A coyote can kill a large deer, and coyote packs prey on deer herds and beaver in the woods. The locals fear that if the timber wolf is introduced, there won't be enough food supply in the forest for both these "wolves" so one or both will venture out of the forest looking for food, and come into direct conflict with humans.

How to Tell If You Have Coyotes

You may hear coyotes or you may see them, or the garbage can may be overturned. They are elusive, slinking nocturnal predators, most often seen at dawn or dusk. Coyotes are not dangerous, except when they are threatened and have to defend themselves and their young, or when they aren't afraid of people. They should not be befriended because your friendship may become their death warrant.

Scientific Information

Coyotes' range is from Alaska to Costa Rica. They are larger than a dog, but smaller than a wolf, with considerable local variation in size and color. They eat just about anything: carrion, insects, berries, apples, rabbits, mice, voles, wood-chucks, and deer. White-tailed deer are the mainstay of the coyote food base in the Adirondacks forest because there is not much variety in the forest; but when other, easier food is available, they take it.

The eastern coyote, or "brush wolf," started appearing about the middle of the twentieth century in the eastern United States. Larger and thicker coated than its midwestern relative (the "prairie wolf" coyote), the eastern coyote has carved out a permanent place for itself in the environment. According to a wildlife biologist in Vermont, it has become the largest predator to walk the hills of Vermont since the timber wolf.

Woods, fields and pastures, deep forest habitats, suburbs, and cities are where coyotes easily naturalize. In the wild they use an area of between four and thirty square miles, but probably less where there is garbage and an overpopulation of small animals.

Coyotes mate for life, breed in February, and give birth in the spring to anywhere from two to twelve pups. They keep one of the pups from the previous year as a baby-sitter, to help with the new little ones. (Better than an English nanny.) The family stays together through the summer, when all the offspring are driven off, except for the one chosen to baby-sit the next year. Their life span is about a dozen years.

Diseases

Coyotes carry rabies. If you find a dead one, carry out careful preventative measures if handling the carcass, the trap, or touching any of the bodily fluids. (See the chapter on animal diseases and the raccoon chapter for more on rabies.)

Control Methods

Exclusion

Garbage is the main attractant, so secure it in cans or sheds or keep it inside. Organic fertilizers with fish and meat scents as well as bone meal should be stored inside too. If organic fertilizers are used, they should be well buried underground, not just tilled in; otherwise use chemical fertilizer. As with all predatory animals, fences are a wise precaution where there are tempting chickens, kittens, or small dogs. Needless to say, children and babies should *always* be well watched and protected. Although coyotes and foxes rarely attack children, they can carry rabies, so one should always be wary.

One problem is interbreeding with domestic dogs, which produces a half-wild animal, not suited to be a house pet. The state wildlife service should be informed if you think your dog has mated with a coyote. (See "Diseases and Interbreeding" in the chapter on wolves.) Better yet, play responsible parent to your dog in heat, and keep it indoors, and just hope the coyotes don't howl at the moon on your doorstep.

Coyote populations are rising because they have wildlife protection plus hospitable habitats in cities and suburbs. Fear of humans has always made them shy, but they may act differently as they become urban animals.

Hunting and Trapping

Coyotes are furbearing wild animals, subject to hunting and trapping laws. However, in Vermont, California, Texas, and many other states, hunting of coyotes has been allowed year round. (Check the laws with your local state wildlife service.) Trapping is often more regulated than hunting and is not a job for amateurs. If you have trouble with coyotes, call your state wildlife service or a professional trapper to rid you of the animals.

DEER

Bambi, please go home. Go home to your sweet doe-eyed mother. Go home to some happy forest. Go home to Disneyland. But stay out of my backyard. This plea can be heard across the landscape in thundered bellows and whispered whimpers in any place where the forest edge meets open grassland. It may be a rural forest where farmers' fields nudge forest remnants. Or it may be where country homes have sprung up on abandoned farms. Or in suburbia, to which city folks have fled to raise their children among trees and lawns and nature. Or it may be in the inner city itself, for deer can easily naturalize in any park, preserve, or urban forest where food, shelter, and protection are available. They will multiply quickly in any small protected area.

In the wild, deer live in natural clearings in the deep forest, eating everything that grows in the sun: trees, shrubs, flowers, and grasses. Deer populations have exploded recently because of the abandonment of farms, for as fields revert to brush, they provide new rich habitats. Suburbs too are ideal deer habitats. Coupled with prohibitions on hunting in populated areas and a dearth of animal predators, deer reproduction rates are currently unrestrained. And as the herds expand, they venture far afield to feed the yearly broods of adorable Bambis.

Much is written blaming humans for the problems deer cause. The rationale is that expanding suburban development is invading their haunts, and they were there first. In some places, including parts of California, this may be true. But in general, providing increased protected habitat increases the number of deer because animal populations are habitat driven. In fact there are probably now more deer in Massachusetts than there were when the Pilgrims first landed. By the turn of the century, in 1900, when Massachusetts was a farm state, there were only a few deer in the western mountain forests. By 1995, they were everywhere, 70,000 of them, eating everything and spreading Lyme disease to boot.

It's the same all over the United States. In Michigan and North Carolina, California and Oregon, the deer are eating well. Gardeners who want to grow flowers or vegetables must fence, electrify, repel, or shoot. Or grow only poisonous plants. So if you see a sweet, lovely deer in your yard (most likely at dawn or dusk), enjoy its grace, its beauty, its shy seductive eyes . . . and look to your bushes.

How to Recognize Deer Damage

The best times to see deer are at dawn and dusk. In winter, when they're most hungry, deer browse whatever they can find. Spring and summer, they're a problem in tender crops and flowers. In fall, ripening apples tempt them. Deer have no front teeth but strip bark by raking their lower incisors upward, making two-inch gouges. When they eat foliage, they tear it off, leaving ragged edges, while rabbit and rodent browsing leaves a clean-cut edge. Also, they eat the lower parts of trees, up to the height they can reach standing on their hind legs, usually between six and ten feet.

Scientific Information

The volume of literature on deer ecology and management exceeds that for any other wildlife species. Deer have been hunted for food since recorded history. In Europe, royalty owned the forests and protected deer for their own hunting pleasure. Lately, however, when Prince William, heir to the throne of England, killed his first stag at age 14, animal rightists had a heyday in the press and branded it a throwback to the nineteenth century.

In the United States deer hunting is a very popular sport. It generates revenues of hundred of millions of dollars when one counts hunters' expenditures for equipment, food, lodging, transportation, and license fees. On the other hand, deer cause enormous crop damage, calculated in 1982 to be $15 million to $30 million, especially to orchards and farms.

Actually deer are the most dangerous wild animal in the United States, causing more death and maiming than any other. How? Auto accidents. The yearly cost of deer-vehicle collision damage in North America was estimated in 1982 at more than $100 million. No one seems to know the number of people killed in accidents with deer, although the insurance industry ought to.

In 1996 in Michigan alone, there were 68,000 auto crashes involving deer, and 6 human fatalities. In one very small Connecticut town, the police keep a "deer kill list" of about three dozen people who will immediately pick up road-killed edible deer for venison. Between 1988 and 1994, 130 deer were run over there. In Kentucky auto insurance may not cover deer damage. In New Hampshire, if the car goes off the road without hitting the deer, the driver gets bad driving points. If the car grazed the deer, the driver doesn't get any points, so it's cheaper to hit the deer.

The main deer species in the United States are the white-tailed deer and the mule deer. The mule deer is the more sociable, friendly animal with large ears which account for its name. Bambi doesn't actually look like either because his face proportions were modified to give him beguiling face appeal. Mother, too, with her long, seductive eyelashes.

Adult deer may weigh between fifty and four hundred pounds, southern ones generally being smaller. Males grow antlers from April to August, breed October through January depending on latitude, then shed their antlers one at a time in winter. One or two spotted fawns are born in May or June. After three or four months, they lose their spots, and when less than a year are forced out by their mother to forage for themselves.

Herds may be small or large, consisting of females, babies, and young males. Mature males form bachelor herds. An assertive deer will flatten its ears against its neck, lower its head, and stare at, or even step on, a subordinate. When a deer senses danger, it raises its white tail like a banner, which is a signal to bound off, at speeds of up to twenty-five miles an hour.

Deer have unpredictable feeding habits. Each animal prefers certain plants and will pass up other perfectly good foliage for what it likes. However, when food is scarce, they will eat anything, even poisonous plants. Each state has a list of deer-resistant plants, mostly based on local observation, not scientific controlled testing. Few of these lists agree with one another. (See the chapter on poisonous plants.)

Diseases

As the population of deer has ballooned, so has the prevalence of Lyme disease. Currently reported in forty-three states, it is now a serious public health problem. Lyme disease was first described in 1975 in the sailing port of Lyme, Connecticut. However, arthritic "potato knees" had been known for quite a while among potato farmers in Patchogue, Long Island, just across Long Island Sound from Lyme. In 1996, a survey by the deer management committee of the town of North Haven, Long Island, found that more than half of the residents carried antibodies to Lyme disease. If untreated very early, and with enough of the correct antibiotics, Lyme disease can become a long-term, debilitating, chronic illness that includes brain memory impairment, pain, and numbness in hands and feet, or arthritis, particularly affecting the knees.

The primary vector, an infectious tick, is spread by the deer tick. In some areas, particularly parts of the Atlantic shoreline and islands of the East Coast, almost all the ticks may be infected, and a high percentage of the population carries antibod-

ies to the disease. Recently it has been shown that the ticks also carry several other, much more serious diseases, including babesiosis and ehrlichiosis, which require stronger antibiotics. These diseases are hard to treat, so prevention is better. A preventive vaccine should become available soon. Not only are hikers and golfers at risk, but lawns and backyards have ticks as well. *So take precautions.* (See the chapter on animal diseases for more complete information.)

To Reduce Ticks on Backyard Lawns

Apply an insecticide to the grass in May or early June. Currently recommended pesticides are chloropyrifos or carbaryl (Sevin). The rate for carbaryl is two pounds of active ingredient per acre. Less toxic insecticides are resmethrin or permethrin, which are sometimes sprayed on lawns and shrubs, but are shorter acting and have to be applied more frequently. Another product, Damminix, has promise. It goes after the intermediate winter vector, the shy white-footed mouse, in whose nests the ticks overwinter. Damminix consists of cardboard tubes filled with cotton balls impregnated with the insecticide permethrin. The mice take the balls to line their nests, and sleep on the insecticide. It doesn't harm the mice but kills the ticks. The tubes are placed approximately ten yards apart around the perimeter of the yard. To catch the tick in both its larval and nymphal stages, the tubes have to be put out twice a year, in April or May and again in late August. While not cheap, they are preferable to putting insecticide on lawns where children play and dogs run.

Control Methods

Most people who have real-life deer problems will say, confidentially, that the only things that work are a tall, good fence or a 30-06 rifle. Otherwise be prepared to weep a little; few folks win many battles with deer. A good barking dog, man's best friend, can be very helpful. Deer will normally shun a large dog. Particularly when backed up by some loud noises that sound like shotguns.

Exclusion

Fences

Deer can leap tall fences if they're hungry enough. Although deer can go over fences, they prefer to walk through them, which is why the fences have to be sturdy or electrified. According to an English book of old farmers' wisdom, a nine-foot masonry wall is the only sure way to keep deer out of a garden. Today, there are many options. Chain-link or very sturdy wooden fences may be used instead. (Sometimes the males will rub their antlers on wooden fences.) Or consider using eight-foot heavy-duty plastic construction fence and snake it among trees. Add fluorescent bows and ties to keep the deer from running into it at night and knocking it down. Attach the fence from house corner to house corner.

Electrical Fences

For deer, electric fencing works second best to a gun, but deer have to touch the wire with their noses or tongues to get enough of a shock to deter them and train them to avoid the fence. The electric shock delivered by a fence with a proper transformer is not harmful, just unpleasant. To keep out deer as well as baby rabbits, large raccoons, and devastating woodchucks, at least three wires are needed, preferably four or five. The lowest is set about three inches from the ground, the next about eight inches from the ground, and the top one about five or six feet for the deer. The wire is mounted on plastic stakes with special hooks to carry it without grounding it. Household electric current may be used with a transformer and a ground fault switch to prevent electric shock. Alternatively, a car or storage battery may be used, although these batteries are expensive and, if outdoors, should be in a waterproof housing.

The main problem with electric fences is they need constant maintenance. If anything touches the wire, such as a plant, it grounds the current, which shorts out. Therefore the area under the wires has to be kept free of all vegetation. Herbicides are the usual way to keep grass and weeds from growing into the wire. However, most home garden and lawn herbicides don't usually last long enough. Also, they can be quite toxic ☠ if used repeatedly in the large amounts needed to keep the fence wires clear. Longer-lasting commercial chemical herbicides may be applied by a licensed pesticide applicator or landscaper. Other long-acting herbicides are motor oil, borax, a thick band of swimming pool filter residue, or a heavy application of coarse salt. These poison the soil so nothing will grow, which is what one wants under wires.

The Best Fence Idea of the Moment

Current recommendations are for a fence five feet high or taller, with an electric wire at the top. The deer are then conditioned to be afraid of the fence by spreading peanut butter or bacon or some other good-tasting thing on the top wire. When they go to eat it, they get a jolt. After a few such shocks, the deer should be wary and stay away.

There is a promising new electric fence now being tested, which is powered by solar energy and uses a braided inch-wide yellow wire ribbon. It may eliminate the battery, the transformer, and fussy precision needed to string the stiff old-fashioned wire.

Other Fences

Because deer can leap quite high, fences typically have to be tall, at least eight feet, and sturdy. For serious designs and construction details for deer fences, contact your state agricultural department. For information on older kinds of deer fences (slanted fence, hog wire fence, electrified fence, "New Hampshire" three-wire fence, "Minnesota" deer fence, "New Zealand" fence, "Penn State" five-wire fence), try to get a University of Nebraska bulletin called *DEER* by Scott Craven, published by the Great Plains Agricultural Council, Wildlife Resources Committee in 1983. It's a classic. Perhaps your local wildlife service can find it.

A slanted fence is one of sturdy wire mesh, built at a 45° angle, that slants away from the area to be protected. It has an overhang that may deter the deer, especially when accompanied by electric wire. The posts have to be at least 6' off the ground and there has to be an overhang.

The deer will walk under the overhang and be unable to jump because of the wire and roof above them. Plant growth has to be kept cut low under the overhang or the deer may not walk under it. (See section on fences in "Understanding Control Methods," Part II.)

Cattle Guards and Hog Wire Deer Fences

Most animals that depend on running fast to escape predators are very much afraid of catching their feet in holes and hurting themselves. They instinctively know that a broken or useless foot means death. Cattle guards and hog wire deer barrier fences have holes that animal feet can become caught in when they step on them. Thus if afraid, they won't cross the barrier.

Cattle grates are put in roads and driveways to keep animals from walking out roadways between fences. Basically, they consist of a heavy metal grating that goes across the road width with spaces large enough for an animal to catch a hoof, but

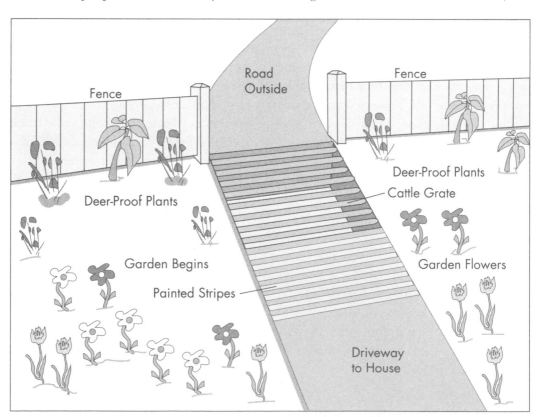

Fence

Road Outside

Fence

Deer-Proof Plants

Deer-Proof Plants

Cattle Grate

Garden Begins

Garden Flowers

Painted Stripes

Driveway to House

EXPERIMENTAL USE OF CATTLE GUARD AND STRIPES PAINTED ON DRIVE

for cars to go over easily. The grates are mounted over a pit (a hole dug in the ground), so if the animals put their feet in a hole there's no bottom. Most cattle grates come in four-foot widths, which is just a hop and a skip for the fleet-footed deer to jump over. However, deer don't see that well, so if white stripes are painted on the road beyond for another ten feet or so, the deer may think the dangerous holes go that far and won't attempt to leap over the grate. As with every deer control method, it may help only until they figure it out.

An untested but interesting idea is a hog wire surface fence. Hog wire fencing (which has about four-inch holes) is mounted horizontally six inches above the ground, for a distance of about ten feet. Then deer-resistant plants (such as vinca, ceanothus, grevillea, corea) are put beneath it. The plants grow to hide the wire, but when the deer try to cross, their feet get stuck in the holes. So they may be afraid to cross again after they free themselves. The advantage of a hog wire surface fence is that one doesn't have to look at the scenery through a tall, electrified, deer-resistant fence. It may be worth a try.

Screened Porches

Sometimes one can grow choice plants in porches with dirt floors and with gardens inside. Paint outside with fluorescent markers to keep deer from tearing through the screens, and perhaps spray the screens with a repellent such as Deer-Away.

Berry Cages

For deer, these must be stronger than for birds, and must have markings for evening. Strong frames are essential. It's not necessary to buy expensive lumber for framing. Cut saplings may be used as building timbers the way they are in underdeveloped countries. However, chicken wire may not stop deer for long.

Row Covers

Another possibility is woven translucent row covers to protect young plants. Deer don't like to get their feet caught in the fabric. This is useful for trying to temporarily protect a vegetable crop.

Tree Protectors—Translucent Plastic Tubes

Several products are on the market, among them Tree-Pro and Tree Protectors, which allow young trees to get a start. They come in heights from two to five feet and are put over the young plant. A stake is placed inside to stabilize the tube. When the tree grows out the top, and the trunk gets thick, the tubes must be cut off, unless they're slit vertically at planting time. There is also a "Supertube Clipper"

eighteen to thirty-four inches tall, originally developed for grape vines, that
comes slit, so plants can be pruned inside
without destroying the tube. The translucent plastic protects the young plants, acts
like a minigreenhouse, and increases the
growth rate. Plants grown in tubes need
less water than plants grown in the open
sun and wind. The tubes also protect
against rabbit damage and mice chewing
the bark in winter. The tubes change
growth habits and some species do better
than others. Experimentation is ongoing.
(For more information, see the chapter on
control methods.)

Repellents

There are two kinds of repellents. Some
are very bitter substances that make foliage
unpalatable. Others produce a smell the
deer can't tolerate. Repellents have to be
reapplied whenever grazing is noticed
again. With many products, this will be after each rainfall. Thus, repellents are a per-
petual battle, in which the plan must be
constantly modified to reintroduce the element of surprise. The smarter the deer, the
shorter the time each repellent works.
Also, the more urban deer are, and the
more used to humans, the less repellents
work. Much testing has been done, but the
bottom line is that some work for a while;
some work in one place but not another.
None of them work most of the time.

Deer, like elephants, have very sensitive smell and taste receptors. They don't
like strong scents or peppery, bitter tastes.
They also generally won't eat strong poisons; however, when they're hungry they
commonly eat poisonous plants like
rhododendron and yew. They think like
elephants—it's better to be sick than dead.

In trials at the Bartlett Tree Research
Laboratory, the two most effective repellents have foul odors, and the third repels
by its bitter taste:

- *Deer-Away*, which is made of putrefied
  egg white solids and can't be used on
  food crops.
- *Hinder*, an ammonium soap that can be
  used directly on food crops. In the trials, Hinder offered less than 50 percent
  protection. (For more on test results,
  see the chapter on control methods.)
- *Thiram*, a very bitter-tasting fungicide.
  Several commercial products contain
  this substance. One is called Ro-pel,
  another Bonide. Thiram is normally
  used on dormant plants during winter,
  because it can harm some foliage; so
  test it first on valuable plants. It should
  not be eaten or used on food crops.

Three other repellents that may work
for a while on some deer are:

- *Plain old Soap*. Irish Spring and Lifeboy
  soap are reputed to keep deer away from
  some special plants. A New Hampshire

orchardist reported that Dial, Safeguard, and Ivory all worked equally well. A tree farmer in Connecticut reported that Ivory worked better and suggested leaving the paper on each bar, drilling a hole, and hanging it up. Soap bars can be hung from branches like Christmas tree ornaments, or impaled on stakes about three feet high, fifteen to twenty feet apart. Small hotel-size bars are cheaper and can be bought in bulk. Researchers report that while soap works in some places, sometimes it doesn't. But it's inexpensive, safe, and easily available. The more urbanized deer are, the less the soap repels them. And in some cases, other animals, particularly squirrels, crows, and even deer, have actually eaten the soap.

• *Bitter Substances.* Hot sauces and pepper sauces are another repellent, but they wash off after a rain and are expensive. There have been instances of deer getting used to them and ignoring them, though perhaps the residues didn't have a high enough concentration of capsicum, the hot chemical in hot peppers. Combining them with a substance like Wilt-Pruf dries to a water-resistant coating that will last longer.

• *Predator Urine.* A new idea that, according to the manufacturer, is selling like hotcakes, is predator urine. It is just what the name implies, not refined or modified. Bartlett Tree Laboratory began testing it, and found that deer eating a row of sweet potatoes, bypassed part of the block when it was sprayed with bobcat and coyote urine. Long used by hunters and trappers, urine may prove to be another useful weapon, but there are surprising complications. It attracts lots of other animals. (For a discussion of the use of predator urine, see the chapter on control methods.)

Hunting

Baron von Clausewitz says of the use of force: "Kind-hearted people might think there was some ingenious way to disarm or defeat an enemy without too much bloodshed. Pleasant as it sounds, it is a fallacy that must be exposed."

This statement applies to hunting, which has always been the main population control for deer. While large animal predators take some animals, the most important predator has always been man.

Since prehistoric times, herbivores such as deer have been a main source of food for man. The Indians hunted deer. So many that they even practiced habitat manipulation (by burning the oak forests) to increase the number of deer. In Maine, they would wait for deep snow to hunt deer and moose, often having to travel twenty, thirty, even forty miles to find enough prey to carry them through the winter.

Hunting is allowed in most states. It serves to cull the herds to a population level that can be supported by an area's vegetation. Each state wildlife agency issues licenses as to how many deer may be taken, at what season, and with what weapons.

White-tailed deer is one of the most sought-after big game animals in the United States. Many people cherish the sport of hunting. Fall and early winter are the usual hunting seasons so that the deer population will be thinned before winter, when the food supply is low, and when they do the most damage to orchards, tree farms, and backyards. If deer damage occurs outside the legal season, a permit to hunt on one's own property may be requested from the appropriate state agency.

Animal rights groups rail at hunters. However, it is not humane to protest shooting deer but then let them suffer and slowly die from starvation and disease, which inevitably follows the overpopulation of a habitat. Nor is it humane to allow them to be torn limb from limb by wild animal predators, often while still alive.

Other Methods

Repetitive Loud Noise

A loud commercial propane exploder, set to detonate at timed intervals, can be tried. The device must be moved every few days so the deer do not become habituated to it. The firing sequence should be changed often as well. It's important to start as soon as deer feeding begins, because once they get into the habit of eating at your place, the habit won't be easily broken. The success of this method, according to agricultural reports, ranges from good to poor. Where shooting is allowed, shellcrackers (firecrackers) can be put in twelve-gauge shotguns, which explode in the air with a loud noise. This is quick but temporary.

Many companies market small electronic devices that make frequent beeping or piercing sounds reputed to repel many animals. Some are sonic, some supersonic. The noise is often annoying to humans, and though it's not supposed to pass solid walls, it does. These devices are usually powered by household current or automobile batteries, which are supposed to last two to three months. Some are available with motion detectors to save the batteries and, one hopes, the peace of mind of humans within hearing distance. When

OLD WIVES' TALES AND FOLKLORE SUGGESTIONS

Since almost everyone is inundated with deer, almost everyone has a trick they swear will work. These range from the somewhat sensible to the sublime. Among them are:

- Bone tar (trade name—Magic Circle) can be used as a perimeter exclusion spray, although it's easier to drape a saturated cord around the area to be protected. It's not for crops or valuable plants and does not weather well.
- The scent of compost fertilizer made from human sewerage sludge may deter them. (One trade name is Milogranite.) Disney World in Florida tried using sludge compost on some experimental rose beds in its nursery. While the fertilizer did repel the deer, the roses didn't bloom well because of the high nitrogen content.
- Tankage from a slaughterhouse may be hung in cans, or feathermeal from chickens can be tried. But not near the house, for they smell powerfully bad. They may also attract carnivores.
- Stuff nylon stockings with human hair and hang among the plants. Theoretically, the scent will repel them (which assumes they've never been out of the woods before). The smell washes out in the rain.
- Fill quart jars with water and put them at the corners of the garden. Supposedly, the deer will see their reflection and be scared away.
- Dog scent, hair, or urine will make them think twice, but probably not without barking and chasing, to make dogs seem a real possibility. The scent washes out easily in the rain.
- Lion and tiger manure has often been recommended because of the scent of the predator. However, the manure of carnivores consists of large chunks of semidigested red meat, which will attract every scavenger for miles around. Dogs, cats, skunks, rats, raccoons—who knows what.
- Another suggestion from a popular book is creosote-soaked rags on sticks. It's a possible last resort, but it is mildly hazardous. ☠ Dip the rags frequently to renew the smell.
- Lavender has been recommended, and a hedge of it would be nice. The scent alone is unlikely to deter deer; however, they may not eat it.

pressed, one company said that half of the deer will be frightened or annoyed away, while half won't. The more urbanized the deer, and the more used to humans, the less likely they are to be scared off. Most wildlife experts rate these devices from poor to useless.

Birth Control and Relocation

If the natural fecundity of deer could be controlled, the passionate pleadings of Bambi lovers who anthropomorphize could probably be accommodated, at least in urban areas and parks. Unfortunately, to date it hasn't been successful enough or cost effective.

The other option is relocation. However, in addition to the high cost of removal, the survival of relocated animals is very poor. In the 1970s there was a park on an island off the coast of California where the deer population had outgrown the habitat so badly that something had to be done. Shooting was proposed. Animal rights groups opposed the plan. Instead, the necessary number of animals were captured, collared, and removed elsewhere. At the end of one year, the population on the island had filled in to the same number. Then chemical birth control was tried, which didn't work at all, so it too was abandoned. Eventually the animal protection groups allowed shooting to control the population, as long as it was done quietly with no publicity.

In the 1990s, there was a park south of San Francisco. The protected deer population grew too large and ate all the vegetation. After a raging controversy, it was agreed that the park department would capture, collar, and move the animals to a ranch. There were twenty-eight animals, moved at a cost of $1,000 a head. The total expense was $28,000 plus another $10,000 to put beepers on the animals and monitor them at the ranch. Within six weeks, most were dead. The main cause of death was mountain lions, because the park animals didn't know how to elude capture, as did their wild brethren. It was like abandoning kittens in the woods. By six weeks, all the beepers were silent. Total cost $38,000. It could have been better spent another way.

Auto Accidents

One needs to drive with great caution in deer country. There is a device called Deer Alert which is mounted on the front bumper of cars and makes a whistle at speeds above 30 miles an hour. Unfortunately, according to auto accident experts, it doesn't appear to influence deer.

Using Plants That Deer Will Not Eat

Creatures of habit, deer are probably conditioned in infancy to prefer certain

In 1994, the National Park Service concluded that unchecked, the deer herds in the park near the presidential retreat, Camp David, would grow so large as to threaten the park's biodiversity. Pity. In 1997, the 6,000-acre park's herd of 600 deer was twice the optimal density. Shooting is not an option near Camp David.

plants. Because of this, the lists of deer-resistant plants rarely agree. Different deer eat different things. A farmer on the island of Martha's Vineyard said his deer ate the herbs but not flowers, while on an adjacent farm, the zinnias and marigolds were all decimated, but the herbs were left alone.

Deer prefer fertilized crops, probably because they are softer, greener, and higher in nitrogen, but they'll eat anything when they're hungry, especially in winter. The list of plants in the chapter on poisonous plants should be considered a suggested starting point for testing the appetites of your local deer.

Roses

Deer just *love* roses. However, deer can only reach about ten feet high if they stand on their hind legs. They do not climb. Climbing roses that are vigorous and grow tall can be trained against sunny walls and up to decks on a second floor.

The stems must be encased in strong permanent wire cages, especially while young. The plastic tree protector cylinders made for starting trees in deer-ridden forests might also work, particularly if two are used, one on top of the other to get the necessary height. When the plants reach ten feet, they can be fanned out for a good display.

The secret to success with climbing roses is to choose the most vigorous, long varieties. Then fertilize them each spring, always adding some extra superphosphate to the soil to make strong stems. Fertilize again in late spring, but not again after that. Summer fertilizing will prevent proper hardening off for winter cold. (In warm climates, roses need a rest period, usually fall, with bloom starting in January.)

Experiments have shown that ample water in times of summer drought will also enhance cold tolerance and hardiness. Mulch the ground well. Ideally, add something deer may not like to smell, such as Milorganite, or other treated sewerage sludge applied in very early spring. It may not help, but it can't hurt. Once the roses are tall and blooming, use regular bark mulch and rose fertilizer, for nitrogen-rich sludge is not properly balanced for best flowering.

All climbing roses bloom on second- or third-year wood, though some, called repeat bloomers, also flower on new first-year stems. When they have reached the necessary height, don't cut off the new soft shoots in midsummer, for they will bear the best flowers the following year. Instead, just shape them by tying them to a trellis or railing. If branches are trained horizontally, more apical flowering shoots will appear along the stems. Remove old side wood as it ages and stops blooming well, but save the trunk and scaffold of main branches.

The longest, most vigorous varieties are listed below, but they are not hardy everywhere. Ask your local agricultural station which are appropriate for your area.

CLIMBING BLAZE IMPROVED. The most popular climber, hardy, twelve to fourteen feet, deep red repeat bloom.

CLIMBING CECILE BRUNNER. Old favorite, cream-pink clusters in spring, eighteen feet.

CLIMBING DON JUAN. Fragrant, dark red, repeat bloom, twelve to fourteen feet.

CLIMBING HANDEL. Bicolor red and white, hardy, repeat bloom, twelve to fourteen feet.

CLIMBING NEW DAWN. Vigorous, hardy, fragrant, pale pink, repeat bloom, eighteen to twenty feet.

CLIMBING PEACE. Yellow/pink bicolor, big flowers, twelve to fourteen feet.

PAUL'S HIMALAYAN MUSK RAMBLER. A mid-nineteenth-century beautiful rose that can grow thirty feet long. Midsummer, fragrant, pink blooms. It can be trained to climb trees if planted far enough away from the tree roots, on the side facing the prevailing wind, where, with a little human help, the long canes can catch their thorns on the bark and grow up the trunk.

Deer populations are growing so fast near the nation's capital that in 1997, three wild deer wandering on the street during morning rush hour caught White House sentries off guard. They finally corralled the deer near the executive mansion.

GOPHERS AND MOLES

These two are the bane of many a gardener's life.

Gophers are voracious animals that drive folks crazy as they stealthily feed below the surface on tubers, roots and plants, killing them. Sometimes plants mysteriously disappear as gophers pull the greenery right down into their tunnels and eat them, leaving just a small hole. Their tunnels cause horrendous problems on lawns, golf courses, and to agricultural fields.

Moles are a tunneling terror, especially to those who love their lawns, raising the soil above their tunnels and killing the grass. While moles feed only on earthworms, grubs, and insects, their tunnels wreak havoc on lawns as well as other plants by destroying the roots with their underground digging. Where preva-lent, they are among the most troublesome of pests.

Scientific Information

The name gopher is applied to two types of rodents: the pocket gopher and certain ground squirrels. Pocket gophers are solitary animals, except for mating and for a few months in spring when the young stay with their mother. After that they begin to dig their own tunnels and cause their own mayhem. Gopher habits are similar to those of ground squirrels; but whereas pocket gophers are silent, the

HOW TO DIFFERENTIATE BETWEEN GOPHERS AND MOLES

Moles

- Eat worms, grubs, insects
- Sever grass roots and raise sod
- Tunnels are three to five inches wide
  Mole tunnels are fragile
- Moles are harder to catch
- Moles can smell a trap

Gophers

- Eat roots and plants
- Sever grass roots and raise sod
- Crescent-shaped mounds
  Gopher tunnels are hollow inside
- Gophers can be trapped
- Gophers exist mainly in the western United States

squirrels make noises from a squeak to a shrill whistle.

There are several species of moles, the most common being the eastern mole, which despite its name lives even in midwestern lawns. Moles usually grow to about seven inches, but the western mole can reach nine inches. Solitary in habit, moles live most of their lives in two-level dwellings, the upper one for feeding, the lower for nesting. The one yearly litter of three to five young, born in springtime, leaves the nest by summer or fall to dig their own tunnels or inhabit abandoned ones. Moles are thought to have a life span of about three years, and their population density is generally not more than three to five per acre.

Moles are small pointy-nosed creatures with small weak eyes, tiny ears, a strong odor, and surprisingly soft, smooth skin that has no nap. It used to be made into a soft, velvetlike, much-prized leather called moleskin. Voracious eaters, if deprived of food they can die in just twelve hours. Moist soft soil is their preferred habitat. They are good swimmers that can withstand flooded burrows, and are rarely found in hard, dry ground. Though moles don't eat vegetation, field mice will often make use of their tunnels to eat the roots of plants and grass.

Both these animals are eaten by snakes, foxes, coyotes, hawks, owls, dogs, and cats.

How to Tell If a Tunnel Is Active

Step on the tunnel, and flatten it halfway. If active, it will be pushed back up in a day or two. Or poke a half-inch hole at several places in a main runway. Moles will repair them in a few hours. If runs aren't repaired, they're not being used.

Control Methods

Trapping, poisoning, and gassing of burrows are the usual control methods.

Exclusion

Filling holes and tunnels with poison gas pellets has been recommended. Because the gas is dangerous, ☠, it is best to have a licensed professional do the job. Also, never use pellets where children may get to them. Poison gas may be effective. But if it were universally effective, gophers and moles wouldn't be the most troublesome of pests. One source said "gopher gas" works only when applied to the nest area, which you have to locate first. Nests are usually located under a protective large stone, tree, sidewalk, or hedgerow.

To exclude moles from the lawn, insecticides may be applied to kill the grubs and earthworms that are their favorite food. This may work for a while, but the insecticides have to be applied as often as the insects and worms return.

Repellents

There are many products on the market that don't work. One that might is castor oil, which is supposed to give the moles upset stomachs. This repellent can be sprayed on lawns and supposedly penetrates the soil as well as coating the grass. Its great advantage is that the residue is nontoxic and not oily. (See "Understanding Control Methods" in Part II.)

Trapping

Trapping is one of the few methods that removes the immediate problem. But it is only a skirmish won. The effort has to be an ongoing war of attrition, for other opportunistic animals will inhabit the empty tunnels. On one midwestern three-quarter-acre lawn surrounded by woods, sixty-eight moles were caught over an eight-month period.

Once one becomes adept, trapping can bring some peace in the garden and eventually clear the area of problem animals. However, long-term control is the same as for rats. It requires continual monitoring and going after each invader before it begins to beget new families. The best time to trap moles is during the spring and fall (particularly after a rain), when mole activity rises and they move up from their deep burrows. Begin as soon as activity is noticed. Early spring trapping may get pregnant females before babies are born.

How to Trap a Mole

This is an exercise for a college professor. One such researcher had this advice:

There are three *P*s. Patience, practice, and persistence.

For successful trapping, first locate the main runways, which are straighter, connect to raised mounds, or connect the curvy runway systems. Main runways usually follow fence rows, concrete paths,

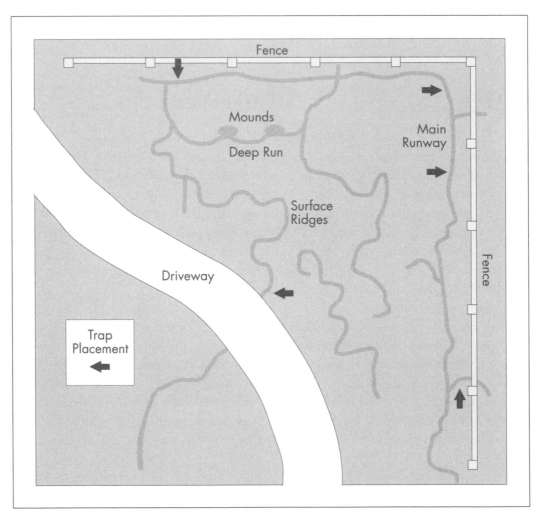

TO TRAP A MOLE

OLD WIVES' TALES

There are many of these, although serious research at universities suggests that they don't help for long, if at all.

For Moles, Gophers, Shrews, and Voles

- Spray on lawns: In twenty gallons of water, combine one cup of liquid dishwashing soap, one cup of castor oil, two tablespoons of the emetic alum (dissolved in hot water). Add an insecticide for grubs, to remove their food supply.

For Moles and Gophers

- Place a mixture of human hair and paradichlorobenzene in small piles along their runs.
- Cut sticks of Juicy Fruit gum into small pieces and place in different areas. Supposedly, if they eat it, the gum gives them indigestion.

For Moles

- Castor oil in the tunnels and holes. (For formulas, see the chapter on control methods.)

To Rout Gophers

- Put foul-smelling substances, such as rotting garbage, dead fish, or sponges soaked in urine, into their tunnels.
- Put a small battery radio in a plastic bag, set to static, and place in tunnels. The noise may discourage them, but not for long.
- Put a vibrating machine of some kind or windmill over or in the tunnels. Knowledgeable researchers say this is a waste of money.
- Electronic or transonic machines that emit sonic or ultrasonic beeps or sounds also are a waste of money.
- Put razor blades or broken glass in the tunnels. ☠ This method is dangerous because the glass and razor blades will eventually work their way up to the top of the soil and injure someone. It's especially unwise in cold areas because the freeze/thaw cycle speeds up the time it takes for these sharp objects to reach the top of the soil.

borders of the yard, a field, or a woody perimeter. Upper-level surface runways are raised ridges, which may be used daily or occasionally or only once. They connect with deeper runways, three to twelve inches below ground. Nests are four to sixteen inches below ground and often in protected places at the edges of property. Trapping where main runways enter the yard often gives good results.

Harpoon traps are best for novices, ☠ but be careful—they're sharp. Don't use such traps where children may get into them. Good brands of mechanical traps are the Nash Mole Trap and the Victor Mole Trap. There is also a *noose-type trap*, which is somewhat safer. (See the chapter "Understanding Control Methods" in Part II.) Set three to five traps per acre. They can be covered with overturned pails to protect the traps and prevent people from getting hurt by them. If nothing is caught in three days, move the traps.

It is also possible to make *pit traps*, which are safer than harpoons and cheaper. Once the main runway is identified, dig a small hole in it and insert a can about seven inches wide by twelve inches deep. The top of the can should be level with the floor of the runway. Lightly stamp down the runway floor about one foot in either direction from the pit. Then cover the area with a board or lightproof material to make it dark. With any luck, something may fall in.

Moles can also be captured (alive) when you see them tunneling. Push the blade of a shovel behind them so they can't retreat. Then scoop them out with a shovel as they dig. If you want to, that is.

Bait

Moles are almost impossible to catch with bait. Even poisoned earthworm bait doesn't work. Because moles eat insects, neither will they be tempted by rat bait dropped in a runway or hole, but gophers might, and field mice definitely will.

Poisons ☠

Poison grain ☠ is the usual bait for gophers and mice, but it should be dropped way down into the hole because birds or children might get it. On golf courses, licensed exterminators may use cyanide pellets, but it is generally against the law for others to buy or use them. Needless to say, cyanide ☠ is very toxic!

The Bottom Line

Moles do good service by helping to keep insect populations under control. Moles and gophers aerate the soil with their tunnels, improving its integrity. So we should welcome their activity on this earth—as long as it's NIMBY, or Not-In-My-BackYard.

MOOSE
LUCY THE MOOSE

A True Story

Lucy was a wayward moose, who started her public saga outside an exclusive shopping mall near Boston. She captured the media's attention with her offbeat antics, flitting through city and suburb appearing, disappearing, reappearing for days on end. *The Boston Globe* has given her more press coverage than any foreign head of state during her brief moment of fame. Multiple police cruisers trailed her marathon run, emergency radios crackling at her sightings. But Bullwinkle the Moose did not come to rescue this distressed damsel. Instead, thoroughly disoriented and no doubt frantic, she was finally brought down with a tranquilizer dart and gently carried to a local zoo. But the zoo

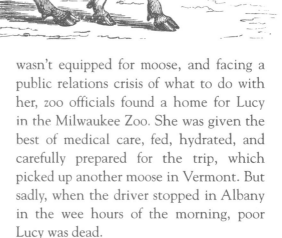

wasn't equipped for moose, and facing a public relations crisis of what to do with her, zoo officials found a home for Lucy in the Milwaukee Zoo. She was given the best of medical care, fed, hydrated, and carefully prepared for the trip, which picked up another moose in Vermont. But sadly, when the driver stopped in Albany in the wee hours of the morning, poor Lucy was dead.

It was known that moose don't easily

tolerate the stress of being moved and seldom last longer than a year in captivity. But the press had made Lucy a person, so they had to find her a home. The real question we should ask is how much money was spent on this wayward moose. And more important, should it have been so spent. We have children whose medical care is rationed in the name of cost control, yet no expense was spared to give poor Lucy loving and complete care.

Moose Damage in and out of the Backyard

At the time of the Lucy story, there were estimated to be about 80 to 100 moose in Massachusetts, with five to eight sightings in urban areas per year. In that state, thirty automobile accidents per year were caused by moose, with three animals killed. Barely two years later, the moose population was estimated at one hundred fifty to two hundred, and Massachusetts moose-vehicle collisions had risen to twelve.

In all of Vermont, New Hampshire, and Maine, there used to be approximately 200 accidents a year. But by 1996, New Hampshire's 4000 animals caused 256 collisions, up from 15 in the early 1980s. Vermont's estimated 1,000 moose caused 100 collisions in 1996, up from none in 1980.

By 1997, approximately 650 of Maine's

35,000 moose were killed in auto collisions. No laughing matter this, for motorist fatalities in moose accidents are estimated at 1 in 80. In Kentucky, auto insurance won't cover moose damage.

Many of the accidents are cars running off the road to avoid a collision. What if you can't avoid a collision? One Vermonter who had been in a moose-auto crash recommended the following: try to hit a moose from the rear, not broadside. The reason is that moose have long legs, and the car hood may travel under the moose's legs, allowing its large body to hit the windshield at full force. So drive carefully and be ready to stop on rural roads in moose country because they're more of a menace on the highway than in the garden.

They seldom cause problems in the backyard, where they will occasionally eat the tips of small trees and shrubs. They may browse, a nibble here or there, but they prefer marshy, water-type plants. Occasionally, during rutting season, when their passions run hot, trees may be badly scarred and the ground torn up. And sometimes fences get in the way of their migration routes.

Scientific Information

Moose are the giants of the deer family. A large bull may weigh more than a half ton and carry sixty pounds of antlers. Soli-

MOOSE-WATCHING TIPS FROM A MAINE FARMER

Moose watching is a favorite pastime of city folk who go to remote corners of the country, like Maine, Michigan, and Minnesota, to see these impressive behemoths. You can recognize city folk by what they're wearing, like a brown cap with stuffed moose antlers on it.

Why do people engage in this pastime? Perhaps because seeing these huge marvelous lumbering creatures is a singular experience of communing with the wild and untouched wilderness and sharing a time before man made his mark upon the Earth. Or perhaps because it's the politically correct equivalent of hunting.

It used to be difficult to sight a moose, but it's much easier nowadays because the population has increased manyfold. To see a moose:

1. Get up at the crack of dawn; that's when the moose get up.
2. Go to some place you're likely to find them . . . like Moosehead Valley or Moose Hollow Lodge, or Alaska.
3. Moose are creatures of habit and regularly follow the same routes in search of food. Find a local guide who knows where the moose trails are and, more important, will tell you.
4. Learn to make moose calls, which are loud, discordant, and ruin your vocal cords.
5. When you find a promising spot, settle in with a good book, lots of beer, blankets, insect repellent, and food. Then wait and read and wait and make moose calls now and then. Moose watching requires great patience—especially when it's cold.
6. If you're lucky, a moose will wander by. Eating slowly. Moose watching isn't very exciting unless you enjoy watching animals chew and chew and chew. It's basically boring after the first half hour or so.
7. To moose, people are even more boring. Moose are not interested in you unless you're very good at moose calls and it's mating season. When they're in heat, you may see the huge males bang their heads together and put on a good show. But don't get in their way.
8. Moose watching during hunting season isn't smart either. Stray bullets whiz by while grown men try to kill one of these gangly giants to get a pair of their huge antlers.
9. Moose antlers are so large that they don't fit in most homes, so it's easy to find them at secondhand shops. This is a lot cheaper and safer than Moose Camp Lodge during hunting season.

tary animals, moose generally stick to one mate. Rutting season is in the fall, and the males fight terrific, noisy battles as they bang their huge horns together. One or two, rarely three, calves are born in May.

Moose are usually not belligerent unless you interrupt their eating, their mating and courtship, get in their way while they're passing through, approach them in a confrontational matter, or shoot at them. However, they are powerful and unpredictable so should be considered potentially dangerous.

Control Methods

Exclusion

Exclusion is nigh impossible. They are large enough to roam where they choose. In Aspen, Colorado, someone cut a rancher's fence to let migrating moose through and unfortunately also let all the cattle free.

Hunting

Because the population of any animal in an unlimited range will increase exponentially, hunting is the usual control method. Most moose, except for a few like Lucy, live in sparsely settled areas or wildlife preserves. As herds grow, game wardens determine how many moose may be taken each year to keep the populations at levels their habitats can support.

Moose hunting permits are highly prized. In New Hampshire, a 1983 moose management study found that the herds were large enough to support hunting. To ensure fairness in awarding the permits, a lottery was created. In 1983 there were 1,600 moose in the state. Despite hunting, the herds had grown to 4,500 by 1995. That year, the lottery raised $193,000 in revenue from the 14,398 people who applied for 500 permits. That's why it's called a lottery.

OPOSSUMS

On a balmy June day in Tumwater, Washington, a man ran over a mother opossum and the babies clinging to her, while she was crossing the road. A policeman who saw the accident arrested him and charged him with cruelty to animals. The district judge dismissed the case, ruling that Tumwater's ordinance of "cruelty to animals" was too vague. For weeks thereafter, possums were the main hot topic in the local paper, with writers evenly split between pro-possum and pro-judge. Are opossums just pests, or do they deserve respect? It was a question of animal rights.

How to Recognize Opossum Damage

Usually you will see them or catch them in traps. They eat everything: fruits, roots, dogfood, insects, and small animals. When too many are around, or there's nice ripe fruit, they cause damage in the garden and often dig up roots. However, they're actually one of man's helpers because they are very efficient destroyers of rodents.

Scientific Information

They certainly are ugly, like big rats with a long skinny tail and a leering mouth full of teeth. Once you see one, you won't forget its toothy grin.

But they are interesting animals because they are the only North American marsupial and thus rear their babies in a pouch. Each year, the female bears about twenty offspring, each about the size of a bee. They climb into her pouch, clasp a teat, and grow rapidly. When they get too big for the pouch, they climb onto her back and with their feet and tail entwine themselves in her long hair. They stay attached until about two months old, when they make their way into the world.

A nocturnal animal, the opossum prefers cold, damp swamps and is rather reclusive. It has a prehensile tail and an opposable thumb on all four feet, like a human hand, which allows it to climb virtually anywhere. However, it is a primitive animal with a small brain. It has the dumb habit of falling down and playing dead when confronted with danger, hence the term *playing possum*. At other times, when cornered, it may growl or screech and excrete a greenish foul-smelling fluid.

Southerners consider its roasted flesh a great delicacy.

Diseases

The main danger is rabies. For more information see the chapter "Animal Diseases (Zoonoses)" in Part II.

Control Methods

The plan is essentially the same as for raccoons and woodchucks, but because opossums are dumb, they're easier to trap. See the chapters on raccoons and control methods.

PORCUPINES

This quaint animal is not bothersome but interesting because it is almost never killed in battle. Thanks to its 30,000 or so sharp, barbed quills, it has few predators. When afraid, it assumes an "on guard" position with its back arched and quills ready in the upright position, like archers of yore in battle. Though lumbering in gait, it can whirl rapidly, always keeping its dangerous backside to the enemy.

If an attacker is persistent, a well-armed clubtail will suddenly lash out with lightning speed and great accuracy and drive some dozen or more quills into the attacker, generally aiming for the face. A quill can work its way into a victim, and mountain lions, foxes, and eagles have been killed by porcupine quills. However, according to folklore, the well-armed porcupine can be easily killed by a strong person with a club, and supposedly it has tasty flesh. If you want to try it, that is.

When a Porcupine Is Likely to Cause Garden Damage

Though unusual, porcupines may damage trees in winter by eating the bark. In summer they feed on green vegetation, preferring clover and alfalfa.

Scientific Information

Porcupines occupy most of the Americas. The North American species are the eastern porcupine, which is black with a white band on its quills. The western porcupine has greenish yellow hairs on its head.

Their large babies are born with open eyes and a full complement of spines. While life expectancy in the wild is about six years, they can live up to ten years, and in some places they are on the protected animal list.

Control Methods

These shuffling armed oddities should be left alone. They do no harm. If you think they're too nosy, plant a patch of clover or alfalfa far enough away to draw them to another area. If necessary, line the path to it with little bunches of greens to help them find their way.

RABBITS

Peter Rabbit may be a friend in the nursery, but in the garden he's just one more mouth to feed. His particular family, including Mother, Father, Flopsy, Mopsy, and Cottontail, the creation of an English lady of refined temperament, was the first single-parent, dysfunctional family to be glorified—and in the nursery yet. Papa was a thief who ended up in Farmer Brown's stew. In her little cottage underground, Mother struggles to care for her little family with love and medicine. Naughty Peter follows in his father's dangerous footsteps, exhibiting a self-destructive tendency.

Is that what we should be teaching our children? Yet pictures of this bunny family festoon children's bowls, walls, food boxes, clothes, and whatnot.

Father rabbit should have stuck to honest work in the hedgerows and grasses and not gone into the vegetable patch. Will Mama stay forever with her little family or will she push them out when her next breeding cycle comes around and find another mate. Such is the reality of rabbit life.

How to Recognize Rabbit Damage

Rabbits will eat flowers and vegetables in spring and summer, and gnaw on tree bark in winter. Usually they are content to eat grass and wildflowers, so rabbits can just be enjoyed—unless you actually see them eating something valuable. They can devastate a flower bed or vegetable garden. On farms, just two rabbits can ruin several hundred head of lettuce a night by taking just a few bites from each. They don't generally eat corn, squash, cucumber, peppers, and potatoes. In winter, you may see their footprints in fresh snow.

Scientific Information

Cottontails inhabit most of the United States. They're gentle, harmless animals that never show anger or aggression.

Though quick and agile, they will often freeze and stand stone still when surprised, thinking that if they don't move, you won't see them—even if you yell at them or bang things. They are a delightful part of the garden scene. Gentleness personified, perhaps that's why bunnies are the most anthropomorphized animal of all for children.

Larger jackrabbits, or hares, inhabit the plains states and the West and do enormous damage on farms. The white-tailed jackrabbit, or prairie hare, has long legs and can easily outrun a fox or coyote, often leaping twelve to eighteen feet at a bound when running. They engage in rig-

RABBITS IN FOLKLORE

The Easter rabbit may come from an old Teutonic legend that the hare was once a bird but was transformed into its present shape by Ostara, the goddess of spring. The word *Easter* is derived from her name. The South American Indians revered the hare as the original creator of the universe, much as the North American Indians looked upon the beaver.

An old Sanskrit fable tells of a hare that lived on the moon and was king of all hares, while devout Hindu lore sees the outline of a hare in the spots on the moon. Among some European peasants, the hare was thought of as the spirit of corn, and the last harvest was called "the hare."

its numbers build up so rapidly. Farmers hunt these hares to protect their crops and have offered bounties. To understand the numbers of hares involved, consider the following: a generation ago, in one year only, a single Oregon county paid bounties for one million tails.

The life span of a hare in captivity may be ten years, while the little cottontail is old at three. In the wild, most cottontails live only a year or a little more. During that time, however, they may have between two and six litters of four to seven young. Their nests are shallow depressions in the ground lined with the mother's fur and covered with leaves. She returns only to nurse them, often in the dark of night. After about a month, the young are able to fend for themselves. Female rabbits are not at all like Peter Rabbit's imaginary, humanized Mother.

Rabbits historically have been an important domestic animal for wool, meat, and fur. They make fine pets and can be house-trained to paper. A well-known writer of children's books kept a pet rabbit on a high floor of an apartment on the Upper East Side in New York.

Rabbits are native throughout the world with the exception of Madagascar and Australia. However, twenty-four rabbits were brought into Australia in 1859 to provide food for foxes imported for hunting. Australia was without other predators, and the rabbits multiplied so rapidly that they threatened to nibble the Aus-

orous mating fights during the breeding season, which lasts from early spring to midsummer. The black-tailed California jackrabbit causes the most trouble because tralian plains bare. The foxes, which were supposed to eat the rabbits, also became a plague, preferring to eat the native animals. Foxes are implicated in the extinction of twenty species of local marsupials.

To remedy the problem, about forty years ago a myxoma virus, which infects only rabbits and hares, was brought in to kill them. It worked on about 99 percent of the rabbits, but 1 percent survived and continued to reproduce while the virus mutated into a benign form. The rabbit population naturally rebounded.

Currently, a new approach is being tried: By inserting a rabbit sperm protein into the virus, they are hoping to trick the rabbit's immune system into attacking sperm, thereby acting as a birth control mechanism. When a fox-specific virus is found, a similar approach for the foxes will undoubtedly be attempted. All of this goes to prove that lots more money is needed for research and testing of new birth control methods.

Diseases

Although rabbits carry many diseases, the main one of concern to man is tularemia (also known as rabbit fever and deer fly fever), which is mostly transmitted from infected animals to humans through abrasions in the skin. Its symptoms include high fever, swollen lymph glands,

and it sometimes progresses to pneumonia. However, it is also carried by infected ticks, can be inhaled, or transmitted in water contaminated by diseased animals. Although rabbits are the most common cause, tularemia can be carried by many other animals, including squirrels, woodchucks, opossums, foxes, coyotes, deer, sheep, birds, and cats. The disease is not common. Prevention involves wearing gloves and masks when handling potentially infected animals, their fur or carcasses, or skinning them. Also, inspect by checking yourself twice a day for ticks.

Control Methods

Exclusion

Fencing is very effective for rabbits, most useful for small areas. Fences should be two feet high, with the bottom tight to the ground or buried a few inches.

For trees, to protect the bark in winter, use the same protection as for voles: cylinders of hardware cloth or wire, two to three feet high and several inches away from the trunk. In areas with heavy snowfall, the wire should go well above the expected snow line, if possible.

More on wildlife laws: Newspaper columnist Ann Landers published a letter from California, where a North Hollywood man was charged with a misdemeanor for beating and choking his girlfriend, which carries a maximum fine of $1,000. He was also charged with cruelty to animals for strangling her pet rabbit, which carries a fine of $20,000. Both charges carry the same punishment—one year in jail.

Repellents

Thiram, a bitter-tasting spray, can be tried. It is most useful in winter to protect dormant twigs, but can harm tender leaves, so test it first. It is also useful for protecting spring bulbs. Thiram should not be used on food crops and has to be reapplied after heavy rains. Don't breathe in the fumes of this powerful fungicide. ☠

Odor repellents do not work. Wolf, fox, or coyote urine has been suggested but may or may not work, and probably will attract other animals. However, if it attracts foxes or coyotes, they may catch the rabbits, and other problem animals as well.

Trapping

Standard Havahart box traps can be used. They should be placed close to food and brush cover, for rabbits will not venture into an open area. In winter, traps should be in areas sheltered from the wind and baited with apple, corn, dried alfalfa, and clover. In summer, try apples, carrots, and cabbage. Move the traps if they fail to make a catch in several days. In many states, relocating trapped animals is against the law. They should be killed humanely. Call your local wildlife service to check the laws of your state, since they vary widely.

Other Methods

Predators are a gardener's best soldiers. Coyotes, foxes, dogs and even feral cats, birds of prey—almost all creatures prey on rabbits.

Another suggestion has been to plant a patch of soybeans at the very far end of the yard. Because rabbits love soybeans, they will theoretically stay away from the garden. Or the soybeans may attract more rabbits, just as Japanese beetle pheromone sex attractant traps attract your neighbor's beetles to your yard.

Hunting

In rural areas, intensive hunting in season can keep rabbit numbers within reasonable limits and reduce damage. This has to be done every year since rabbit populations recover quickly. An early-twentieth-century book, written by the American Museum of Natural History, said that 20 million rabbits were killed annually by hunters.

The Bush-Browns, famous Philadelphia garden writers in the 1950s, wrote, "A good shotgun seems to be the most effective control for rabbits." They also recommended powdered aloe "as a most satisfactory repellent. Dusted lightly from a salt or flour shaker." Reapply after a rain.

RACCOONS

Raccoons are really cute-looking animals, entertaining, and not shy. They are easily recognized by the charming dark mask around their eyes, which makes them look like aviators or party goers. 'Coonskin caps with the ringed furry tails were part of American rural folklore and the staple costume of Davy Crockett.

Reality is different. Raccoons in the attic or the chimney are not so cute, and not an animal to be messed with unless you know what you're doing. They are smart, large animals and will fight to defend their babies or themselves if cornered. During winter, when they usually come indoors, they semihibernate and rarely go out. But they're not asleep, and often there is more than one. Because they are one of the main carriers of rabies, they should be considered a pest to treat with caution. When they nest indoors, calling an exterminator, though pricey, is your best bet. (When you clean up after them, be aware of roundworm eggs, discussed later in this chapter, as well as ringworm.)

Sometimes you see them at night, particularly if the outdoor lights are on. They are not afraid of humans and will just sit and look at you, even if you scream at them or bang things. You actually have to throw stones or shoot at them to get them to move away. Then they'll just wait in the shadows until you leave.

How to Recognize Raccoon Damage

While raccoons eat many plants, their favorite is corn, corn, corn. One can recognize raccoon damage on corn because they break the stalks climbing up them and leave many half-eaten ears with the husks peeled back. One farmer reported that a 1,400-foot row of corn, which normally yields twenty-five bushels, produced a harvest of only eight bushels after the raccoons attacked.

Raccoons have long, sensitive fingers and can tell better than most humans when the corn is just at the "milk stage," which is its sweetest. (The kernels make a tiny pop when the husk is squeezed.) That's why raccoons always manage to pick the corn exactly one day before you planned to harvest it yourself. Guarding the corn from these thieves was a chore of Native American maidens of yore, who built a platform above the cornfields and spent the entire night guarding the harvest. Let's hope the bear grease they wore kept the mosquitoes at bay.

Many garden crops appeal to raccoons, including tomatoes and apples. When these heavy animals climb small fruit trees, they often break the branches. With watermelons, they dig small holes, then hollow out the inside by raking with a front paw. They tear up the lawns looking for grubs and will even roll back sod to look for these fat juicy insects. Raccoons also attack small animals, wild birds, and domestic poultry. A distinctive raccoon trait is that they bite off the heads of adult birds and leave them some distance from the bodies.

Scientific Information

Found throughout North America, raccoons prefer a habitat in the hardwood forest near water. However, they will live anywhere. Dens may be in the ground, hollow trees, stone walls, clumps of cattail, brushpiles, barns, abandoned buildings, chimneys, and attics. Intelligent animals, they readily adapt to living in close association with people. Because raccoons are opportunistic feeders, they thrive especially well in cities, where there is garbage available. The urban population density of these animals can reach 500 per square mile.

Long, bare-skinned, agile fingers allow them to open any lock or any garbage can. They have a habit of repeatedly washing their food in water as though afflicted with an obsessive-compulsive disorder, but they don't wash all their food and are probably just playing with it.

Raccoons are strong, large animals, sometimes reaching forty pounds, and they're not afraid to fight. The males are territorial. One litter of three to five is produced each year between April and August. The offspring stay with the mother for about a year, so it is common to see family groups. Though the life span is about twelve years, the survival rate is poor. Half of the autumn population generally consists of animals less than one year of age.

Raccoons are nocturnal animals. When they're out during the day, especially if they're acting odd, one has to be concerned about disease, particularly rabies.

Diseases

Raccoons carry many diseases such as rabies, canine distemper, trypanosomiasis, coccidiosis, toxoplasmosis, tularemia, tuberculosis, listeriosis, leptospirosis, ringworm, roundworms, and mange. Their fleas, ticks, lice, and mites may also transmit diseases. Children and pets are particularly at risk. Because raccoons comfortably inhabit the same space as man, they are more of a risk in spreading disease than shy wild animals that shun human contact. If trapped or found dead, carry out careful preventative measures when handling them, the traps, or touching any of their bodily fluids.

Roundworms

This rare but serious illness, Baboascaris procyanis, can be spread by raccoon feces and causes an encephalitis that presents with fever and stiff neck. The eggs of the roundworms remain viable for ten years, but they have to be ingested. Children are most at risk because they play in dirt and put their hands in their mouths. If a raccoon gets into a house and poops indoors, the house has to be thoroughly washed out, and any soiled furniture should be recovered, for dry cleaning or soap and water will not kill the eggs. If you catch a raccoon in your Havahart trap, the eggs remain where feces touched the ground and the trap. To kill the eggs, professional exterminators sterilize the trap bottom with a blowtorch.

Rabies

Before the mid-twentieth century, rabies in wildlife was not a major public health threat except in a few animals, mainly bats, some mountain squirrels, some skunks in the Midwest, and raccoons in a few places. Dogs were the main reservoir. Dreaded canine rabies was largely eradicated by the 1950s, along with the elimination of the many stray dogs that dotted the landscape.

However, the incidence of rabies in wild animals, especially skunks and raccoons, has increased every year since then. In the eastern United States, raccoons are the main carrier. In the Midwest, Southwest, and along the Pacific coast, skunks have that dubious honor. In Alaska and Arizona, foxes are the main reservoir of the virus.

In the late 1970s an outbreak of rabies began in the Virginias, inadvertently brought in with raccoons imported for hunting. It was left unchecked and within six years had become well established in the neighboring states, which provided the reservoir for continued spread.

It is most unfortunate that these amusing animals were allowed to become infected. Now they are the primary rabies vector on the East Coast. The disease perhaps could have been prevented from spreading if strong control methods had been taken early on. The accompanying chart shows the East Coast time line of the spread of raccoon rabies. It has blossomed into an epidemic so widespread that even Herculean measures probably can't affect it now. The financial expense of rabies outbreaks in wild animals is enormous. When the disease reached Maryland, several counties alone spent over $1 million, mostly to vaccinate all the dogs, cats, and other pets.

In 1995, just a decade later, the Centers for Disease Control and Prevention reported that raccoons accounted for half of the 7,881 cases of animal rabies in the country. In Massachusetts alone, 476 (out of 695 raccoons tested) were found to be rabid. The outbreak that started in 1977 had reached New Hampshire and northern New York, and south to North Carolina. Once it reaches the Ohio Valley, fears are that it will rapidly spread westward because there are few natural obstacles such as rivers and mountains to impede it.

A major factor in the spread was the previous unchecked explosion of raccoon populations in all cities, suburbs and towns. Then, when rabies came along, this dense population became a veritable highway of infection. The disease was able to travel along it, like wildfire, throughout the entire eastern United States.

Unfortunately, all mammals are susceptible to rabies. No longer is it possible to feed the friends of the field or be safe in the forests, as it was a few years ago. Spreading from raccoons, rabies has infected the entire wild fauna. The lack of vigorous public health response, compounded by a conspiracy of silence in the media about problem animals, has allowed a once relatively benign landscape to become perilous.

Once rabies infects a wild population, the reservoir of infection remains for a long time, perhaps forever. This scourge of humankind was essentially wiped out in inhabited areas, but now our woods and wild places are all contaminated and will always be suspect. Worse, pets and domestic animals, once safe, are now again at risk.

RABID RACCOONS BY STATE, 1977–1983

State	1977	1978	1979	1980	1981	1982	1983
West Virginia	1		8	14	22	43	89
Virginia		3	4	7	102	645	545
Maryland					7	118	735
Pennsylvania						25	81
Washington, D.C.						5	158
Totals	1	3	12	21	131	836	1,608

Source: "Mid-Atlantic Raccoon Rabies Outbreak," Centers for Disease Control, 1984.

In southern France, in one small forest, the local inhabitants said that when rabies was discovered in the foxes, they were all killed. When the area was rabies free, healthy foxes were reintroduced. For about fifteen years in Europe, modified live virus vaccines have been used successfully to both control and eliminate rabies whenever an outbreak occurred.

It has taken the United States two decades of galloping spread before trying to contain the disease and start using vaccines. Treatment in this country began in the mid-1990s, using dead virus vaccines, which are theoretically safer but more expensive. And because the infested area is now so vast, it will cost a lot to cover it all.

Baited vaccine is finally being dropped and tested in the northern woodlands to keep the disease from crossing the Canadian border, and in Massachusetts to keep it from crossing the Cape Cod Canal and infecting Cape Cod. Several other states, including Texas and Florida, are also conducting experiments. It remains to be seen how well this will work, what rates of application and frequency are necessary, and if it will be cost effective.

The eastern rabies episode is a glaring example of what happens when animal populations are allowed to explode unchecked. In nature, as in history, overpopulation is corrected by the Four Horsemen of the Apocalypse: pestilence, disease, famine, and war. For raccoons, disease has temporarily reduced their numbers. Unfortunately, man also becomes a victim of so-called natural law when he allows Mother Nature to make decisions for him.

In the United States, all dogs and cats now have to be immunized as well as all people who handle animals regularly. People who are exposed or bitten have to take an expensive course of repeated shots to prevent the disease. (Once contracted, rabies is fatal.) The cost of these measures is enormous. Over $300 million is spent yearly for rabies prevention, mostly for inoculating pets, and another $15 million is spent for postexposure treatments.

Concern for animals must be coupled with honesty about potential problems. Wanting all sentient creatures to be preserved, at whatever human cost, has led us to this tragedy. The worst losers are the wild animals that might have been spared.

Precautions to Be Taken in Areas Where Rabies Is Endemic

Now and forever, one has to be wary and cautious if an animal approaches or acts strangely. It could be infected. So might roadkill. No longer can a sick animal be simply picked up, taken home, and nursed back to health. Wild animals should not be fed. Pets should be fed indoors, and no food should be left outdoors for them. Bird feeders should be off the ground (which is unfortunate because some of the nicest birds are ground feeders).

If one sees a raccoon is out during the day, or acting oddly, avoid it. They are nocturnal animals and must be suspect if out during daytime. Leave it alone and take the children and pets inside. If such an animal approaches you, back away. If it jumps at you, beat it off with anything that's handy. If you are scratched, bitten, or come into contact with saliva or any bodily fluid, report it immediately to your health department and your doctor. If the animal cannot be caught and its tissues tested for disease, you must have rabies shots. Not all raccoons carry rabies, but because of its long incubation period, which can be months, one should always be cautious.

Control Methods

Exclusion

To keep raccoons out of houses, their entrance holes have to be found and covered, and chimneys covered with wire mesh. To keep them out of the garbage and garden is more difficult. Garbage cans should have raccoon-proof locks, if such things really exist. Otherwise, build a sturdy storage shed or keep the garbage indoors. (It smells in hot weather.) A rag heavily soaked in ammonia inside a closed can might help. Try to remove their food, water, and destroy their shelter, especially the wood piles where they nest.

Fences are often recommended for this wily marauder, but he's an excellent climber and ordinary fences don't work that well but they are worth a try to discourage him from exploring for food. Raccoons also use overhanging branches to jump inside if they're fenced out. A "hot" electric wire on a fence will increase its effectiveness. Place the wire on top or set it eight inches away from the fence and eight inches above the ground. To protect corn, use a double hot-wire arrangement, turned on at dusk and off at daybreak. Often a fence, with a trap inside, works better than just a fence alone

Trapping

There are many kinds of traps that can be used, but since the animals are large, traps must be sturdy. The most common for backyards is a Havahart or live animal trap. In traps with two doors, one should be secured closed with a sturdy stick or pipe. Bait should be put in the farthest end. Since raccoons dig up all the dirt beneath the trap and pull it inside, it's useful to put traps on a flat piece of wood. (If a raccoon is caught, dispose of the wood to get rid of diseases and worm eggs left from the animal's waste.)

As soon as the trap is sprung, the door or gate should be secured with a metal rod or strong piece of wood to stay closed. Otherwise, as the animal jumps and shakes and turns the trap upside down, it will open. You can usually hear the trap snap shut at night, then the rattling that indicates something has been caught. It's best to boot up and go out right then and there, to secure the trap.

Traps should be placed in animal runs, which can be identified by watching the animals for several days. Bait the trails with tempting bits of food leading to the trap. Raccoons, woodchucks, squirrels, opossums, and skunks occupy similar habitats, so you may be surprised at what you've caught.

Because wild animals are likely to have fleas or ticks, it's wise to spray them with insecticides before handling the traps. Most of these animals, especially raccoons and skunks, may carry rabies. If trapped or found dead, use the best sanitation and health precautions when handling them. Wear sturdy gloves covered with a plastic bag or protect your hands with a couple of layers of plastic bags. When finished, thoroughly wash your hands and any other exposed areas with lots of soap and water. If you are scratched or bitten, wash the affected area thoroughly with soap and water, and see a doctor immediately. Save the animal for testing.

In areas with rabies, it may be worth getting a licensed animal exterminator to dispose of the animal. If you can, get him to torch the floor of your trap (to kill roundworm eggs) as part of the job. Soap and water or disinfectant won't do the job.

Bait

Raccoons like everything, especially dog food and fish. However, to prevent pets from being caught, use fruit, berries, vegetables, raw eggs, or peanut butter. The addition of a piece of wadded aluminum foil inside the trap may stimulate their curiosity, but food remains the main attractant.

Poisons ☠

None are registered for use with raccoons. Using poisonous ☠ antifreeze inside the trap is against the law in most states. Never leave poison around, particularly something like antifreeze because it has a sweet taste and could be eaten by pets or, worse, children.

Hunting with 'Coon Dogs

Specially trained 'coon dogs tree raccoons, which are then shot. Don't have your untrained dog attempt this; it could get badly hurt fighting with raccoons, which are not timid animals.

Repellents

According to wildlife services, no approved repellents work with raccoons. Using naphthalene ☠ or paradichlorobenzene ☠ in closed areas may help temporarily. These compounds are all poisonous to humans and pets, and should not be used in food gardens.

Predator Urine

Marking a territory with fox, coyote, wolf, or bobcat urine will probably attract raccoons rather than deter them. It also attracts dogs, opossums, and foxes, sometimes pet cats.

Other Deterrents

A good barking dog that marks the yard with its urine scent is the best deterrent.

Frightening raccoons with other deterrents may delay them, but not for long. They're smart. They figure out what's a threat and what's not. Temporary deterrents include radios, scarecrows, plastic or metal streamers, aluminum pie pans, tin can lids, plastic windmills, night lights. Rotating the different deterrents may help some as the animals become accustomed to and unafraid of each one.

SILLY OLD WIVES' TALES

- To keep raccoons out of garbage cans, put ammonia, Lysol, or Tabasco sauce on top of the cans.
- Hang a few articles of sweaty clothing over the fence. Replace them as the odor wears off.
- Get dog's hair from a pet groomer and put it in mesh bags and set them around your property. This won't work any better with raccoons than it does with deer.

RATS AND MICE

A True Story

Pied Piper, Where are you?

Once upon a time, there was a town described in the fashionable magazines as "fine white wine." It had many famous folks, giants of industry, professors, and a goodly share of Nobel prize winners. It prized itself on its fine schools and liberal thinking. There was an excellent high school on the edge of a park in the center of town, situated on a beautiful pond that children fished in. An arboretum of ornamental trees and shrubs was another feature of the park, which had neatly-cared-for grass and paths.

Then the Wetland Protection Law was passed, and the conservation commission, which administered it, decided that the pond in the center of the town should be-

come a wildlife sanctuary. Not a people park. They refused to allow any lakeside vegetation to be cut or trimmed, and they planted invasive wild food plants using state grant money. Around the once beautiful pond, weeds and wild seedlings grew, which restricted access to the pond edge and in places hid the water from view.

The rats loved it. They produced little rats by the score, along with a muskrat or two which shared the rat condos on the pond. The problem was that the rats liked to go to school. And soon the school became overrun with rats too, just like the park and the pond. When teachers wanted quiet during study hall, they stamped their feet to shush up the scratching and scampering rats beneath the floor.

The conservation commission stead-fastly refused to allow any weeds or shrubs or trees to be trimmed or the rats to be trapped or poisoned. Poison ivy climbed up trees. By day, emboldened rats skittered around the park, unnerving joggers and children. Few famous folks sat on the grass anymore.

The health department's response was to buy expensive garbage cans and badger the children not to litter. All the while, the rats thrived feasting on the invasive wild food plants and Canada goose drop-pings. The conservation commission fi-nally allowed the use of rat poison, but only for two weeks and only at the walls of the school, not near the overgrown rat habitat by the lake.

Parents, citizens, the local newspa-per—all called for the Pied Piper to come and rescue them from the plague of rats. But the Pied Piper never came. The pro-tected rats still live in their comfy wildlife condos around the pond, and still scamper under the school. The teachers still stamp their feet for silence.

Rat History

There are black rats, and there are larger brownish gray Norway rats. Black rats reached Europe in the thirteenth cen-tury, imported on ships returning from the Crusades. The rats had fleas. The fleas car-ried bubonic plague, which wiped out a third of the population. A painting by Rembrandt shows a rat catcher hawking dead black rats, whether to rid houses or for food is not quite clear. In China, rats have long been a dietary delicacy. Ugh.

The brown/gray Norway rat probably originated in central Asia, migrated west-ward in the eighteenth century, reaching England by around 1730, and America by about 1775. Rats thrive everywhere man lives, and eat everything, even each other. Rats are a great worldwide army. Quick learners, they swiftly master the rules of battle in each of man's efforts to destroy their army. They even recognize a poi-soned rat as a warning of concealed dan-ger. Remorseless rat divisions harass man all over the world. And man never wins.

Problem Rats and Mice

These two rodents are the biggest prob-lem animals of all. Rats live anyplace they can find food, including in sewers, where they eat raw sewerage and, the stuff of nightmares, they can actually come up into houses through the toilet. They go af-ter garbage, animal feed, stored foodstuffs indoors or out, and are attracted to mulch piles that contain vegetables or refuse. Mice are more likely to be inside build-ings, where they can find food close by.

How to Recognize Rodent Activity

Both are nocturnal animals so if, when trying to sleep, you hear scratching and the patter of little feet, be suspicious. If populations are high, they will run about during daytime as well. When you see rats foraging during the day, you have a BIG problem because there are lots and lots more than you see.

Rodents leave fecal droppings, small dark pellets, which once seen, you will recognize forever. Often droppings are discovered in cabinets, drawers, attics, cellars, garages—whatever places they frequent in their daily search for food. Outdoor burrows can be identified by the freshly dug soil around a hole. To test if a burrow is active, cover it with dirt and wait a day or two. If it's dug open again, you know it's being used by hungry occupants.

Field Mice

There are many kinds of wild mice that usually stay outdoors, away from humans. In winter some field animals come indoors for the warmth, including squirrels and raccoons, sometimes field rats and field mice. Field rodents are generally not a problem inside houses except during cold weather. And since there are usually only a few of

them indoors, they can be caught and eliminated or set free outside in a sheltered spot if one prefers.

Field mice, also called voles, are small, gray, shy little creatures. They cause problems in the garden, where very quietly and unobtrusively they eat the tops and roots of many tender plants. They're particularly partial to grass. Weighing about an ounce, they look sweet but can be quite aggressive if cornered and will bite. In the spring, grass has a chemical that stimulates their sex organs and makes them more aggressive as they fight over territories and mating—hot-blooded, these little guys.

They reproduce at a prodigious rate, which is necessary because they are eaten by foxes, cats, snakes, coyotes, and birds, particularly hawks and owls at an equally prodigious rate. In the wild, their average life span is only three months. Still, there are always lots and lots of them and, because they eat their weight in food every day, they do enormous damage to crops and orchards. They have population cycles that rise and then crash about every four years. You rarely see these little fel-

lows, but they are out there. You may see their one-and-a-half-inch-diameter tunnels hidden under tall grass.

Another charming, shy field rodent, the white-footed mouse, is believed to be a carrier and winter reservoir of Lyme disease. These creatures inhabit the tall grasses at the lawn or forest edge and keep the Lyme disease tick warm and protected in their winter nests. Fawn colored and adorable, they have large ears and long whiskers, and perhaps are the model for Mickey of Disney fame.

A favorite fall food of the white-footed mouse is acorns, which they strip from the trees and bury in small caches, called "scatter hoards," the locations of which they don't seem to remember at all. They can smell where acorns are underground, and for some reason they constantly re-bury nuts each night. In one research experiment, 1,000 marked acorns were buried. By the next morning, every one had been moved. Which is good, because these forgotten buried acorns, protected underground from insects, are the ones from which mighty oaks grow.

Not so charming is the damage that all outdoor mice do to trees in winter. Tree bark is very tasty to them, especially the bark of fruit trees, which they chew and frequently girdle all around. This kills the trees, which is a *big* problem in orchards as well as backyards. Even partial stripping of the bark can do permanent damage. In areas with large mice populations, their damage can be prevented by physically protecting the trunk with wire mesh or special stiff plastic spiral wrap.

Scientific Information

Fierce and cunning, rats are the most adaptable of animals and have spread throughout the world, causing destruction, loss of food crops, and disease. Known for their predacious habits, omnivorous diet, and great fecundity, they may lose a battle here and there, but have never lost the war, and probably never will.

Rats bear young four to six times a year, producing litters of four to ten. The young are able to reproduce in about six months. They rest during cold weather, eating food stored in their burrows, or venturing out to forage when it's not too cold. Mice are equally fecund and produce litters of one to eighteen at a time. The young are ready to reproduce at two to three months of age.

The normal life span of most ordinary rats is about nine months, and about a year for house mice. Rats have more scales on their tails (up to 210) than mice (never above 180), but the real question is who ever bothered to count them? There is complete information on every aspect of rodent life available from your local health department. If all they talk about is how you wrap your garbage, call the state department of health for more complete information.

Both of these rodents are the main despoilers of agricultural produce the world over. Incidentally, the level of rat and mice contamination in popcorn that is considered acceptable by the U.S. Food and Drug Administration is:

1. one rodent pellet per sample or one rodent hair per two samples *or*
2. two rodent hairs per pound or twenty gnawed grains per pound *or*
3. hairs in 50 percent of the samples.

Check your popcorn next time!

Diseases

Remember rodents can carry over thirty diseases, and they usually have fleas. Serious diseases that must be reported to health departments are plague (now confined to southwestern locations), hantavirus, and leptospirosis (which has infected people in cities, Baltimore and Philadelphia among them). Rodent droppings, their urine, and their fleas may transmit infections, so practice good public health sanitation when you deal with these animals. If you catch these animals in the traps, spray them with an insecticide or flea spray before handling them be-

cause most fleas find people more attractive than dead rats. (See the chapter on animal diseases.)

If you handle traps, wear disposable gloves or put plastic bags over your hands. Then turn the bags inside out as you peel them off, and dispose of them in the garbage. When disposing of dead rodents, put them in secure paper or plastic bags and throw out in the garbage too. Flushing them down the drain is not such a good idea, particularly if they get stuck in the pipes and you have to pay the plumber.

Control Methods

Exclusion—Outdoors

To protect trees: In winter, field mice crawl through tunnels in the snow and quietly eat the bark of many trees. To prevent girdling of the bark, enclose the trunk with a closely woven wire mesh cylinder. This cylinder should go down to the soil line and be roomy enough to allow the tree to grow for a couple of years. It should also enclose the root flare and be high enough to be above the snow line. The cylinder must be removed or enlarged before the trunk starts to grow into it as the tree thickens.

Another easier but not quite so effective method is spiral plastic fruit tree wrap. It is not too difficult to use, and should be removed in spring to prevent fungus and insects from breeding underneath. It may take two sections to get above the snow line.

Sometimes mowing the grass very close will help because field mice shun areas where they can't hide in tall grass runways and are exposed to predators such as hawks.

To protect underground roots and tender crops, exclusion is virtually impossible because many rodents stay completely underground. If you see damage, you can set traps, but there are so many you probably won't make a dent in the population.

Exclusion—Indoors

Buildings can be made rat and mouse proof if one can find the hidden, small entrance holes—no easy task. It's best to engage an experienced exterminator who can make recommendations. Rats can gnaw through most anything except metal and concrete.

Trapping

"Build a better mouse trap and the world will beat a path to your door." So the old advice goes. Perhaps this originated in Amsterdam, when folks got tired of waiting for the rat catcher or Pied Piper. Deal with rats and mice the same way. Trap them.

Traps

There are many kinds of traps. They usually work best when two or three are used together, and placed in animal runs or corridors. If an animal eludes one trap, the next one usually catches him as he jumps back. Multiple traps are also useful if there is more than one problem animal, which there usually is.

For mice, sticky traps are easiest and the safest if there are children or pets present. Put them in the runs where the mice travel, which are usually along the walls. Sticky traps are easy to buy and use, particularly the kind that open into a little covered triangle. Several in a row are better than one or two because the mice have to actually walk through them to be caught. When the mice die inside, they stick, and so don't fall on the floor when you try to throw them out. There are larger, stickier ones for rats. Sticky traps can, of course, be baited, the same as snap traps.

Snap traps are older and do a fast guillotine when they work. They're more difficult to set than sticky traps, and often they can painfully snap down on a finger while the bait and the spring are being set. They are reusable, but one has to remove the dead animal first, a disgusting job that isn't worth the cash saved. Moreover, any fleas or disease organisms might remain on the traps.

On more expensive traps, there are all kinds of special improvements, which allow easier emptying, more efficient catching, or some other gimmick. You can buy and try them, but I've never noticed much of an improvement over the more basic ones.

Animal rightists feel that snap traps are better than sticky traps because the rodents die quicker and don't suffer. However, if you still suffer from guilt, check the traps twice a day, particularly early in the morning, and dispatch the trapped animals quickly and humanely.

If these thoughts bother you, but you still want to have the ease and convenience of sticky traps, you can always do what the Jains do. The Jains are a sect in India, whose followers so cherish all life that they won't kill intentionally, not even insects. Naturally, they are vegetarians, but since they must eat something, they ask forgiveness when they kill plants, forgiveness of the spirit of plants in general, and the particular plants they are eating.

To assuage your guilt at killing mice and rats, you can create your own forgiveness rituals, even incantations to the rodent goddess somewhere underground. In animistic religions, all things have spirits, and surely there must be a spirit goddess somewhere, even for rats and mice.

Or, if you prefer, you can go to see that classic Christmas ballet, the *Nutcracker* by Tchaikovsky, and watch the brave and handsome nutcracker vanquish the swaggering evil rat king, thereby providing you with folklore justification for rat killing. The dance of the sugar plum fairies helps too.

Where to Set Traps

Mice are homebodies and stay fairly close to their nests. Their range is about 5 to 30 feet, often spending their entire life in 10 square feet if food is available. Their runs are usually along the wall. Rats stray farther and are more daring. Their usual range is about 100 to 200 feet, but they'll forage 300 to 400 feet from their burrows to find a good food supply. Rats and mice can enter buildings through very small holes, often finding an entrance where pipes come through the walls. Mice can squeeze through a hole the size of a dime.

Put traps as close as possible to their nest holes in walls or in the ground. If you aren't sure where they nest, set the traps in their runs (which can be discovered by patient observation, by listening, watching, or finding droppings). Indoor runs usually follow the walls and are often inside cabinets and behind appliances. If you're not sure where the runs are, put the traps where you find droppings. Once you get the hang of it, it's not so hard.

Indoor areas can be made rodent free by adequate trapping and occasional poisoning. Field mice and rats are much harder to control because new animals will quickly move into empty areas.

Bait

Good baits for rats and mice are cheese, bread, birdseed, peanuts, and peanut butter.

For voles, or field mice, use grain or pelleted baits. For pine voles, which burrow and eat underground, use apple baits. The best time to bait for field mice is mid-October through November in northern areas, which is after the grass cover is down from frost, most dropped fruit has rotted, and just before snow cover.

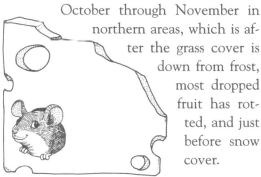

Disposal of Rats and Mice

One way to dispatch live trapped animals quickly and humanely is to drown them. Fill a garbage can with enough water and do the dastardly deed. Keep them submerged at least ten minutes. Then throw the water away far from the house, and not on the vegetables or where pets or children play. Finally, wash the garbage can outdoors with detergent. Wear disposable gloves or double plastic bags on your hands. To be extra cautious, spray the animal first with flea powder or hold it far away from you.

Poisons ☠

Many people use poison bait, but it carries hazards. Whether used for mice or large animals, it's very dangerous because a pet or worse, a child, could easily eat it. ☠ Poison should be used sparingly and with great caution. It's too easy to forget about it until someone inadvertently eats it next summer. Another problem with poison is that often a mouse or rat will die somewhere inside the wall, giving off a smell that's even worse than that of decaying squirrels. This smell lasts for weeks and weeks until the body decays and dries up. Once one has suffered the unforgettable perfume of putrefying mouse, one doesn't crave a repeat experience.

There are special locked box traps for use with poison. Exterminators have these special safer traps and in many states, only a licensed exterminator can legally use poison. If an infestation is heavy, it's worth hiring an experienced exterminator to clear it up quickly, which takes about two weeks. Then the area should be monitored every three or four months to keep new arrivals and their new litters from filling up the empty habitat.

There are basically two types of toxicants. Single-dose poisons kill only the target animal with one dose. They are dangerous because other animals can eat them. The other kind, anticoagulants, have to be eaten for several days and are used to control bait-shy animals. Gener-

ally, eco-sensitive controls don't work well for indoor rodents. There is a story about a famous medical school that implemented the elegant biological theories of ecological animal control propounded by one of its professors and yet was overrun with mice for years and years. Finally, a licensed exterminator was brought in, and the school was rodent free within a month.

With a little perseverance, it's not hard to keep rodents under control if one adopts a sensible battle plan and follows up with regular monitoring.

Mousers

Cats are good mousers. A good barn cat is worth twice its weight in sticky traps. Cats not only keep vermin out of the house and garden, but, if they have good genes, are delightful, loving pets as well. Feed them in the morning, so they'll be in the mood to hunt at night when mice are out and about.

Rats are larger and can intimidate cats. However, a big dog will scare them, and they may leave the area. When a good hunting dog species, particularly a male, marks a territory with urine, most small animals will respect the scent and look elsewhere for a comfortable home. One hopes.

Be cautious, though. Your pet can catch diseases from rodents, so be wary for his health and your family's. Be sure to vaccinate your pets against rabies and give them all their medical inoculations. Both cats and dogs add a happy dimension to our lives, in addition to their animal-deterrent value, so consider getting a trusty dog or cat.

Other Methods: Long-term Rodent Control

There are three absolutely essential parts to any successful, long-term rodent program. They are regular trapping, sanitation, and habitat control.

Sanitation

To control rodents, cut off their food supply and make your area unattractive. Keep garbage in tightly closed containers, or rats will surely find them (as will coyotes, foxes, raccoons, and bears). Garbage put out on the street in plastic bags for an early morning pickup can become a regular breakfast buffet. Use metal cans—determined rats can gnaw through plastic. Store foodstuffs in rodent-proof cans or jars as well as edibles like grass seed, bonemeal, and organic fertilizer, particularly bonemeal and ones made with fish or chicken.

Habitat Control

Rats often live outdoors in burrows under trees and shrubs, in open sewers, as well as in manure and mulch piles. They like nice moist soil, especially clay, for their burrows, also pond edges and brooks. They do not like to burrow in stone or sand, so occasionally changing the top several inches of soil to sand or stone may discourage them.

Keeping plants low makes it easier to find burrows. If there are multiple nests in brush or overgrown clumps of bushes or under roots, it's useful to pull the whole mess of plants out using a rope attached to a heavy-duty machine. Then regrade the area and monitor regularly for fresh burrows, which will be easily seen. Rats will also nest in planters and window boxes, so cover the tops and insides with hardware cloth to exclude them.

Integrated Pest Management

This is the latest theory. It involves tolerating a low level of infestation. (See last

Many laws are idiotic. There was a rat case in New Jersey. It seems a man trapped a rat in his garden, but it wasn't dead, so he beat it to death with a shovel. It was reported to the police as a felony under the wildlife protection law. The man was booked, charged, and prosecuted. He had to hire a lawyer and to defend himself in court before a judge, who had the good sense to throw the case out. Pied Piper, where are you?

section of the chapter "Understanding Control Methods," Part II.) Although not even one rat or mouse is acceptable in a restaurant or hospital, theoretically, a few can be tolerated in the garden. While the thought of having a few rodents around may be yucky, it's easier than constantly battling to eradicate every single rodent around.

Skunks

A True Story

Once upon a time, there were two brothers. One lived in the city, and he came to visit his brother in the country, arriving weary and famished on a Friday evening. The table was set and resplendent with hearty country fare.

The visiting sister-in-law went into the garden for a smoke, when, lo and behold,

she spied a skunk newly caught in the Havahart trap. She announced that dinner could not begin until the skunk had a home, because no skunk should be in a trap over dinnertime.

The Animal Rescue League, the Audubon Society, the Association for Prevention of Cruelty to Animals, the wildlife service, and the local veterinarian were all called to find it a home. But no one in animal welfare was remotely interested in helping, particularly late on a Friday. Instead they recited the law, which required that the animal be kept in a trap for no more than twenty-four hours, and while confined was to be fed and given water. Such are the wildlife laws.

The reunion deteriorated into a group of ill-tempered, hungry people, while the dog waited sullenly under the table for scraps. The cat was unhappy, locked in the bathroom to prevent it from getting sprayed with Eau de Skunk.

In desperation, a friend named Ray was called. He came and announced that since the skunk was young, he would take it home with him to be a pet. He named it Rosebud. "Nice Rosebud," he crooned, slowly picking up the trap of the totally mystified creature, which had never been exposed to so many people before. If raised by humans from childhood, particularly with their smelly glands removed, skunks make fine pets, loyal and pleasant. And they are excellent mousers, better than cats.

How to Tell If You Have Skunks

You can tell by smell, especially when they frolic under an open bedroom window. Or when the lawn has lots of small holes in spring, as they dig for grubs. Then more holes from August to October after the second generation of grubs hatch. Skunk lawn damage appears as turned-up chunks of dirt and grass, three or four inches wide, and funnel-shaped holes three to four inches deep. It's as though they pushed through the sod with their noses. Squirrel holes are usually smaller and rounder. Raccoons are more inclined to roll up the sod.

Often you will see skunks. If you do, slowly and quietly walk away. Pick up the dog and carry him away. (If skunks are out in midday and sit and look at you, they may be sick.)

Scientific Information

The striped skunk, the hooded skunk, the spotted skunk, and the hog-nosed skunk are all members of the weasel family. Their range is from Mexico well into Canada, and from sea to sea. They usually live in clearings, fields, and forest borders, where home may be a hollow log or a protected shelter, sometimes a burrow in the ground. These nocturnal, slow-moving animals are active most of the year, except for a month or so during the coldest part of winter. Skunks protect themselves by discharging nauseating musk from the anal gland. They can shoot the spray nine feet or more. The smell can carry half a mile.

Their normal feeding range is one-half mile to one and a half miles, although males, during breeding season, may travel five miles to find a mate. The four to eight babies born each year are weaned in about two months, and leave to find a territory of their own in late summer or early fall. The young usually start poking around in early summer and may cause problems at that time. However, they are easy to catch when young because they're not yet wary of traps, bait, and humans.

Skunks eat both plant and animal food, but in spring and summer they prefer insects, and bird's eggs. Mice, rats, rabbits, and small mammals are also eaten, particularly when other food is scarce. Only about five percent of their diet is made up of garden plants or vegetables, and in general, they are useful at ridding the world of unwanted pests.

Skunk Damage

Skunks can identify a grub-infested lawn in the dark better than the most knowledgeable horticulturalist can in the daytime. Lawn grubs are fat, white, inch-long, C-shaped delicacies that are a favorite food of skunks, raccoons, and moles. When the grubs are near the surface, animals tear up the lawn to get these insects, which are the larval stage of rose chafers, European and Japanese beetles, all of which feed on grass roots. To prevent skunk damage to the lawn, kill the grubs with a strong, fast-acting insecticide. Do it as soon as you see the skunk holes.

Since squirrels also dig up lawns looking for nuts—they can't remember where they planted them—it's wise to check for the presence of grubs before using a pesticide. To test for grubs, cut a one-foot square in the lawn. Roll back the sod and count the number of white grubs you see. A lawn can tolerate ten Japanese beetles per square foot or about eight of the other grubs. Fewer than those numbers are not usually treated, because healthy grass can tolerate them. However, if skunks are tearing up the lawn and you find several grubs, you may want to get rid of them.

If you don't find any grubs, you don't have them, and pesticides won't help your skunk (or lawn) problems. If you do find grubs, ask your local nursery or agricultural extension agent for the currently allowed chemical treatment for the common lawn grubs in your area. As some chemicals are outlawed and other new ones are released, the recommendations change frequently.

The timing of pesticide applications is very specific. In spring, *fast-acting* knock-down chemicals are applied, usually when the forsythia bloom, to catch the grubs as they rise to the warming surface to feed on the grass roots. To catch the fall grubs, apply fast-acting pesticides in mid-August or as soon as the damage is noticed.

Slow-acting chemicals, most particularly the new, less toxic, insect hormones like Merit, need a long lead time, so check the instructions and follow them carefully. They are usually applied in late May or early June, so that the spring grubs can't mature to egg-laying adults (usually late spring), or from eggs to larvae (usually late summer). The late spring application lasts through summer. The advantage of Merit is that it is safer than fast-acting chemicals for children and pets that play on the lawn.

If you miss the proper time period for applying pesticides, wait until the next proper season occurs. Applying pesticides too late is like locking the barn door after the horse is stolen. Just sprinkle grass seed in the torn-up areas.

after chicken coops and eggs. Occasionally they'll eat corn, but their damage is confined to the lower ears since they don't climb.

In general, because they eat insects and rodents, they are beneficial animals and become problems only when their digging or feeding habits conflict with man. Or when they frolic too close to the open bedroom window in August and perfume the night air.

Diseases

Skunks carry rabies in many parts of the country, particularly in the East, the Midwest, and along the Pacific coast. In the Midwest, they are the main carrier. Along the Atlantic coast, as the rabies epidemic spread in the raccoon population, skunks became infected as well, and have become a permanent reservoir of infection. Because of the risk of rabies, you

Other Skunk Problems

Skunks are also likely to cause problems when the young start looking for their own permanent digs. Once they become established, they don't interact much with humans, except to go after the grubs in the lawn. On a farm they may go

HOW TO HANDLE A SKUNK IN A TRAP

Very carefully! Skunks spray when they are frightened.

To move a skunk in a trap, quietly drop a sheet over the trap, pick it up gently without shaking or jerking. Crooning "Nice skunkie" in a soft, soothing voice is very helpful to humans, though whether or not to skunks has never been documented.

In order to spray, skunks have to raise their tails, haunch up and aim. If the trap is low, and they can't raise their tail or turn their back to you with the tail up, they usually won't spray.

Do not let the skunk spray a dog or cat. It takes a long, long time for the smell of skunk spray to go away. For the same reason try not to upset a skunk that's under the house, porch, or in the basement. Just leave it alone with the door open and wait quietly. By nightfall, it will usually find its way out, but if it doesn't, call an exterminator. If a skunk gets frightened under the house and sprays, plan to go to Disneyland for a long visit.

Theoretically, the scent of a skunk musk can be neutralized with a mild acid such as tomato juice or weak vinegar, although one exterminator says it doesn't do much. A dog lover's suggestion is to mix a quart of 3% hydrogen peroxide with ¼ cup of baking soda and 1 teaspoon of liquid soap, bathe one's pet and rinse well. However, the honest truth is that when the day is damp, the dog will still smell like Eau de Skunk for a long, long time. Neuotoleum Alpha, an aromatic hospital deodorant, applied to cotton balls, may be helpful in masking the odor when scattered about in garages or basements.

must be very careful if you trap a skunk or find a dead one. Carry out preventative measures when handling them, the traps, or touching any of their bodily fluids. See the chapters "Raccoons" and "Animal Diseases (Zoonoses)" for more information.

Control Methods

Exclusion

Prevention is best. Wire mesh fencing is useful to keep skunks out of gardens and from digging under buildings. Two feet above ground is high enough. To prevent burrowing under the fence, use three-foot mesh and bury six inches, with another six inches bent outward at the bottom below ground. To discourage skunks, rid the lawn of grubs, as described in an earlier section.

Repellents and Fumigants

Moth flakes may be tried, but they have to be renewed frequently, and there must be enough to vaporize and the smell has to blanket the area. Results with moth balls are spotty. Ammonia-soaked cloths are repellent and may be useful in a closed garbage can. Sometimes gas cartridges are used for fumigating skunk dens, but be prepared to run fast after lighting one.

Trapping

Traps should be set near the entrance to dens or along trails commonly used by the animal. Setting two or more traps at the same time is useful, particularly if there is more than one animal, which there often is.

Kinds of Traps

Use live traps, such as Havahart traps. (See the chapter "Understanding Control Methods.")

Bait

Skunks will usually go for fish flavors such as fish-flavored cat food. Other good baits are bread crust coated with peanut butter or sardines. Young skunks often will walk into a trap with no bait. Since many animals and all pets are attracted to these baits, it is not a good idea to ever lace them with poison. Moreover, skunks that are suffering from poison are likely to give off a powerful unpleasant odor. Baits don't work when skunks are digging for grubs; it's almost like a feeding frenzy and they won't go after any bait in a trap, not even one made of ground-up grubs.

Other Methods

Electrical or electronic yard guards that give off sounds of beeps or high-frequency pulses may deter animals for a short while, but once they realize that the sounds don't hurt, they ignore them. Skunks have been caught in unbaited traps with a $100 electronic Yard Guard Protector with motion sensor mounted right on top of the trap.

SQUIRRELS

Certainly part of the enjoyment of the garden is seeing squirrels running, jumping, chasing each other. Often a pair will scamper together in a seemingly romantic relationship. Their little tails twitch as they sit upright on their little haunches and eat acorns. We all love these furry friends of the field, as long as they stay in the field. But too often, upon opening the attic door to find the Christmas ornaments, one is greeted by the unmistakable sickly stench of . . . squirrel. Once smelled, it's never forgotten.

Winter is cold outside, and many animals, squirrels, rats, mice, voles, and raccoons, like to come into our heated houses. The problem is we don't like them to. While squirrels are fun to watch in the garden, they are a definite burden indoors. As they try to get closer to the warm ceiling and walls, they do damage, chewing holes in walls and insulation and shorting out electric wires. They also ruin stored clothing and blankets in which they choose to nest.

Though charming to watch in the garden, they are actually a menace, severely damaging trees, shrubs, orchards, and crops. The only small comfort is that they are even worse in England. Many bird lovers also hate squirrels because they raid bird feeders and gobble up all the seed. Some people put out special squirrel food in special feeding stations to woo them from bird seed. Others spend their time trying to shoo them away, which is an exercise in utter futility. Squirrel perseverance will outlast any human's, and their gymnastic feats of leaps, jumps, and tightrope walking are legendary. These acrobats can easily jump ten or more feet and hang on to whatever they hit. They will walk on clotheslines, under and over twirling baffles, leap onto tiny moving feeders—anything for a nice bird seed.

How to Recognize Squirrel Damage

Indoors, squirrels like to nest and raise their young in boxes of your best stored clothing, where they make a mess. If you find a cache of seeds and your wedding dress has a rotton brown spot, mother squirrel has been there.

Outdoors, they love fresh greenery when they can find it, young leaves, twigs, flowers, seeds, and vegetables. Most infuriating is the disappearance of spring bulbs, especially tulip and crocus buds, making gardeners ready to kill when roundly robbed of spring's anticipated joy.

Squirrels will strip tree bark to get the sap beneath. Also, in certain seasons, they clip twigs and drop them to the ground to get the seeds; however, their greatest economic damage is to fruit. They love fruit! They can strip a crop or damage an ornamental in no time flat. When they can get them, squirrels eat birds' eggs and, though rarely, insects. They scavenge roadkill, and some cannibalize their own kind.

As fall comes, they gather nuts and acorns, storing them in their cheek pouches until they find a suitable spot to store or bury them. They can bury up to twenty-five nuts an hour. The problem is they have bad memories and can't remember where to look. So they dig all over the place hoping to find them, which is great for the propagation of trees, but rotten for the backyard.

They also have a tendency to dig in newly turned soil and softened areas. If bulbs come up in the oddest places, it's often because a squirrel has dug them up and replanted them only to forget them. Other squirrel problems are accidents caused when people and horses trip in the holes of burrow-digging ground squirrels. Their tunneling weakens levees and earthen dams, undermines roadways, and causes erosion. When they burrow in irrigation ditches, they cause leaks, wasting precious water.

Scientific Information

There are twenty-three species and 119 subspecies of squirrels in the United States, at least ten of which cause agricultural or public health problems. Most squirrels are not problem animals, except when they eat backyard plants, damage trees, and get into houses.

A squirrel's main preoccupation is eating. The time of peak feeding activity in summer is the first two hours after sunrise, and midafternoon. In winter, when it's cold, they forage more during midday. They eat about sixty species of plants, although about 10 percent of their diet is animals, mainly birds' eggs and chicks. They follow regular lanes marked by scent, both on the ground and through the trees. These can be discovered by careful observation or by footprints in the snow.

Two litters are born per year, sometimes more in warmer climates. In the wild, their survival rate is about 50 percent, and their life span about one year; as pets, however, they have been known to live up to ten years. Their predators are many: dogs, cats, owls, hawks, weasels, foxes, raccoons, cars, and hunters, which accounts for their brief life span in the wild. When the acorn crop (called mast) is low, squirrel populations decline.

Squirrels that are trapped and taken somewhere else will come back unless the distance is several miles or across a wide body of water. However, moving wild animals is against the law in many states.

Diseases

Squirrels carry several serious diseases including capillaria, mycosis, leptospirosis, and, in the Southwest, plague. Most of these are transmitted by their fleas, so if trapped squirrels are handled, take appropriate precautions to avoid getting fleas. For example, before handling trapped animals, spray them with an insecticide to keep the fleas from jumping onto you. Squirrels also get rabies but seldom transmit it to humans.

Control Methods

Exclusion—Indoors

They may be kept out of buildings using the same techniques as for rats, mainly covering entrance points with metal or cement. Yearly inspection is wise because they chew different places to get inside. Finding their entrance holes is not easy, but by observing them for several days, especially when there's snow on the ground, you may be lucky. If not, ask an exterminator to help you.

Look behind drainpipes, under eaves,

check the space between the lowest clapboard and the foundation, and any weak areas that can be chewed open for additional entrances. For persistent squirrels, tack sheet metal over corners or edges that are not flush and could be chewed.

Many species do not hibernate but go outside foraging whenever the sun is out, so close up their entrance holes with tin, hardware cloth, or concrete while they are outside. Also, whenever possible, remove any trees within ten feet of a building, and cut any overhanging branches that give easy access to the roof. Chimneys can be covered with hardware cloth.

Exclusion—Outdoors

Fencing is usually not effective except for berry cages. (See the chapter "Understanding Control Methods" in Part II.)

Trapping

Most squirrels are not problem squirrels. They are charming creatures that make the outdoors alive and amusing. Only squirrels that actually cause problems should be trapped. To get rid of them, use a live trap such as a Havahart trap. A gluttonous appetite makes squirrels easy to catch. See what route they take and set the trap in an appropriate place. Although other squirrels will eventually refill an empty habitat, trapping may give a season of relief. It's usually necessary to trap several squirrels to end the problem. You may think there's just one, but there are always many more. They just all look alike.

Squirrels are nervous creatures and will often die if left in a trap overnight. Sometimes carnivorous animals will eat them while they are in the cage. Wildlife laws require that they be disposed of in a humane way, so contact your state wildlife agency or health department to find out what laws apply to your state, or hire a licensed trapper to dispose of them.

Bait

Use peanut butter and peanuts. Scatter bits of broken peanuts around to attract them to the trap area. Also useful are seeds, grain, small fruit, though some ground squirrel species prefer fresh succulent greens.

Poisons ☠

Because of their feeding habits, poison should not be used for squirrels. They are very likely to move it or bury it somewhere and forget it where another animal or even a child could find it. Squirrels will eat rat poison cakes, though it's ☠ dangerous to put them around outside.

Hunting

Shooting or using a slingshot are time-tested control methods. They're challenging, though, as squirrels are so fast and so agile.

Repellents

Most chemical taste and odor repellents are ineffective with squirrels. However, some bitter-tasting ones containing Thiram can protect succulent shoots and are very useful for spring bulbs. It will damage some leaves, so use only on the plants specifically named on the container label. If in doubt, test a few plants first and wait to see if the leaves develop brown areas. Of course, brown areas are better than no leaves at all. Do not use Thiram ☠ on edible crops.

Keeping Squirrels out of Bird Feeders

Another approach is to prevent squirrels from getting into the feeders. Total ingenuity is necessary to devise squirrel-proof bird feeders, so be forewarned. A few have won battles; no one has ever won the war. Squirrels who raid bird feeders are always fat and hated, and it's hard to outwit these acrobats.

Supposedly, squirrels don't like hot red pepper, so it can be smeared on anything you want them to stay off. Special bird seed coated with red pepper is available because birds are immune to hot pepper.

A few bird feeders have been successful in keeping squirrels at bay. The best one has a weight-sensitive platform that closes when a fat squirrel or heavy bird like a pigeon alights upon it. However, it stays open when small, light birds come to feed. The spring-balance mechanism can be adjusted to the weight of birds you want to exclude. One brand is called "The Absolute Feeder." If you ask anyone who has one, "Does it work?" the usual answer is "Absolutely!"—which is probably how it got its name.

Another feeder has an inner feeding tube surrounded by a widely spaced vinyl-coated wire grid through which small birds can pass, but larger birds and animals cannot. It is most useful for feed like suet stuck with sunflower seeds, which doesn't spill. If a squirrel can't get into a bird feeder, it will shake the feeder vigorously until the seeds fall on the ground.

Some folks have devised a long clotheslines arrangement so they can pull

Squirrel-safe bird feeder. Use suet for best results.

BUT WHAT IF YOU LIKE SQUIRRELS

Many people like to feed squirrels because they're amusing to watch and can be trained to recognize you. They're smart enough to know whose hand feeds them! An open hanging feeder where they can sit and you can see them is most fun. However, remember, squirrels are wild animals and should not be fed out of your hand. Additionally, in areas where rabies exists, it's not advisable to scatter food on the ground. Squirrel feeding stations should always be hung like bird feeders or nailed up on trunks of trees so that other animals, particularly raccoons that may carry the disease, will not be attracted to the yard to raid them.

the feeders in and out to a porch. Baffles may be needed to keep the squirrels from executing an elegant tightrope walk to the feeder. Aluminum pie plates with holes in the center or old records may be used as baffles. Round film containers that turn and spin when strung on the rope will also cause them to lose their footing.

Another technique is to hoist a feeder up high in the air, hanging from a high, long, isolated branch with a long rope weighted with a rock. When the feeder is hoisted up, it is left raised in the air between ground and branch, at least ten feet out from the trunk. It can be hoisted up and down like a flag to be refilled.

The Audubon Society suggests feeders be mounted on tall poles, at least ten feet high and freestanding, possibly greased. (The grease has to be applied often. A ten-foot ladder is needed to fill the feeder. Besides, who wants to grease a pole?) Slippery baffles may be tried to keep squirrels from climbing up poles and also from getting a hold onto hanging feeders.

If you like battling with metal weapons, like knights of old, there are squirrel

and raccoon baffles on the market that go over poles. There are two basic types of baffles: either they are large round metal plates, turned down at the edges, that are supposed to prevent the animals from climbing poles to bird feeders. Or they are hollow tubes, open on the bottom and closed on the top, that fit over poles. The animals crawl up into the tube, and when they get to the top it is closed.

Some suggestions range from the ridiculous to the sublime. One book that lists "101 cunning stratagems" to outwit squirrels suggests digging a moat around your feeder and filling it with water, then adding piranha (carnivorous fish). We will not cover the other 100.

A simpler approach is to put out a single handful of seeds at a time in an open platform feeder when birds appear looking for food. They will soon become accustomed to your schedule and will appear whenever they see you. And they will learn to peep at you if you don't notice them, even indoors through a window. These welcomed friends will gobble up every morsel you put out, leaving nothing behind to attract squirrels. You will also have the fun of choosing the birds you want to visit you.

WOLVES

As infants, Romulus, the legendary founder of ancient Rome, and his twin brother, Remus, were thrown into the Tiber River but were saved, and suckled, by a she-wolf. An unlikely story, but the kind of improbable story that primitive people turn into myth by repetition. Perhaps to assuage their fears of both abandonment and wolves. Little Red Riding Hood is a similar story, possibly meant to teach children to be wary of the dangers in the forest, much as we teach our children to look carefully before crossing streets.

In England in the Middle Ages, wolves were so common and dangerous that at the time of Alfred the Great, January was called Wolfmonat, or wolf month, and was set aside for hunting them. They were also significant carriers of rabies. They became almost extinct in most of England in 1500 and eventually on the continent. Perhaps the wolves in Europe became so dangerous because they lost their fear of and respect for man, possibly through interbreeding with domestic dogs. When the Puritans settled in America, they levied a one-cent bounty on wolves.

Our new wilderness fantasy of somehow running with wolves creates another myth. But it's mostly modern media mush suggesting that somehow these socially well organized packs of predatory wild animals are not that different from the family pet dog. Wolves look like dogs. They howl in unison, like good watchdogs. They signal with their tails up or down. And that's about where the similarity ends. According to recent DNA tests on 67 breeds of dogs and 162 wolves on four continents, dogs and wolves took different evolutionary paths 100,000 years ago.

These hunters, wolves, though fascinating, are motivated by wild animal basics—eating, reproducing, and surviving. As predators, they serve a useful purpose in natural ecosystems by keeping down the populations of herbivores like deer, elk, and buffalo.

Extremely efficient hunters, savage and fearless, wolves work in packs with a plan of attack that would make von Clausewitz proud. Their strategy is designed to lead to the "total defeat of the enemy," even including that "no victory is effective without pursuit." They follow their prey with a relentless "emphasis on the essentials." You'd think they had read his book on war.

A well-disciplined battalion, wolves act together, supported in their cooperation by frequently reinforced pack bonding rituals. The dominant (alpha) male or female leads a charge that is both vicious and determined. It continues, if there are enough reinforcements, until victory is achieved.

Wolves chase animals much larger than themselves: deer, caribou, bighorn sheep, moose, and even follow buffalo herds. The "enemy," or prey, is carefully chosen for weakness and vulnerability. Like lions, they pick one animal on the edge, probably noticing a slowness or infirmity.

Wolves have only their teeth to fight with, so several will grab and hang on to the animal's rear, where they cannot be bitten, or gored by a buffalo's sharp horns. They swarm and circle, attacking again and again, in waves. Finally, they exhaust the larger animal, unless they themselves are spent first, in which case they retreat in defeat to try again another day.

The dominant males or females enforce discipline in the packs. (They walk with their tails up, whereas the lesser members keep their tails down.) Alphas are the chieftains, exercising control as long as they're strong enough to fight and beat all challengers. Eventually, as they age or weaken, they're replaced, with no pity and no medals for valiant service to the pack. As an African saying goes, "The chief must go behind his shield or be carried out on top of it."

To quote the popular television series *Nature*, "The wolf is forced by nature to kill, which is hard for our human sensibility" because, the voice-over explains, we haven't had to kill for our food for a long time. This statement actually accompanies a scene showing a pack of wolves eating a buffalo while it is still alive.

The way wolves hunt is graphically and correctly depicted in Walt Disney's *Beauty and the Beast* cartoon movie. Many children have had nightmares, and some adults are a bit dismayed as well, because a child, Beauty, is made into wolf bait to sell the movie. Beast, who rescues Beauty, even looks a little buffalo-esque. Red Riding Hood's comment, "What big teeth you have" may only be in a fairy tale, but it is based on fact.

Because of their liking for domestic livestock, wolves were hunted almost to extinction in most of the United States and were placed on the list of endangered animals. In the mid-1990s, however, several packs from Canada were reintroduced into Yellowstone National Park in Wyoming.

After two years, they had settled in, were breeding successfully, and were changing the park's wildlife hierarchy and animal behavior. Coyotes had been the top predatory animal in the park, but the wolves challenged them, attacked, and often killed them and their pups. Other changes are that elk are now huddling in large groups, bears are fighting wolves, and coyotes are retreating and being attacked by bears.

In the past, the absence of wolves changed the natural balance of predator and prey, which allowed a population explosion of species such as elk and deer. Wolves are expected to kill about 1,200 elk, deer, and moose a year, which will help control those populations and keep them in better balance with the herbivore-carrying capacity of the park. Unfortunately, some wolves roam beyond the park borders onto ranches. In the first year they were introduced, no livestock were killed. The second year, more than a dozen were killed, and the next year several dozen, but the ranchers were compensated for the loss from a wildlife fund.

As wolves are introduced into wilderness areas, their populations will rise and fall in accordance with their food source, but when hungry, they will extend their territory onto ranches and inhabited areas. As long as the wolf populations are kept in balance with the food supply in the parks, and if people hiking, living, or farming in nearby areas take precautions, the problems can be managed. However, if too many wolves breed too successfully and become the main problem themselves, it will upset the planned population balance envisioned by the wildlife experts.

The United States Fish and Wildlife Service expected enough wolves to naturalize so that by 2002 they could be removed from the endangered list. However, the wolves have been breeding so well that they should be off the list much sooner.

Traditionally, in America, gray wolves (also called timber wolves) generally did not attack people but were wary of humans, probably because they recognized them as dangerous. However, if the romantic "wild mythology" is put ahead of human safety, accidents and tragedies will happen as these hunters lose their fear of man and become bolder.

How to Tell If Wolves Are in Your Area

Ask. Don't wait for an accident. The wildlife service of every state can advise you, although its biologists, who understand animal ways and are instinctively cautious, may downplay the risk. Find out how to conduct yourself in wilderness areas.

When a Wolf Is Most Likely to Cause Problems

Wolves normally are creatures of the wild and don't approach human areas unless very hungry, usually in times of drought or famine. Then pets or even children may become vulnerable. Livestock is always vulnerable near parks or preserves, and wolves that stray outside the parks should be reported as soon as possible for capture and removal, or elimination. When hiking in woods or fields inhabited by wolves, people should take every precaution and probably carry firearms for defense. Never approach wolf pups because there most surely is a parent or watchwolf guarding them nearby.

Wolves in the Garden

Wolves aren't a problem because they're not into onions and cabbages. However, the same scents that tempt dogs and cats might attract them. Garbage and organic fertilizers with fish and meat scents, as well as bonemeal, should be kept inside. If these are used in the garden, they should be well buried underground. Or stick to chemical fertilizers. Female dogs that run free might attract wolves, especially when they're in heat.

Scientific Information

One of the largest living canids, a large northern male wolf may measure five feet in length, including its two-foot bushy tail, and stand three feet high. Females are smaller. Prior to their reintroduction in Yellowstone Park, they were found only in Alaska and Canada, and they are extremely rare in Europe.

The wolf's first call of the evening is an unforgettable long, deep, tremulous sound. Actually the wolf has several calls. One is a high, soft, plaintive call; a lusty, throaty howl is a mating call; and a deep, loud, guttural roar is the call of the chase.

Though wilderness animals, they inhabit both open and forested areas. However, when hunted, they become wary and stay in dense timber and thickets. They usually hunt in small packs, rarely large groups, using their speed and endurance to win. They gorge when hungry.

Wolves often mate for life. Breeding is from December to April. Pups, four to fourteen to a litter, are born about two months later in dens on banks or rocky crevices, usually with a sunny exposure. The young mature in two or three years and often remain with the family group. Members of the pack are friendly to each other but will drive off or kill almost all outsiders. While a wolf may live twenty years in the wild, it is old after but a dozen years. Old wolves are called "gummers" by trappers because their teeth are usually worn way down.

Diseases and Interbreeding Problems

Wolves rarely transmit diseases to humans, but they can carry rabies and most of the illnesses that affect pet dogs. Another danger, though not a disease, is that wild wolves may breed with domestic dogs that run loose. The resulting offspring will inherit the genes that make wolves wild and dangerous. Half-breeds make unpredictable pets. Wildlife services generally want these half-breeds registered with them for safety and control as they really come under the wild animal laws. Half-breeds born to wild females may have a genetic tendency to approach and befriend people, which can be even more dangerous.

Control Methods

Exclusion

In areas that have wolves, sturdy fences are a wise precaution in residential areas, and are essential if there are tempting treats like livestock, chickens, kittens, or small dogs. Needless to say, children and babies should always be well watched and protected in such locales. In parts of Alaska that have wolves, mothers always stay in the backyard with their children and often keep firearms handy.

Despite all the modern mystique of running wild, finding our inner savage selves, humanized cartoon characters, and anthropromorphizing, Red Riding Hood's danger still is the reality. Wolves are strong and can be dangerous.

Trapping

Trapping is not a job for amateurs. When wolves, coyotes, or even wild dogs run in packs, they can become a public health threat. Some years ago, in the Bronx, the ultimate urban environment, packs of strays dogs were threatening people and had to be eliminated by the health department.

When wolves stalk around a residence, the wildlife service should be contacted immediately. It can decide whether the animal is a danger and should be trapped, relocated, or possibly shot. That's the law. It's also common sense. Bear in mind that a normal-looking animal may be diseased or hungry. In any case, never, never approach a predator stalking a house or a person.

Hunting

All states have complex rules for hunting, especially for endangered or threatened species. If you kill such an animal, there are all kinds of complications. Obviously, you can shoot to save your life, but if possible, get inside and use the telephone first. You may save yourself a court appearance or a hefty fine. If you report a threatening animal and your wildlife service won't help, you might have to contact a lawyer to protect yourself. Wildlife laws are not always sensible.

WOODCHUCKS

Woodchucks are Mother Nature's lawn mowers. And weed wackers. And leaf strippers. Woodchucks are the absolute worst pest in gardens and on farms. More people have given up, in disgust, on growing a variety of things, because weeks of effort and care were demolished in one evening by this despised marmot. It is the only animal for whom there can be no quarter in the battle for the backyard.

Although not picky eaters, these groundhogs instinctively know which is your most cherished plant or vegetable, and they start there. They proceed to anything else that's green. When they're done, it looks as though a

drunken lawn mower has gone through. Everything's cut down to short stubble. Sometimes, the 'chucks don't eat the flowers but instead just strip off all the tender leaves, leaving naked, naked stems.

It is war! If one is to garden, the woodchuck must be excluded. The battle plan needs to use all the strategies gleaned from generals, political strategists, warriors, even old Maine farmers, for woodchucks

are a formidable foe. Of course, as the good Baron von Clausewitz says, "In war, the result is never final." There is always another year, with another wandering four-legged lawn mower that settles into your backyard. And then the battle plans must begin anew.

Is it worth the effort? Well, after a while you'll begin to wonder.

How to Tell If You Have Woodchucks

One morning all the beautiful beans will be nibbled nubbins, or the prize phlox just bare stems, or the violets entirely disappeared. Sometimes the tree or shrub bark is clawed or gnawed, and fruit may be eaten.

If you look carefully, in the early morning or evening, eventually you will see a lumbering gray/brown mound munching. Or more likely, a flat head, with eyes and ears on top, will appear above the grass or weeds, standing upright and looking all around as if to smell the air. Woodchucks are not shy. In fact, they like sunbathing during the day, often stretched out on a nice warm rock.

Another hazard is their burrows. The large entrance holes (six to twelve inches) and adjacent mounds of fresh earth can waylay equipment, horses, and people.

When Woodchucks Are Most Likely to Cause Problems

On the Fourth of July! Patriotic animals, they kick their babies out of the nest around Independence Day. As the young look for a new territory, any garden is inviting. The young move into abandoned dens and begin to feed. Because they're not yet worldly wise and wary, they are easiest to catch at this time. The new burrows that appear in late summer are usually dug by older animals.

Scientific Information

Woodchucks, also called whistling pig or groundhog, will make use of any location where the eating's good and their population can become quite dense. If you see one woodchuck, there are usually several more, or will be by next year. They weigh on average eight pounds and eat approximately one third of their weight in vegetation each day. And that's a lot of violets!

Common noises are a "tchuck," a "phew," and a whistle (hence the nickname whistle-pig). Their predators are hawks, owls, coyotes, foxes, bobcats, weasels, dogs, and humans.

Woodchucks are found in most central and eastern states and Canada. Each spring, they produce a litter of two to nine young, though usually just four. Adults weigh four to twelve pounds, come in varying shades of gray to brown, rarely albino or black. Life span is about five years.

Their burrows are large and long, with two or more entrances. The many chambers can go as deep as five feet and spread from eight to fifty feet in length. Well-drained knolls are the preferred burrow sites, but they may be dug under a stone wall, a ledge, a fallen tree root, or along fencerows. Good housekeepers, woodchucks frequently bring up new soil and leave it around the entrances. And that's how you know they are active burrows.

A woodchuck's range is not enormous, 50 to 100 feet from the den, yet when smitten with passion, they may travel miles to find a mate. Though slow and lumbering, they can move with quick agility, jumping into their burrows when alarmed, and they fight to defend their territory. They also can swim, climb trees, and easily scramble over walls and fences.

One of the few mammals that hibernates deeply, these animals may remain in a true torpor for several months, awakening only to mate in February or March, then to sleep again until spring.

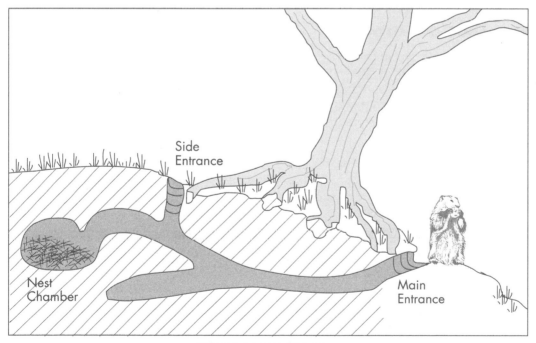

WOODCHUCK BURROW

Diseases

Woodchucks carry rabies. If they are trapped or found dead, carry out careful preventative measures when handling them, the traps, or when touching any of their bodily fluids. For more information on rabies, see the chapters "Raccoons" and "Animal Diseases (Zoonoses)."

If you see an animal on your property acting strangely or threateningly, immediately call the police, take your pets, and go inside. It may be sick. Healthy animals are afraid of humans and will run if you shout or clap, make loud noises, or throw a rock at them.

Control Methods

Let's start with what doesn't work.

Screaming works for about a half hour. Once. Blasphemy doesn't help. 'Chucks are very persistent and return the minute you turn your back.

Noisemakers also don't work for long, nor do expensive electronic beeping devices. These critters learn quickly that noise alone won't hurt them. Fox scent does not scare them, nor predator urine.

Because they have sensitive noses, they don't like the prickly vines of pumpkins, squash, and cucumber. If planted around the beans, they may move on to eat other things. Then again, they may not. They like to eat pumpkins.

One frustrated agricultural extension agent published an article asking for suggestions and new ideas. Not one useful thing came back.

Exclusion

Fencing will deter woodchucks. Since they generally amble along the ground, they may just go around the outside of the fence. Particularly if you plant the least tasty and desirable flowers and vegetables around the inside edge of the fence. (For plants, see chapter on poisonous plants.)

Fencing should be sturdy, at least three feet high, and ideally buried in the ground. Bend the top of the fence outward to make scaling more difficult. Woodchucks can climb when the spirit moves them. To make fencing more effective, one can also use electric wires about four inches to the outside, and four to five inches off the ground. Keep all vegetation from touching the wire, or it will short out. Use a herbicide, salt, motor oil, very thick ashes, or the chalky residue from swimming pool filters to prevent vegetation from growing into the wire. (For more details, see the chapter "Understanding Control Methods.")

The Old Maine Farmer's "fence" is worth mentioning. If a man, with lots of testosterone, pees along the edges of the garden each night, he will mark the territory as his, and theoretically no woodchuck will cross his scent. This has never been subjected to controlled scientific testing.

Repellents

There are none registered for woodchucks, but hot red cayenne may keep them from nibbling. Bitter Thiram-laced animal repellents will work, but since woodchucks prefer tender greens, Thiram may harm these. Still, it's worth a try. Apply Thiram only to those plants listed as safe on the label, and never to vegetables or edible crops. ☠

Trapping

Properly baited Havahart traps work quite well, although as the animals age, they become wary and harder to catch. For this reason, it's best to trap them as soon as you see them each year. Once ensconced in a nice den, the females will produce a sizable new litter each spring, and you'll just give up.

If you had a woodchuck last year, you'll have more this year. So set out traps as early as possible in the season, as soon as the grass begins to grow, and they are hungry. One wants to catch the females early before they produce the new litter. If the population is low, trapping is an effective way to keep the problem under control. Where the population is large, help from a professional trapper or exterminator may be needed.

Set traps in the travel lanes or as near as possible to the burrow entrance. (The entrance is where the fresh dirt is piled up.) Sometimes two traps close together are better than one, so if the critter backs out of one, he rushes into the next one.

Near the nest, placing logs or wood to define a path to the trap helps. Or a path can be created with small bits of bait, leading to the trap. Baiting the ground in front of and behind the trap with small bits of bait helps too. After all, the animal has to *want* to go inside. And he will want to if tempted outside with tiny bits, but with more food he can see or smell inside the trap.

Woodchucks are strong animals. When caught, they'll wrestle and turn over the cage until they spring the trap and free themselves. If you catch an animal in a Havahart trap, you will hear it rattling the trap. As soon as possible, secure the gates with crossbars of metal or strong wood at each end. (For more details on traps, see the chapters "Raccoons" and "Understanding Control Methods.")

Remember to exercise caution when handling traps with animals. Don't put your hands anywhere near where they might be scratched or bitten. Always wear disposable gloves or plastic bags on your hands, because the animals may carry rabies. Also beware of the hordes of fleas, which are hard to avoid.

OLD WIVES' TALES

Frustrated gardeners and farmers have tried everything they could think of. Most of these ideas are on a par with the Old Maine Farmer's fence. None have ever been tested with proper placebo controls, nor have results been replicated with any statistical accuracy. Just think of them as psychotherapy for backyard frustration.

- Put dog droppings in the entrance of the burrow.
- Collect predator scents, such as lion, fox, coyote, etc., and put them down the hole. Or put them in the garden. (You may not like the fragrance.) Ditto predator urine.
- Fill a can with gasoline and put it inside the entrance hole. The smell may drive them away.
- Spray powdered aloe on plants. Reapply after each rain.

Who knows, one of these methods may work for you. Or perhaps the woodchucks will leave because of disease, predators, old age, better eating elsewhere, sun flares, the early arrival of the monsoons in the Himalayas, or the elephants stampeding in India.

Bait

Apples and broccoli are recommended by some experts. Carrots and lettuce by others. Change the bait daily. They like it fresh. Strawberry sugar cookie wafers and peanuts are the universal favorite of one successful exterminator. Woodchucks are opportunistic eaters and will take the food that's closest to home. Baiting the trap with some of the plants they are eating is useful, especially if they don't take the bait you put out. But be forewarned; mature woodchucks are one of the most difficult animals to catch in a trap.

Disposal of Trapped Animals

Because of the wildlife laws in most places, disposal is much more difficult than trapping. Call your U.S. Fish and Wildlife Service or your agricultural extension agent and find out what the law in your state is before you set the trap. All laws are different. Agricultural states usually are more helpful than urban ones, even though woodchucks (as well as raccoons and skunks) are urban problems too. See the chapter "Understanding Control Methods" for more information on disposal.

GROUNDHOG DAY

Lore says that on February Second the woodchuck will come out of his burrow to look for his shadow. If the day is sunny and he sees it, winter will be six weeks longer, so the woodchuck runs back in to hibernate. If it's cloudy and there's no shadow, he thinks it's spring and stays above ground. In fact, if the creature is stirring at all, he's probably just waking up to mate, at least in the warmer part of his range. Then, that job done, he clunks out again.

Now, each year, on February Second in Punxsutawney, Pennsylvania, people gather to forecast winter's length by watching a man in a cutaway coat, striped pants, and top hat hold up a hibernating woodchuck for the media. In 1997, 25,000 people actually showed up for the event. Perhaps there's not much else to do in them parts in winter. The woodchuck, named Punxsutawney Phil, correctly forecast the weather in three of the previous six winters, about the same odds as tossing a coin.

This old myth stems from religious beliefs associated with Candlemas, an early primitive celebration of the midpoint between the Winter Solstice (December) and the Vernal Equinox (March). An old English song goes:

> If Candlemas be fair and bright,
>   Come, Winter, have another flight.
> If Candlemas bring clouds and rain,
>   Go, Winter, and come not again.

The original animal myth, which involved groundhogs, badgers, or bears, came to the United States with the German settlers to Pennsylvania.

Poisons ☠

Because these animals are often in close proximity to people and pets, poison should not be used in the traps or pushed down into the holes. The woodchucks might just shovel it up again in their daily housekeeping. Putting poison automobile antifreeze, which is sweet, inside the traps is against the law.

Get a Dog

A big barking dog. Man's trusty friend is a good deterrent. But don't let the dog actually tangle with the critter, because woodchucks will fight and can hurt pets and spread diseases. If your town has a leash law, keep the dog in the fenced-in yard.

Gassing the Burrow ☠

For farmers, a commercial gas cartridge, usually containing carbon monoxide, is the most common way to get rid of woodchucks. The poisonous ☠ gas floods the burrow, making it uninhabitable. The cartridges usually also produce smoke to serve as a marker.

Carbon dioxide from fire extinguishers, and unlighted propane, ☠ both of which are heavier than air and will settle in the tunnels, have been used. However, they haven't been tested as have the commercial cartridges, and it takes a lot of gas to fill up the large burrows. Road flares ☠ whose active ingredient is sulphur may work, if lighted and shoved into the burrow. Another possibility is pouring diesel fuel into the burrow and setting it on fire.

☠ *Great caution must be taken when gassing!* This can be done at any time, but is usually done in spring before the young emerge. A government wildlife bulletin advises the following precautions:

1. The fumes must never be breathed. All gases can kill people, ☠ and propane and diesel fuel are flammable.
2. Never use gas in, near, or under buildings. In the dry season, even the commercial cartridges may be a fire hazard ☠.
3. Find the burrow openings. There may be several. Dig up a piece of sod to fit completely over each. Cover all but one. Have a few extra sod clods on hand for other openings that you didn't know existed.
4. ☠ Carefully follow the instructions on the label of the gas cartridge.
5. Kneel at the burrow opening, light the fuse, and immediately place (do not throw) the cartridge as far down the hole as possible. Quickly cover the

hole with a piece of sod. If the sod is placed with the grass side down, dirt will not shake off and smother the cartridge.

6. Watch for nearby holes where smoke escapes. Reseal those.
7. Active burrows will have freshly dug soil at the entrances. Treat each burrow independently.
8. Burrows may be reoccupied by another animal, and may have to be retreated. Gassing the burrows is not that easy, but it works.

Shooting

Because they're slow, woodchucks are easy targets using a rifle, especially with a telescopic lens. But you have to get them with the first shot, or they'll dive into their hole. When shooting outdoors, the bullets can ricochet and harm someone, so great care must be taken. Note that firearms are prohibited in many towns. In most states, woodchucks are considered game animals, and a hunting license may be required.

INSECTS AND INVERTEBRATES
BUGS, BLIGHTS, AND OTHER BLOKES

Any garden battle plan needs to address pests of the smaller variety, since they can provoke just as much agony and frustration.

If it's not one problem critter, it's another. For every plant, there is a bug . . . or two . . . or more. They come early, they stay late, and in the evanescent moonlight, they busily produce families of thousands. No matter how unusual or rare a plant may be, some insect will discover it, take up housekeeping, and maybe even eat it. Floating fungi spores will settle in. Viruses will attach and replicate their genes. It's a devil of a battle to control insects and diseases.

Control is more complicated these days because the long-acting pesticides have been taken off the market, and the safer ones are not effective for very long. For ex-ample, DDT (now outlawed) could control insects for months. But this very toxic chemical had to be banned because it lasted forever in fat cells, the food chain, and the environment. Plus insects adapted with genetic mutations and quickly became immune to it.

Today, it's a constant battle to develop safer substances that will control insects and fungi before they develop resistance to them. When they become immune, additional new products have to be developed.

Pest Management Theories

Many ideas have been tried to lessen the use of pesticides and increase plant health. Making use of all the cultural sophistication we know and using as few pesticides as possible is now well accepted by farmers and professional landscapers.

The theories have gone by different names over time. About twenty years ago the concept was called Integrated Pest Management (IPM). This theory finally became accepted and at least partially understood by most of the public, though they probably don't know its name. A few years ago Plant Health Care (PHC) came along and now Low Input Sustainable Agriculture (LISA). These theories make use of all the pesticides and fertilizers available but as safely and as sparingly as possible. Organic farming uses the same concepts but allows absolutely no chemicals, only natural substances.

The main thrust of all these approaches is to manipulate the growing ecosystem in such a way as to discourage insects and diseases. And to promote healthier plants because it is believed that vigorous plants can better withstand predator attacks and environmental stresses. In other words, one tries to build biological control into pest management strategies. If ever the wisdom of those old war horses von Clausewitz and Sun Tzu was needed, it is in the current battle, where one fights problem pests by turning their own biology back on themselves. Information and understanding are essential for success.

Insect Life Cycles and Pesticide Use

Current scientific advice is to start with the least toxic remedy for a problem, and if it doesn't work, only then go on to stronger stuff. If you examine any plant, it always has insect and fungi visitors. The current philosophy is to only treat particular plants, and then only where you see insects causing significant trouble.

Not all bugs eat everything all of the time. Each bug has its favorite victims. Understanding insect life cycles tells us when each bug should arrive, mature, lay eggs, and depart. Scientific measurements have produced, based on weather temperature analyses, Growing Degree Days (GDD), which predict exactly when each bug will emerge or each blight will appear. State agricultural extension services can provide the GDDs for each area, often as a manual that includes identification of fungi and insects plus proper treatments.

The time to control problems is just as the bugs or blights first appear. Waiting until insects are large or too numerous make control more difficult. So keep your eyes open and catch 'em quick and early. When they are young, they are more vulnerable and so more susceptible to control strategies. Reapply when they return.

Cultural Practices

By changing the planting times or pH of the soil or watering schedules, certain problems can be lessened. For instance, the cabbage family prefers a sweet soil (around pH 7), which retards the disease called clubroot. Potato, on the other hand, does best in an acid soil (around pH 5.3), which helps prevent potato scab.

Some crops are planted early or late to avoid the hatch date of certain insects. Rose bushes, when pruned very early in spring before the buds swell, generally will not attract cane borers, which lay their eggs in the pithy center of freshly cut stems. The adult stem borers don't hatch until just about the time the buds swell.

Decoy plants, insect sex attractants (called pheromones), and similar strategies that aim to draw insects away from desired plants are useful ideas. Nasturtiums, for instance, are reputed to attract aphids, so these flowers are often grown in vegetable gardens to keep the aphids away from other plants. However, they often just act as breeding ground for more aphids. Baited traps have been developed, though they are most useful for monitoring population growth. Pheromone-baited Japanese beetle traps, which are widely used, have been shown to attract more beetles than might come without them. The current

> ### BUILDING BIOLOGICAL CONTROLS INTO THE BATTLE
>
> 1. Focus on key pests, the ones that cause major problems.
> 2. Identify and protect the natural enemies that attack these problem fungi and insects.
> 3. Don't overuse chemicals that harm the helpers.
> 4. Recognize that biological controls alone can't solve all problems.

recommendation is to place Japanese beetle traps 100 feet or more from the garden area to be protected.

There are many good ideas for manipulating the environment, but their effectiveness is mostly anecdotal. Much has been written about companion planting, in which one plant is supposed to retard insects or disease on its neighbor. One English old wives' tale for retarding clubroot disease on cabbages is to bury a few sticks of rhubarb here and there at planting time. Although many people swear by some of the techniques, university testing has not shown significant benefits.

Insects

We currently believe that accommodating to the natural world is better than trying to zap every bug in sight. We can live with many—and in fact almost all—of the insects in the garden. As with troublesome animals, insects should just be controlled when they cause significant problems. Usually, only certain plants will be bothered at any one time.

Like animal populations, insect populations rise and fall, depending primarily on the weather. Many insect explosions recur at rather regular intervals that relate to rainfall. There has been speculation that these weather cycles may be connected with sun flare activity. First, heavy rains provide an abundance of food, and a population explosion begins. Different insects seem to be on different cycles, and when the numbers get too large, they outgrow their food supply.

When hungry and malnourished, insects become stressed and weak. The females produce fewer and weaker offspring. Finally, natural population controls kick in, which are usually virus or fungus diseases that attack the bugs in their weakened, stressed state. The insect population collapses, and it is soon followed by a collapse of the disease organisms that attacked them. Then they all wait around, innocuously, until the next weather cycle and the next population explosion. This is why some years there are huge numbers of one kind of insect, while at other times they seem to disappear. A population explosion usually lasts for three years from its beginning to its collapse.

To Spray or Not to Spray

Blanket spraying of pesticides is out. Today, people must consider the health of their children, their pets, and themselves before they douse the air and ground with pesticides. It has been documented that when the lawn of a house is sprayed with pesticides, the concentration of poison in the rugs of that house is many times more than what is allowed by law outside. Shoes are the villains. In addition, it's important to only spray the right pesticide at the right time for a particular problem. Applying chemicals after damage has been done or at the wrong time in the life cycle of an insect or fungus is a gigantic waste of time and money.

There are, however, circumstances when selective spraying of the least toxic pesticide on limited target plants at risk may be necessary and desirable. Mother Nature's choices may not be ours.

For example, there are some chemicals, called systemics, that are applied to the soil and absorbed through the roots directly into the tissues of plants. These are usually for sucking insects only but can be very useful in certain situations. Also, us-

---

IMPORTANT SAFETY PRECAUTIONS ☠

There are many insecticide choices. Although some insecticides are safer than others, remember that if they kill insects, they probably aren't good for you either.

- Don't breathe in the spray and wear a proper protective mask if the exposure is longer than the time it takes you to hold your breath.
- Wash any residue off your skin in the shower, and don't put contaminated clothes in with the family's, and especially the children's, laundry. Be aware that pesticides may have effects on human fertility and disease that we don't know about yet.
- Read the instructions on all pesticide ☠ packages carefully. Most of the insecticides in current use are short lasting and may need to be reapplied, sometimes in a week or ten days for continued control.
- Always check the current guidelines as new knowledge changes our thinking and the products recommended.

---

ing a rose fertilizer that contains a systemic insecticide makes growing these bug-ridden beauties much easier. Systemics are also useful for houseplants because they can be watered into the soil, instead of spraying chemicals into the indoor air. Note, however, that systemic pesticides are poisons and can never be used on food crops or where children or pets poke around in the soil. ☠

Where to Begin

Basically, there are chewing insects and sucking insects. Chewers are easy to recognize by the clean-cut edges and neat holes they leave. (Slugs tear and shred when they eat.) Sucking insects, such as aphids, mites, and white flies, make the foliage crinkled or yellow. Sucking insects, being soft-bodied, are generally easier to control safely than are chewing insects.

What's Out There Today

The list that follows will change yearly as government regulations change and as new products are licensed and old ones retired.

Chemicals

Made in factories, these have been around a long time and are now falling out of favor because of the long-term side effects both to people's health and to the environment. However, at times, they are useful and remain part of the available armaments to be kept in reserve. Much current research by large chemical companies is to synthesize the active poisons into safer, organic pesticides. The pure substances then can be used, without the many other complex chemicals that exist in natural substances.

Organic Pesticides

As our understanding of the effects of chemicals on humans and the environment increases, agriculture is turning to less toxic ways to control insects and diseases. This has sparked a new interest in "organics," which are mainly soaps, oils, and botanicals (products derived from plants). However, these organics are complex to use because each one has certain limitations and peculiarities which must be understood.

Generally, organics are not as effective as man-made chemicals. Their range of uses is more limited, and they have a short residual. They must be used according to directions and reapplied as needed, usually in seven to ten days as long as the problem pest persists. But just because a pesticide is

organic or biological doesn't mean it's safe for people. Some, such as ryania and tobacco, though botanicals, are not safer than man-made chemicals. Nicotine sulfate, made from an extract of tobacco leaves, is very toxic to mammals and has actually been outlawed by some organic farmers' associations.

Biorational Pesticides

These make use of biological processes like good bugs eating bad bugs, or insect hormones that only affect certain insects at certain stages of development. There are many new engineered insecticides, which are based on chemical analogues of the active ingredients in natural insecticides or insect hormones. They are meant to be less toxic to people and the environment and more selective in which insects they control. Because their activity is so specific, each has to be used exactly as the directions state and on the plants listed on the packages. People tend to get all excited about them when they're first introduced, without understanding how to use them properly and effectively.

Though many biological controls exist, not all are convenient for ordinary gardeners. For instance, Disney World in Orlando released about 50,000 predator wasps each week to control marigold leaf miner. It also released 13,000 good predator mites per week to eat the bad mites in its vegetable greenhouse. That's a lot of bugs for a private homeowner's backyard battle plan. Incidentally, good insects that eat other bad insects generally don't bite people. Disney's wasps are nonstinging insects that look like very tiny flies. They lay eggs in the bad bugs, and their larvae devour and kill them.

Some Safer Insecticides That Are Available

A Stream of Water

Surprisingly, a strong stream of water will knock off some insects. It's useful for mites, aphids, and some small ones that can't hang on. If repeated often enough, it may be a deterrent to population buildup of some insects.

Insecticidal Soaps

Soap is safe for people. It's useful against soft-bodied, sucking insects like scale aphids, whiteflies, mealybugs, leafhoppers, thrips, and adelgids. It kills them (particularly aphids) by clogging their breathing holes and disrupting their metabolism.

Once the soap dries, there is no residual effectiveness, so you have to hit the critters directly and it's necessary to spray under the leaves as well as on top. Soap also helps other pesticides by serving as a sticker-spreader (particularly when combined with summer oil, discussed below) and by stressing insects that it doesn't kill. Moreover, soap does not kill bees, wasps, beetles, or good predator bugs.

You can buy horticultural soaps, or you can make your own much more cheaply. Use one tablespoon of liquid dishwashing soap to one gallon of water. In a scientific experiment testing different soaps, mild Ivory liquid dishwashing soap performed best. The addition of onion, garlic, or pepper to the solution did not improve insecticide activity, as some anecdotal information has suggested.

Leaves may suffer some leaf tip burn from soap, especially young or nonshiny leaves. It is possible to test a lower concentration such as one teaspoon to one gallon. Damage is more likely if applied in very hot or sunny weather. Plants that are very sensitive to soap sprays are Japanese maple, horse chestnuts, sweet gum, tender new growth, some ferns, succulents, begonias, and azaleas. Test on a section of the plant first.

Pyrethrum

Made from an African daisy, this is an old remedy, for sucking insects, most of which are soft-bodied. Pyrethrum is nontoxic to humans, but don't breathe it in or douse your skin, as it can cause allergies and a stuffy nose. It is deactivated by soap or lime. Pyrethrum is a contact poison,

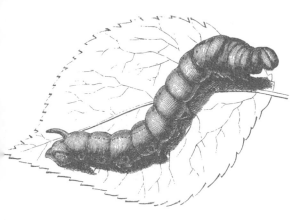

which means it kills when the insects come in contact with it. It is usually combined with rotenone to cover a wider spectrum of insects. There are new synthetic pyrethroids that are more potent and last longer and may be used as a short-acting mosquito spray.

Rotenone

Rotenone (sometimes called derris root or cube resins) is both a contact and a stomach poison, so it kills chewing insects as well and causes them to stop feeding. It is useful against some beetles, worms, thrips, and as an adjunct where a systemic insecticide (for sucking insects) has been applied to the soil. Repeated application is needed for thrip control, especially on roses. Rotenone breaks down rapidly in air and sun and is toxic to fish, so it shouldn't be used where it can get into wetlands. When you're not sure exactly what's doing a job on the plants, a combination of

pyrethrum and rotenone gets both chewers and suckers.

BT

Bacillus thuringiensis is a bacteria that releases a stomach poison for insect larvae but is safe for humans and beneficial insects. There are many strains of bacteria, each specific for certain insect species. One kind controls caterpillars on plants like cabbage. A different BT kills mosquito and blackfly larvae. Another improved strain is being tested for Japanese beetle grubs in the lawn. BT is relatively easy to buy and use effectively. It works best on small caterpillars when you first see them eating leaves. Large caterpillars often require stronger chemicals (rotenone or carbaryl). But identify the caterpillars first so you don't kill valuable butterfly larvae.

Neem

This is a new product from an old plant, the neem tree of India, which has been used as a pesticide for years. It's an insect hormone that upsets the maturation process. Neem kills many insects, though it takes several days to work and has to be reapplied as needed. It also acts as an insect repellent. Some trade names are BioNeem, Azatin, and Margosan-O. Neem is safe for humans, although an oil from the seeds has been used as a male contraceptive in India.

Summer Horticultural Oil

An improved version of another old remedy for scale, mites, and other sucking insects and also is a fungicide. This lighter-weight oil is less damaging to green leaves and is relatively long lasting; read the directions carefully, and remember, it's oil, so don't breathe it in.

Sabadilla

Usually supplied as a dust, sabadilla is safe for most humans except for some irritated noses and sneezing bouts. It does kill some hard-to-control adult insects, particularly aphids and mites. While it's OK for mammals, it's very toxic to honeybees. Since their population has been threatened by bee diseases, anything that harms them should be avoided.

Merit

This product belongs to a new class of insecticides on the market that stop insects but should be safer than chemicals. It acts on insect metabolism, causing them not to develop properly. It has been promoted against Japanese beetle grubs in lawns but must be applied at the right time to work. (See the chapter "Skunks.")

The Least Dangerous Chemical Insecticides

When the safer ones won't work, try:

Carbaryl (trade name Sevin)

This carbamate is a good insecticide for chewing insects, especially hard-shelled beetles. It harms bees and some plants, including ivy. Spray after sunset, when the bees are in their hives.

Diazinon

An organophosphate, Diazinon is useful against many insects, both chewers and suckers.

Malathion

Though much maligned, Malathion is an old standby that kills on contact; useful for most sucking insects, some chewers, and mosquitoes resting in bushes.

Chlorpyrifos

is a newer organophosphate.

For More Information

Unbiased, scientifically accurate information is hard to come by. The best source is your state extension service or a state university that has an agriculture department. There are many books, magazines, and circulars, but most have abbreviated information, as does this book. Complete identification of pests and the damage they cause is best found in large garden encyclopedias available at libraries and nurseries.

Pesticide Hotline

A National Pesticide Telecommunications Network (NPTN) has been opened to the public to answer questions about pesticides. Started by a university, it is staffed by qualified pesticide specialists in toxicology and environmental chemistry, who will help callers find local resources. Information comes from sources such as Environmental Protection Agency documents, cooperative extension publications, and scientific literature, and the NPTN maintains a pesticide product database. This hotline is a much-needed service, so let's hope the government will continue to fund it. There are a variety of ways to make contact:

Telephone: 1-800-858-7378
Fax: 541-737-0761
Web site: http//www.ace.orst.edu/info/nptn/
Email: nptn@ace.orst.edu

Learn to Recognize and Protect the Good Predator Bugs

There are many good bugs that eat bad bugs. They are dragonflies, spiders, ladybugs, ant lions (doodlebugs), aphid lions (lacewings), praying mantis, predator mites, nematodes, and tiny black parasitic wasps, among others.

One can buy many of these from catalogs, and it may be worth a try to establish them in the garden. However, if there is not enough to eat, they will die or fly away to someone else's house.

The best approach is to protect and encourage those that are in the garden already. While they will not control all insects, they will keep the populations of many down. To protect them is another reason to spray very selectively when using pesticides. Bees should also be protected, and all labels should be read carefully to learn which are harmful to them.

Save the Butterflies Too

Many caterpillars, especially large or colored caterpillars, are the larvae of beautiful butterflies, so if you see some caterpillars and don't know what they are, save them. For instance, the monarch butterfly larvae have black, white, and orange stripes and often can be found on milkweed plants. If you treasure them, they may grace your garden with beauty.

Blights

Anything that harms plants without actually eating them is loosely called a blight or disease. Problems may be caused by a fungus, a bacteria, a virus, herbicides, a combination of all of the above, or the unknown. Blights are hard to separate out and identify, even for experts. And they're even harder to treat.

Blighted leaves may get spots or may turn gray, yellow, or brown. Blighted plants may look streaked or wilted, or fall over, or just curl up and die. Most blights are not curable, although some may be controlled with preventative spraying (usually of fungicides) or by changing cultural practices. The good news about blights is that not all plants get them, and most don't die. But they can be upsetting.

Fungus Infections

Damage usually shows as brown, black, or gray spots or blotches, sometimes with a different colored rim. They're generally worse in wet weather. It takes only eight moist hours for a fungus to insert its feeding tube into a plant and infect it.

To retard fungi, water in the morning so the foliage can dry. Or water only on the ground and don't wet the leaves. Increase air circulation by judicious pruning, and throw all diseased leaves in the garbage, not on the mulch pile, so as not to inadvertently infect next year's garden. On valuable plants, you may want to use a commercial fungicide to get problems under control. However, fungicides only retard future damage and don't repair damaged plant tissue.

If using fungicides, read the label carefully to make sure your plant and its problem are specifically listed. Identification of the exact fungus is often difficult and may require the help of an expert. Putting the wrong chemical on the wrong species won't help and may kill the plant. Remember that fungicides are chemicals, so use proper health precautions and consult with a sophisticated nursery on correct usage.

One treatment that is now being touted is safe for people, but it too only works as a retardant. Old-fashioned baking soda (sodium bicarbonate) deters mildew, perhaps black spot and other fungi. Use three-quarters of a tablespoon to one gallon of water plus a few drops of Ivory dishwashing liquid to make it stick. There have been reports of damage to leaves, so test it first on a small area and wait a week or so to see if the leaves turn yellow. Unfortunately, nothing is perfect. Another promising retardant being tested is summer horticultural oil.

After struggling for many years with fungi, most people finally learn to live with them because it's just too much trouble to constantly spray. Fungus-prone plants can be moved into open, sunny places where they should be happier. Problem plants can be replaced with varieties that have resistant genes.

Some plants live perfectly well despite frequent fungus infestations. American plane tree, for instance, gets anthracnose three years out of five in some areas, but can grow to be a giant. The variety "Bloodgood," however, is more resistant and a better choice for people who don't like the look of brown leaves falling off in spring. Lilac leaves often have gray powdery mildew by season's end, and old-fashioned late summer phlox usually lose their lower leaves. But both bloom bravely on, year after year.

Viruses

These produce streaks on leaves or stems, lack of vigor, odd branching, and strange, stunted growth. Viruses can't be cured, and infected plants usually just peter out after a while.

Cleanliness and good sanitation are important with all blights, especially viruses. Infected stock should be pulled up and thrown out in the garbage. Check plants you buy, especially those subject to virus infections, so you don't bring infected ones into the garden. Ask for guaranteed virus-free stock, particularly for strawberries and raspberries.

Virus infections are often transmitted by insects and even by people. Just smoking in the garden can infect beans with mosaic virus, which is spread by tobacco. Unfortunately, once some viruses are in the soil, they can infect future plants of the same variety. Since there are no practical cures, practice prevention. Switch to resistant varieties. Where possible, rotating crops, usually on a three-year cycle, helps keep these diseases from getting a foothold.

Herbicide Damage

This produces stunted leaves with odd whitish streaks. Using herbicides is a complex science. Each chemical targets specific plants, must be applied at certain times, in certain ways, and sometimes repeated.

Herbicides are carried in groundwater and can damage plants downhill from target species. Herbicide sprays carried downwind can damage sensitive plants. Lilacs are very sensitive to the least air-borne drift of certain chemicals. Beech trees and honeylocust are very sensitive to some weed control herbicides applied to the grass over their roots. What have you used on your lawn lately?

Some of the chemicals have long residual activity and have been implicated as health hazards. In backyards, herbicides should not be used routinely for weed control that could be handled in a safer way, nor where weed control is not absolutely essential. Another way to control weeds is to use mulches. Many, many choices exist, but bark mulch is the most common. Some other weed barriers are black plastic, nonwoven weed fabric, or wads of thick wet newspaper. One of these is often put beneath the loose mulch for better protection. However, newspaper should not be used in vegetable gardens because of the possibility of heavy metals dissolving from the ink.

Soil may be permanently poisoned (nothing will grow again) by borax plus a detergent soap, heavy motor oil, salt, or diatomaceous earth debris from swimming pool filters. Some of these will leach through groundwater into other areas, so be careful where and how they are used.

Salt Damage

This looks like a disease but is purely environmental. It often shows as a crisp dry brown leaf edge or tip that becomes more obvious as summer wears on and during droughts. There are many kinds of salts that can cause damage. Some are residues from chemical fertilizers. Some are precipitates from the soil itself caused by changes in soil acidity or evaporation. In desert areas, as water evaporates, calcium salts can cause the formation of a cementlike layer under the soil. However, most salt damage comes from salts used on ice in winter in northern climates, especially sodium chloride (common table salt). Maple trees are quite sensitive to this salt.

To prevent deicing salts from desiccating plants, one can substitute less toxic calcium chloride or fertilizer for the cheaper sodium chloride. Other possibilities are kitty litter and wood ashes, though these track damaging grit into the house. Sand is useful, though it quickly freezes into any melted water and has to be reapplied frequently. Salts may work longer but also have to be reapplied as needed to prevent accidents.

Long, deep watering helps to wash salt out of garden soil. In northern climates, it is especially useful in April, which coincides with the spring rains.

Air Pollution

Air pollution often shows as brown or yellow blotches, sometimes with a purple rim. Don't fret. What the plant absorbs, you don't have to breathe in. Plants are excellent pollution sinks and absorb or adsorb many air pollutants, including ozone, sulfur dioxide, nitrous dioxides, carbon dioxide, and particulate ash. And because they produce oxygen, the air is always better where there are lots of trees.

Slugs

Let's start with the bottom line. There is no perfect solution to the problem. Slugs are a problem to tender seedlings, many flowers, vegetables, fruit, or almost any nice soft plants. You can recognize their damage by torn leaves, ripped seedlings, holes in tomatoes and strawberries, chewed-up blossoms, and vegetables. Most insects create neat holes when

they eat. Slugs tear holes and leave their telltale mark—a slimy trail. You know the damage is not earwigs or ground beetles by the shiny trail. Slugs are gray, fat, squashy globs of protoplasm like their relatives the snails, but without the shells. Indians ate them, so do the French. Chickens love them. They are pure protein.

Slugs thrive in cool damp weather. Bad times for the gardener are June (strawberry time) and September (tomato time). During the dry heat of summer, and in frozen winters, they are inactive, except under protective mulch or compost. Slugs are a much worse problem in the Pacific Northwest, where the climate is always cool and moist. No fools they, slugs' preferred meal times are dusk and dawn, when the temperature is pleasant. Population levels depend on whether they have a supply of food and a cool, moist place to live.

Chemical Control

Scientific field tests with actual total slug counts were done some years ago. They showed that only a chemical pesticide-laced bait (using metaldehyde) made any dent in the damage level. There are two formulations of such slug bait, one for vegetables using metaldehyde alone, and one for nonedible plants that uses metaldehyde in combination with a stronger pesticide, usually carbaryl. The bait, generally in pellet form, is spread around plants at risk. New pellets have to be added frequently, especially after rains. ☠ The bait is very poisonous, so don't use it where there are children or pets.

"Natural" Control Methods

There are many control methods; some are based on biology, others are old wives' tales, most are wishful thinking. Fortunately, slow-moving slugs are easy to catch and kill. Most of these methods may lower the population, but keep in mind, the aim is not to reach a world record of the number of slugs caught but to prevent plant damage.

- Slugs must have a smooth surface to slither along on. Thus anything that roughens surfaces such as a salt is effective. Ashes, rough gravel, calcium chloride, granular fertilizer, or lime, sprinkled on the soil surface, deters them.
- Anything hot and dry is uninviting to slugs as well, such as a dust mulch (a well-cultivated, dry, soil surface) or full sun exposure on the soil.
- Slugs love beer, and they will crawl in and drown in low pans of it sunken into the ground. The idea is to woo them to the brew before they get to your plants.

New agricultural studies seem to indicate they really favor the hops and are more attracted to the smell of beer than to sugar, yeast, plain alcohol, or commercial metaldehyde slug bait. In the past, stale beer was recommended. However, the alcoholic slug population is only a percentage of the wiser ones, which stick to tomatoes, strawberries, and favorite flowers.

- Spear them at dusk or dawn. You can find hundreds. This is a good remedy for people who have anger to vent at day's end, or who just can't sleep. All that's required is a sharp stick, lots of mosquito repellent, and neighbors who don't think you're crazy to be out there in your pajamas at 5:00 A.M. You can catch what seems like thousands. While this technique definitely must lower the slug population, it may or may not lessen the damage level. If spearing turns you off, just sprinkle the slugs with salt (which ruins their body fluid balance) or pick them up with tongs and toss into strong detergent.
- Trap them. Slugs like it damp and cool during the heat of the day and will rest under any old piece of wood, damp newspaper, upside-down half grapefruit, flowerpot, or under mulch.
- Some natural gardeners theorize that wounded pests release chemicals warning of danger, so leaving dead slugs around serves as a natural repellent. This has never been proved in con-

trolled studies, but it can't hurt to give it a try.

- Egg clusters (which are transparent or cloudy) may be found under debris or soil and can be destroyed before they hatch, though you'll need luck on your side to find them.
- Slugs like to eat what we like, especially fermented sugars. Old classic bait was bran and molasses laced with now-outlawed, and very poisonous, arsenate of lead (which is not good to have in the environment). Federally approved bait now uses metaldehyde in place of the arsenic and lead.
- Slugs supposedly love marigolds and zinnias, which can be planted far away as a decoy crop. According to one list, slugs will pass up alyssum, daylilies, mint, cosmos, ivy, bamboo, ferns, and foxglove. However, as with animals, any list of favorite and rejected food is purely local. It depends on the particular acquired tastes of the slugs involved.

The Bottom Line

Try what you will. You can spear 'em, salt 'em, boil 'em, poison 'em, or intoxicate 'em. But it's a holding action at best and you rarely win. There are always more to move into the place you've just cleared.

SECTION TWO
The Battle Plan

Understanding Control Methods

The Basic Facts

All animals are habitat driven. This is the basic fact that determines success or failure of any control method. Populations expand as much as the habitat allows. Gardens are part of the habitat, and as long as an edible garden is within reach, a hungry animal will find it, make a home of it, and bear young. How long it causes problems, however, depends on how long you tolerate it.

To control animal problems, you must either change the habitat or get rid of the animal.

The long-term solution is to change the habitat. However, this may not be possible or even desirable. One changes the habitat by removing the food supply using fences, by changing the plants, or by eliminating nesting sites. It takes continued efforts to keep it from reverting back to an animal-attracting place.

One gets rid of animals by the use of repellents, fumigants, trapping, poisoning, and hunting. This is not a long-term solution. Getting rid of the problem animals of the moment will solve the problem for a while, sometimes a year or two. But as new generations of animals find you, the removals have to be repeated.

Baron von Clausewitz describes it thus: War does not consist of a single short blow. War is countless duels, but to understand the whole picture, imagine a pair of wrestlers. Each tries through physical force to compel the other to his will. In war, the result is never final. But always remember your original goal.

The goal is to grow one's garden in peace. At least for a while.

Information—A Necessary Weapon

Before you go into battle, you have to identify the animal and know its ways. Each animal has certain peculiarities and has special requirements for effective control. To win, says Sun Tzu, you have to know the enemy. Information is the first tool.

Where to Get Information

The best place for accurate, concise information is your state fish and wildlife service or APHIS (which stands for the United States Department of Agriculture Animal and Plant Health Inspection Service). APHIS has a division called ADCWS (which stands for Animal Damage Control–Wildlife Services). This division has information sheets on every pest animal in the country, and will mail you the ones you need. Different areas of the country are served by regional APHIS offices.

The tone of government publications depends on whether your state has more rural farm areas or large urban centers, and by what's politically correct the year you call. Farm states are more honest in their appraisals of animal problems and have more complete damage prevention and control methods.

In cities, where wildlife personnel are subject to criticism from animal rights groups, they are more tentative with their information. This is especially true on the East and West Coasts, where many wealthy socialites and media personalities enforce their own brand of political correctness, which is understandably intimidating to public servants. The closer you are to the ultimate politically correct metropolises of New York City and Los Angeles, the more timid information may be. If your state information isn't useful, try getting information from a state where farming is an important industry. Or consult your state department of agriculture or a professional exterminator or trapper.

Colleges and universities are another source of good information, particularly in states with agriculture. Most states also have extension services funded by universities, the federal government, or the state, and they usually have position papers on subjects of interest. Most good research is done by state universities, extension services, and the United States Department of Agriculture.

Biased Information

Unfortunately, many garden and animal books, as well as almost all publications of wildlife groups, hunting societies, animal protection groups, and even boards of health usually proselytize a particular philosophy or point of view. Rather than an unbiased overview of animal problems and a frank appraisal of all possible solutions, the information may include hopeful hints and sometimes passionate pleas. Most of these publications contain some truths, some half truths, and sometimes a political wish list.

Control Strategies

Exclusion

Fences

Fencing is a long-term cure. If a food supply is fenced off, animals usually stop coming, eventually. Everything else has to be repeated. Fences against animals are like the Great Wall of China against the Tartar raids, unable to prevent every raid, but incursions are made more difficult and therefore occur less frequently.

Von Clausewitz adds that no engagement is decided in a single moment, although in each there are crucial moments that are responsible for the outcome. The most important time to start fencing is when animals first appear. This keeps them from developing feeding habits at your backyard table, because prevention is better than trying to break feeding habits once they're formed. You may fence before problems start if you know lots of problem animals exist in your area.

Fences need not be limited to utilitarian chicken wire. They can be beautiful or architecturally interesting or visually open or closed. They should serve not only to keep animals out, but to provide privacy and define garden spaces. Fences can be made of brick, concrete, decorative metal, wood, wire, plastic, or reinforced screening, including any combination of the above. The sturdier the fence, the less repair it will need.

Different animals climb, dig, or jump better than others, so fence designs have to take this into account. Electric wires, which shock but don't harm animals, are often used in conjunction with fences to make them more effective barriers. Or electric wire fencing can be used alone. Poisonous plants put around the perimeter, either inside or out, will help to discourage investigation by animals. See the poisonous plants chapter for lists.

Recently, the government has been testing an electric fence powered by solar cells that will be self-charging and not require any external electric source. Contact your local agricultural service for details on the best designs and where the parts can be located.

FENCE DESIGNS

- *Rabbits, skunks, and woodchucks* do not climb, so low fences deter them. However, they will dig, so fences to exclude them often have wire buried underground. Use a three-foot mesh and bury six inches with another six inches bent outward at the bottom below ground. Two feet will be above ground.

- *Chipmunks and mice* need a smaller-size hole to be kept out. Sometimes a low fence will have a low bottom row with mouse-proof fencing. Theoretically, they can squeeze through spaces the size of a dime.

- *Squirrels* cannot be effectively fenced out.

- *Birds* are even more difficult to exclude. Several things can be done to protect fruit and sometimes sprouting seeds. For protection of fruit crops, temporary plastic or nylon bird netting is often put over trees and shrubs while the fruit is ripening. Sour cherry and blueberries will be totally eaten if they're not covered. Other stratagems are used to protect buildings from the roosting and nesting of pigeons, swallows, woodpeckers. A kind of sharp-pronged strip called porcupine wire can be put down to permanently exclude them. (See the section "Bird Traps and Exclusion Methods" later in this chapter.)

- *Deer* can jump up to eight feet high and can leap across a barrier nine or ten feet wide, so they need tall fences. Serious deer fences are often electrified as well because deer are so relentless. When using electric wire alone as fencing, the deer have to be conditioned by a shock; otherwise, according to one wildlife professional, they have limited value.

- There are several kinds of deer fence. Most usual is welded wire, which lasts the longest. There is also special seven- to eight-foot-high green or black plastic (high-density polypropylene) fence, which usually comes in large rolls of several hundred feet. It is ultraviolet stabilized and supposed to last seven to fourteen years. Also possible is nonstretching, plastic mesh, which is easier to install and can be snaked around trees. These rolls of fence are most useful where the ground is fairly level.

- The latest recommendation is to use a six-foot fence with a "hot" wire on top, which is baited (with peanut butter mixed with peanut oil) to condition the deer to be afraid of it and not just jump over it. For more information on deer fences (slanted fence, hog wire fence, electrified fence, "New Hampshire" three-wire fence, "Minnesota" fence, "New Zealand" fence, "Penn State" five-wire fence), try to get the University of Nebraska 1983 bulletin called *Deer* by Scott Craven from your local wildlife service.

- *Raccoons*, because they climb, are difficult to fence out. Therefore electric wire is often used either alone or in conjunction with chicken or hog wire fencing, as well as traps.

- When using electric fencing, which only shocks but does not harm animals, the wires must be kept free of vegetation. Anything that touches the wire can carry the electric current into the ground and eventually short out the system or use up the electric source.

- A herbicide must be used to keep the ground below the wires vegetation free. Borax plus a detergent soap makes a good herbicide. Other permanent plant killers that poison the soil are motor oil, heavy salt (which will leach away eventually), and residue from swimming pool filters. Commercial chemical herbicides may also be used, but each has different residual activity, so choose one that will last through the growing season.

- If the fence is around a vegetable garden, one does not want to use weed control substances that would contaminate the food. Very thick wads of wet newspaper will suppress vegetation and last about a summer. Sometimes boards are used to smother plant growth.

- If contemplating electric fencing, consult your local state agricultural service for detailed specifications. See also the deer chapter.

FENCE DESIGNS: SEE-THROUGH LATTICE FENCING AND PICKET FENCE

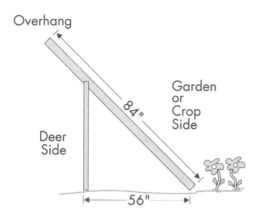

A slanted deer fence. It can be constructed as an electric or non-electric fence.

Other Exclusion Methods

Various kinds of products and materials can be used to keep animals away from particular plants. They may be wire frames, plastic enclosures, netting, and inaccessible planters, among others. These are useful for particular plants that are always eaten, or to protect particular trees (especially their trunks), or to protect a crop at harvest time (such as blueberries, grapes, or field vegetables).

Chicken Wire Columns or Cones

To keep out animals, chicken wire can be made into round columns or cones, tall enough and wide enough to enclose individual plants. They can be moved from plant to plant. If birds are the problem, the holes in the wire or mesh have to be much smaller, because a bird can get inside a hole the size of a fifty-cent piece, which is about one inch round.

Netting

On fruit trees and bushes, netting is commonly thrown over the whole plant and tied at the bottom to keep birds out. It is put on when the fruit become partly ripe, then removed when the crop is harvested, and the net is stored for use again the following year. Nylon, jute, plastic, or cotton are common materials. This is probably the easiest way to control bird predation on individual trees and shrubs in the backyard. (For larger areas, see the chapter on birds.)

FRAME TO PROTECT SPECIAL PLANTS

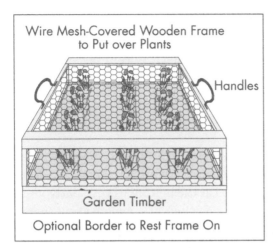

Wire Mesh-Covered Wooden Frame
to Put over Plants

Handles

Garden Timber

Optional Border to Rest Frame On

MOVABLE WOODEN FRAME

Critter-Proof Cages

If certain beds are lined with something like treated wood ties, then a wooden box frame screened with chicken wire or hardware wire can be built to fit directly over those beds. These frames can be used when certain crops are ripening (such as strawberries) or when rabbits and woodchucks are prowling about. If regular mosquito screening is used, it will keep out pesky insects too (good for cabbage, carrots, and spinach) but will screen out pollinators as well (not good for strawberries and squash).

Berry Cages

Such cages are more commonly used in England, where birds and squirrels are a much greater problem than in the United States. Most people in this country can get crops of raspberries and blueberries without them. However, when netting individual bushes or small trees fails, a berry cage can be built. If deer are the problem, the cage has to be very sturdy and needs night reflective markers to keep the deer from running through the wire.

A berry cage is a major construction project. It has to be tall enough for the plants to stand in comfortably, have a convenient, easy-opening door, and a sturdy frame well anchored in the ground. It's essentially like a greenhouse except the top and sides are covered with wire mesh. To keep birds out, the holes have to be less than one inch in diameter. Chicken wire will keep squirrels out, but deer may break through it.

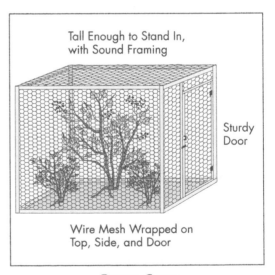

Tall Enough to Stand In,
with Sound Framing

Sturdy
Door

Wire Mesh Wrapped on
Top, Side, and Door

BERRY CAGE

Tree Protectors— Translucent Plastic Tubes

These items are useful to protect young plants and trees from deer, rabbits, and mice chewing the bark in winter. The translucent plastic acts like a minigreenhouse and enhances the growth rate. Sometimes the plants stay too warm in fall and don't harden off for winter, so the tubes should be half opened during September, October, and possibly November in cold climates. Then they are closed again for the winter to protect the tree trunk and leaves from browsing. When the tree grows out the top, and the trunk gets thick, the tubes are cut off.

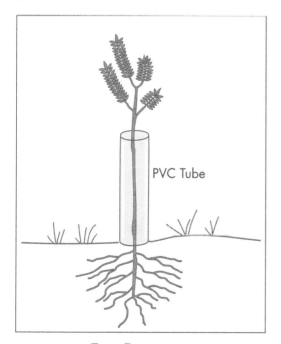

PVC Tube

TREE PROTECTOR

There is ongoing research into the effects of tree protectors on plants grown in them. The trunks do not thicken as much in relation to height as with trees grown in the open. Therefore, when the tree is above deer browsing height, it may need staking for a few years until the trunk thickens properly and develops the necessary flare at the root line. Some reports have indicated more tree loss in cold climates, although in areas with warm winters this does not seem to be a problem. Summer heat buildup inside the tubes can be a problem in southern areas. Although these problems exist, it's better than no tree or shrub growth at all because of animal browsing.

Some brand names are *Tree-Pro* and *Tree Protectors*. The tube by *Tree-Pro* is a pliable plastic sheet that is wrapped around the tree and tied closed. It can be tied half open in fall for hardening off. A stake stabilizes the tube. A small piece of bird netting is included, which is put over the top so birds don't fly down into the tube after insects. It comes in sizes from eight to seventy-two inches high and makes a tube three and half inches wide. Two tubes can be tied together for a wider diameter. It is supplied by Tree-Pro, 445 Lourdes Lane, Lafayette, IN 47905. Telephone: 1-800-875-8071.

Tree Protectors come in two-, three-, four-, and five-foot heights and are solid tubes that are slipped down over the young tree saplings. Vitaculture Supertubes, developed for grapes, are slit longitudinally and are eighteen to thirty-four inches high so they can be pruned without being removed. All are three and a half to four inches in diameter. A stake is placed inside to stabilize the tubes. Minimum order is a package of five, all in one size. The supplier is Treessentials, River View Station, P.O. Box 7097, St. Paul, MN 55107. Telephone: 1-800-248-8239.

Plastic Milk Bottles, Protection for Seedlings

Some plants just need a start and once established can fend for themselves or become tough and unappetizing. For them, the old milk container trick is cheaper and recycles otherwise wasted plastic. Take a plastic milk bottle and cut off the bottom with strong shears. After planting seeds or seedlings, push one such bottle into the ground around it. A stick inside will stabilize the bottle and keep it from falling over. This technique works best with one plant per bottle.

The bottle will cut out some light but acts as a minigreenhouse to protect the plant from frosts. It is especially useful for early peas and spinach, and to protect sprouting seeds from birds, rabbits, and usually woodchucks.

When the plants are big enough to be safe and are ready to grow through the top hole, the bottles should be removed. Do this on a cloudy day, for the leaves would burn if suddenly exposed to full sunlight. Then the bottle can be turned over, inserted into the ground with the small end down, stabilized with a stick, and used for delivering liquid fertilizer and irrigation water directly to the roots of the plant for the rest of the season. In hot climates or in midsummer, a quart-size paper milk carton with the top and bottom cut out works better because there would be too much heat buildup inside a plastic bottle.

Underground Wire Cages to Protect Bulbs and Underground Roots from Field Mice

Sometimes field mice, or voles, eat bulbs and plant roots underground. Other times, squirrels dig up bulbs and move them around to random places. Where this has been a problem, the only long-term solution is to plant underground wire cages made of hardware cloth. A hole is left on the top for the foliage to come through, but otherwise the planting is enclosed in wire mesh.

Repellents and Fumigants

There are many products on the market. All are temporary at best, but at least it's something to do. They are most useful for protecting particular plants or to protect a crop at harvest time. The following have been tested (mostly by their manu-

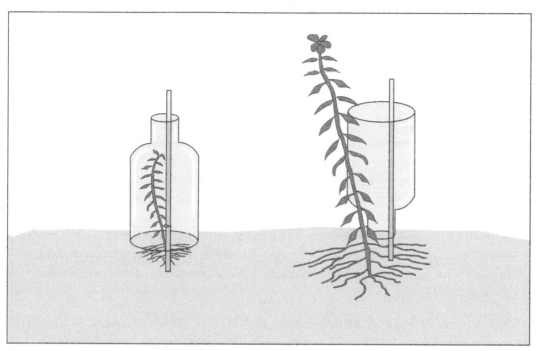

Bottom is cut out of a plastic milk bottle. The bottle is placed in the soil over a seed or a seedling plant and stabilized with a stake. When the plant grows larger, the bottle is turned over, again stabilized with a stake and used to deliver water or liquid fertilizer.

facturers) and may be promising enough to test in your garden.

For deer, the most troublesome of all problem animals at this time, the following products are generally considered better than most others, although people who have constant deer problems usually don't get much relief from them. They have to be reapplied often. However, if mixed with a sticker-spreader adhesive (such as *Wilt-Proof*), they should last longer.

- *Deer-Away spray*. Made of egg solids, it's a little messy to use because it has to be mixed. One forestry researcher says it lasts several weeks. It is available in many garden catalogs or from the supplier: Deer-Away, 8500 Philsbury Avenue South, Minneapolis, MN 55420. Telephone: 1-800-468-2472.

- *Hinder* is another deer repellent, mainly 15 percent ammonium soaps, also available in many catalogs. Or contact Necessary Trading Company, 422 Salem Avenue, New Castle, VA 24127.

- *Thiram* is a bitter-tasting fungicide, the taste of which repels rabbits, squirrels, woodchucks, and deer. Unfortunately, it

OLD WIVES' TALES AND OTHER GADGETS

Most of the old wives' tales and folk remedies rely on repellents, few of which are tested using impartial scientific methodology and control plots. Successes that are attested to or guaranteed by those who sell the products usually stem from personal experiences and observations. The number of tests, if any, is small. However, some of the old wives' tales may work, at least initially. If animals are kept off guard by frequently changing repellents plus things that frighten them, they may be deterred. For low-density populations of any animal, a few scares, bad tastes, and bad smells may send them elsewhere. Particularly if they are harassed when they first arrive. It's worth a try. However, since animals come to eat, removing their food supply is more effective. You may test any of the following, but don't waste much money or expect repellents to solve all your animal problems. Most serious research scientists don't think much of them.

- Electronic or transonic machines that emit sonic or ultrasonic beeps or sounds don't work for long, if at all. They are very expensive and not worth the money.
- Moth flakes may be tried, but they have to be reapplied frequently, and there have to be enough to vaporize and fill the area. Results with mothballs are spotty too.
- Ammonia-soaked cloths are repellents and may be useful in closed areas like garbage cans with tight lids.
- Radios left on loud or on static or tapes of barking dogs
- Scarecrows
- Plastic or metal streamers, aluminum pie pans, tin can lids mounted on lines, fences, or poles
- Plastic windmills, particularly ones that make noise
- Lights that come off and on
- Fake snakes, owls, balloons, with or without eyes
- Old farmers rubbed the trunks of trees with bars of soap to repel rabbits in winter. Mice will eat soap.
- One repellent advertised for dogs and cats uses methyl nonyl ketone, which has a very strong, persistent, sweet industrial / perfume–type odor, though not unpleasant. However, it is very poisonous, cannot be used on food crops, and is absorbed through the skin. Hands should be thoroughly washed with soap and water after using. One such product is called "Get Off My Garden" (Supplier: Rudducks USA, Inc., 5760 Shirley Street, #11, Naples, FL 33942). ☠

EFFECTIVENESS OF DEER REPELLENTS

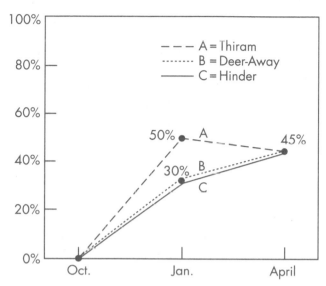

Replicated plots of yews treated once in fall at the Connecticut Agricultural Station.

Percent reduction in deer browsing compared to untreated plots

damages some tender green foliage, so is best used to protect dormant twigs and evergreens during winter. However, some plants will tolerate it: test it if in doubt. When mixed with a sticker-spreader adhesive, it will last longer. One source says several months. Available in many products, or contact Gustafson Inc., P.O. Box 660065, Dallas TX 75266. Thiram also deters squirrels, sometimes woodchucks and rabbits.

Soaps

Hanging small bars of soap among trees and shrubs is reputed to deter deer, though reports are spotty. Some deer are repelled, others are not, occasionally the bar is eaten. If trying soap, hang small hotel-size bars, in their wrappers, with holes drilled in the paper. The scent may last longer when held in the wrappers.

Gas Fumigating ☠

Sometimes a gas cartridge may be used for fumigating woodchuck, gopher, and skunk dens, but be prepared to run fast after lighting it because it can be quite dangerous, particularly if an enraged skunk comes tearing out.

Before considering use of gas, see chapter on woodchucks for safety precautions and contact your state agricultural agency

MOLES

Many things have been proposed for moles, which are virtually impossible to control. One may be worth a try, however. The active ingredient is castor oil, which may stick to their fur and is supposed to give the moles upset stomachs. It's safe, nontoxic to humans, and can be sprayed on lawns. One product has supposedly been researched at a university, but the supplier wouldn't supply the research protocol or results.

There are two formulas for preparing castor oil repellents at home, though neither has been tested anywhere. Both are watered into the grass above and near the raised run.

- Formula 1: Mix six ounces of castor oil with two tablespoons of dishwashing liquid and one gallon of water.
- Formula 2: Mix four ounces of castor oil with eight ounces of dishwashing soap and two ounces of human urine. Use one tablespoon of this mixture to a gallon of water or one teaspoon to a quart of water.

for further details, applicable laws, and sources of supply.

Predator Urine

Marking a territory with fox, coyote, wolf, or bobcat urine is an old idea that's become popular again. Animal urine scents have long been used by trappers to attract animals. Dispensers containing animal urine are hung from plants. They are exactly what they are called, not an extract or refined product. Though they smell quite strong and very gamey, the odor is only noticeable to people for a short distance. (It usually takes some soap and water to get the scent off one's hands, but toothpaste can be used to clean smelly fingers as a last resort.)

Currently being tested by Bartlett Tree Company, predator urine does seem to deter deer and probably rabbits, at least during the first year of use. However, it can attract and excite foxes, raccoons, and opossums, dogs and sometimes even cats, so these urines aren't a good idea where one keeps pets. Perhaps the attraction of predators to the area will deter the deer and other herbivores. The question is, do you want predators in the backyard?

The best use of predator urine, at the moment, is in locations at the edge of the property or around vegetable gardens, to protect plants that are browsed by deer and other animals. It's a promising idea but needs more research to be effective.

Reminds one of the Old Maine Farmer's "fence"; this remedy for woodchucks calls for a man to pee around the garden every night and mark it with the testosterone in human urine.

Although the idea is fashionable these days, the fact is that animal pee on a cottonball doesn't work very well in most gardens. Better to train your dog to mark the garden daily with its scent.

Dogs as Deterrents

Man's best friend is a friend indeed when it comes to keeping animals out of the garden. Barking and chasing are most effective. Attacking is not recommended because the dog could be hurt or could be exposed to diseases, especially rabies.

For Canada geese, one of the few helps is border collie dogs, specially trained to chase geese but not attack them. (The dog should not chase the birds in the water, where the latter would have the physical advantage.) On one golf course, where this technique was used for three years, the Canada geese population was reduced by about 80 percent. However, the dog has to make the rounds every single day all year, and the birds must be chased and routed. If they are not chased constantly in spring before they lay eggs, nothing will move them until the chicks can fly in about June.

Trapping and Bait

Eventually, most serious gardeners trap, particularly if growing fruits or vegetables. Trapping eliminates the particular animals that are causing problems that season. Others come, over time, but trapping keeps the populations low and the damage tolerable. Also, trapping targets only the problem animals that come into the garden and leaves blameless ones alone.

Ideally, start trapping as early in the season as possible to catch animals before they produce the current year's litter of new animals. If you had problem animals last year, there will surely be more of them each year, so the sooner you start the fewer they'll be. For success, traps should be set near the entrance to dens or along trails commonly used by the animal. See individual animal chapters for more specific information for each. Setting several traps at the same time is useful, particularly if there is more than one animal (which there usually is by the time you're having a problem).

Bait is helpful for attracting animals to traps. However, many animals will enter a trap without it if the placement is correct. Scatter bits of bait around the trap, a trail to the entrance, and put a nice bunch inside so it can be seen. Another trick to using bait is to pick a handful of the plants that the problem animal is eating and use that to bait the trap, as well as one of the other common baits. Universal baits are

RECOMMENDED BAIT

Bait	Raccoons	Skunks	Woodchucks	Squirrels	Field Mice	Rabbits
Alfalfa & clover			x (greens)			x (winter)
Apples			x (mash them)		x (pine voles)	x (winter)
Broccoli			x			
Carrots			x			x (summer)
Fruit/melon	x		x	x		
Vegetables	x		x			
Grain				x	x	
Peanuts & Peanut Butter	x	x		x		
Dog food	x					
Cat food	x	x				
Chicken	x					
Fish flavors	x	x				
Cabbage			x			x
Marshmallows	x (in cities)					

peanuts and strawberry sugar cookie wafers, for nuts and fruit are favorite foods of most plant-eating animals but will generally not attract dogs and cats. The wafers are a very visible bright pink, smell like strawberries, are cheap to buy, and can be crumbled around the trap as well as tossed inside. Various other baits may be used. Many animals are attracted by the same bait, and raccoons, woodchucks, squirrels, opossums, and skunks will come to the same trap. For most vegetable eaters, change the bait frequently so it is fresh, and change it daily for woodchucks, which are very fussy eaters.

Sometimes animals need to be acclimatized to bait. Start by putting a nice mound of it outside a trap, as well as inside. Get the animal used to easy access to the good-tasting food for several days.

Then put it in the trap only. To test which bait to use, start by putting out a selection the first day, then on subsequent days repeat the one that's been eaten. The identity of the animal is often revealed by the bait that's chosen.

However, even more important than bait is placement of the trap in a frequently used run between the animal's nest and food supply.

Kinds of Traps

Live Animal Traps

These are the most humane because when the animals are trapped, they are held unhurt inside. Many companies make them. One common brand is Havahart, which offers several different sizes for animals ranging from small rodents to large raccoons and beavers. They may have one or two doors and can be rigid or collapsible. Live traps are sold in most home centers, farm and hardware stores. To locate one in your area, call the Havahart company at 1-800-800-1819.

Other Traps

There are many other types of animal traps available. Some are illustrated here. Others can be found at trapper supply houses. Many can be dangerous. Leghold traps are outlawed in some states because animal activists feel they are cruel, even with padded legholds.

Moles and gophers need special traps that either harpoon them or snare them as they pass through their tunnels. Harpoon traps are most common, but they have the disadvantage of being hard to set and have sharp prongs. Scissor traps and noose traps are other options. Water traps, dug inside the burrows, are a safe, do-it-yourself option. Moles have a sensitive sense of smell, and if they catch human scent they won't come near the traps. People who have moles say they are very, very, very difficult to trap, but sometimes you just can't stand it anymore. (See the moles chapter for details on where to set traps.)

ANIMAL TRAP FOR LIFE CAPTURE

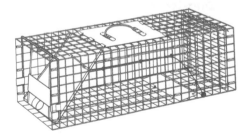

COLLAPSIBLE CAGE

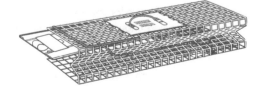

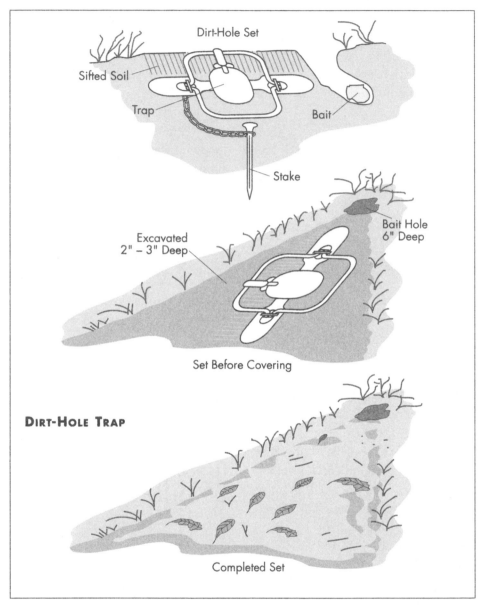

Dirt-Hole Set

Sifted Soil

Trap

Bait

Stake

Excavated
2" – 3" Deep

Bait Hole
6" Deep

Set Before Covering

DIRT-HOLE TRAP

Completed Set

Dirt-hole sets are effective for raccoons. In the dirt-hole set, a bait or lure is placed in a small hole and the trap is concealed under a light covering of soil in front of the hole. A no. 1 1/2 coilspring trap is recommended for this set. It is important to use a small piece of clean cloth, light plastic, or a wad of dry grass to prevent soil from getting under the round pan of the trap and keeping it from going down. If this precaution is not taken, the trap may not go off.

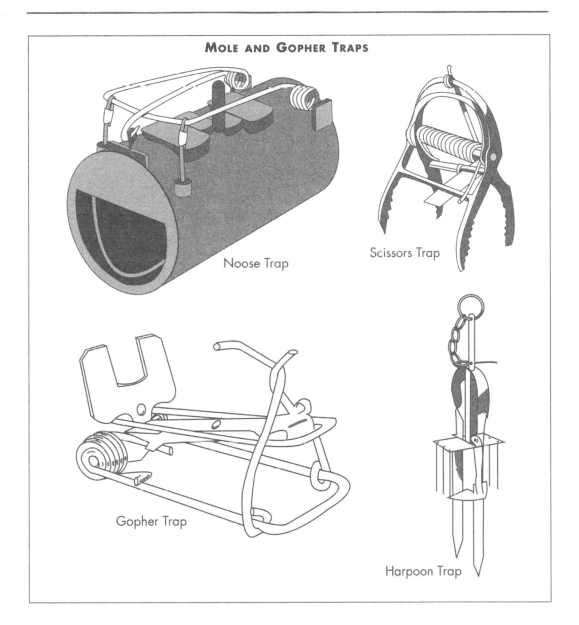

MOLE AND GOPHER TRAPS

Noose Trap

Scissors Trap

Gopher Trap

Harpoon Trap

Bird Traps and Exclusion Methods

Funnel traps are commonly used for pest birds. Sometimes a sieve trap is used, but it requires someone to pull the stick holding up the sieve in order to trap the birds, which isn't practical if there are very

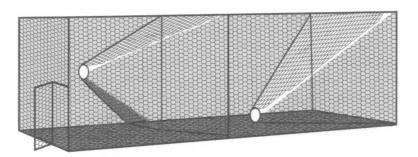

FUNNEL TRAP

many birds. Unless you have nothing bet-ter to do than sit on the porch and wait for birds to come. To keep birds from roosting and nesting on buildings, porcupine wire and other strategies are used.

Disposal of Trapped Animals

Federal or state fish and wildlife services will inform you about the methods allowed by law. Also, most health departments will advise, though some are more sensible than others. They usually can supply a list of people able to dispose of the animals for you, most of whom will be licensed by the state as trappers or exterminators or wildlife officers. They may euthanize (i.e., kill) the animal, or they may (rarely) find it a new home. One thing is sure. They will cost you a pretty penny. Veterinarians will dispose of animals too but for a stiff fee. Sometimes humane societies will euthanize them if you bring them the animal and insist.

The old-fashioned way was to drown them, in the trap, in a lake or a big 55-gallon drum, or to shoot them. The wildlife service will give you suggestions if you ask. One wildlife offi-cer suggested drowning, but the only place avail-able to the gardener was his bathtub. So in the dark of night, he let the animal loose five miles away. When things become too complicated one takes the easy way out.

In many states, it's against the law to move a wild animal from your property to any other place, although that's what most people do because it's easier and cheaper. It is not neighborly though to give your problem animals to someone else to cause problems, and it can also spread rabies. It's not humane to the animal either, because it won't easily find a new home; as an in-terloper in another animal's territory, it will have to fight to find food and shelter in the new place.

Hunting and Other Methods

Hunting and Shooting

Machiavelli wrote 500 years ago, "If we must choose, it is far safer to be feared than loved." Animals that are hunted

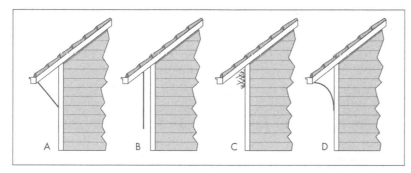

Four methods that may deter cliff swallow nesting: (A) Netting attached from the outer edge of the eave down to the side of the building. (B) A curtain of netting. (C) Metal projectors attached along the junction of the wall and eave. (D) Fiberglass panel mounted to form a smooth, concave surface.

TO DETER CLIFF SWALLOW NESTING

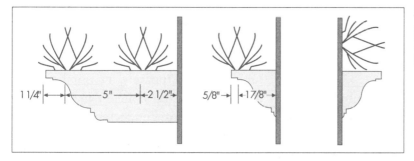

Metal projectors called "porcupine wires" can be attached to ledges or rafters to prevent birds from roosting.

TO DETER BIRDS FROM ROOSTING

learn to fear humans, so they keep their distance and are less likely to become problem animals. This protects them as well as us. Hunting is a source of great political debate. Poor Prince Charles of England was roundly chastised in the British press by the powerful English animal rights groups for taking his son deer hunting on his ancestral lands. Not even an heir to the throne of England can blithely engage in this sport of kings anymore.

Some people love to hunt, as their for-

bears did before them. Humans respond to the thrill of the chase, the excitement of pursuit. A new archaeological dig in England found well-balanced wooden javelins 400,000 years old, along with the bones of some eaten wild horses. Today some people hunt with rifles, some with bows and arrows, some on horseback. People who object to "blood sports" hunt on foot or from cars with cameras and binoculars, or on horseback while chasing only the fox scent dragged over a course.

Most animals are protected by law, particularly if fur-bearing. Hunting requires a permit in most states, and certain seasons are allowed for different animals and different times of year. However, one can sometimes obtain a permit to hunt problem animals out of season on one's own property. Many localities, particularly suburban and urban ones, outlaw the use of firearms entirely, often bows and arrows too. Check with your local game warden or state wildlife service.

Lethal Injection

This is the way most unwanted animals are euthanized. Lethal injections can only be done by a licensed person, and there is usually a fee. It is not widely known that many humane associations will do this for free when an animal is brought to them, although they don't like to.

Carbon Dioxide Chamber

Probably the most humane way to dispose of small problem animals is by using a carbon dioxide box. The carbon dioxide box is less expensive and probably less painful to the animal. There is no need for needles, nor squirming animals that might have saliva or blood with unknown rabies or other diseases.

Most dog officers or exterminators that deal with animals use an airtight box fitted with a carbon dioxide canister. A regular metal live trap fits inside. If you want a captured animal to go more contentedly, give it some nice food. When the canister is turned on, the problem animal will peacefully fall asleep while eating. It is always sad to kill an animal. Better to develop effective birth control methods so this won't be necessary.

Animal Birth Control

Obviously, this is the wave of the future, but unfortunately it's not here yet. Research is being done in many places. One experiment, conducted and financed by the National Park Service, has been ongoing for several years at Assateague Island Park in Maryland, which has a carrying capacity of about 150 wild horses. They were reproducing too rapidly, overrunning the area. However, their population growth has been reduced by using a contraceptive that tricks the female animals' immune system into attacking sperm as a foreign body. The contraceptive is delivered by a dart given twice a year to each female horse. It's not inexpensive.

On Fire Island, in New York, the same twice-a-year darting technology is being tested on deer, helped by a resident who can distinguish between different animals. So far the birth rate has been lowered by 50 percent.

In Australia, which is overrun with introduced rabbits and foxes, a different birth control technology is being tested. It's delivered in bait, which contains a rabbit-specific virus that causes the females to attack sperm as a foreign body. Tests are also under way for an appropriate fox-specific virus for fox birth control.

Another experiment started in 1992 involved putting Norplant, a contraceptive, in urban skunks, which carry rabies and disrupt garbage. The philosophy is that if you kill a skunk, another will move in and inhabit that empty space; however, if an infertile animal remains, it will defend its territory and not allow another fertile skunk to move in. Then, ideally, the population will stabilize. Let's hope it works.

Integrated Pest Management

Called IPM for short, this philosophy has been used for many years in landscaping and farming to control plant insects and diseases. The theory is now being applied to the control of pest animals.

The basic approach is that a certain level of damage can be tolerated, and only when that is passed is anything done to control the problem animals. For instance, rather than immediately killing every rabbit in sight, controls are started only when they threaten to become a serious problem. Then the least dangerous control methods are tried first. This philosophy only works if:

1. One understands *all* the control methods available, including habitat modification.
2. One monitors regularly and catches problems early before animal populations grow out of control.
3. One is prepared to use whatever control methods are best suited to the problem.
4. One is willing to tolerate a certain level of damage.

While practicing IPM is complicated and requires a lot of information and a good understanding of ecosystems, it is a reasonable intellectual approach to problem animals in the backyard if one is willing to tolerate its shortcomings.

POISONOUS PLANTS ☠

A True Story

Once upon a time, there was a Canadian ornithologist, stationed in Africa, who wanted to grow a tropical garden, dripping with flowering vines and exotic blooms. But he had an animal problem. A big animal problem. Elephants. It wasn't that they ate so much; it was their big feet. For when they walked through looking for goodies, they destroyed his dream garden. He wanted a garden the elephants wouldn't eat.

Now there is nothing so incredible as watching wildlife during the powerfully beautiful tropical sunset on the African savanna. The sky is gold and black and orange. Flashes of sheet lightning illuminate the insides of the heavy cumulus clouds like 1,000 lightbulbs.

Silhouetted against the vibrant sky one might just see a herd of elephants, drunkenly reeling, three sheets to the wind. Why? Because they love fruit. There is a native African palm whose fruit resembles hard croquet balls, which nobody would consider nibbling except the elephant. And when the woody balls ferment and smell like fruity wine, the elephants gorge on them until they become lurching black behemoths.

In the battle to design a garden the elephants won't eat, one needs to use strategy, for no fence will contain them. Baron von Clausewitz says, "Strategic theory deals with ends which bear directly on the restoration of peace." For all animals, look at their eating habits as a way to restore peace in the garden. It's easier than waging continual war. Elephants illustrate both the principles and the limitations of this approach.

Elephants are very picky eaters, and they have a highly developed sense of smell. They like nice greens (especially lettuce), fruits, grain, and fragrant flowers (which the hapless ornithologist was growing on a flimsy fence).

Elephants are also very wary eaters. One tiny bitter taste is enough to send them looking elsewhere. And therein lies one secret of keeping animals out. Elephants won't eat poison plants, usually because most such plants taste bad. Nor will most other smart animals. Also, elephants don't like strong scents, sharp flavors, and pungent herbs, even eschewing marigolds.

However, when food is scarce, they *will* eat unpalatable, even poisonous plants. In one overpopulated game park, the grass was chomped low, and there were few trees because the elephants had stripped the leaves and bark, killing the old trees and preventing young ones from getting a foothold. Yet many large, green, healthy shrubs dotted the vast savanna. The lush bushes were comifera, a bitter, moderately toxic plant. The elephants won't touch it, except in times of drought or famine. Then they eat it. Better sick than dead.

Poisonous Plants of East Africa, a slim volume of witch doctor herbal medicines that had killed people, identified poisonous plants for the frustrated ornithologist. By choosing the ones that had beautiful blossoms, it was possible to design a garden dripping with flowers that the elephants wouldn't eat.

After about six months (things grow fast in the tropics), the happy man was able to send his friends a photo of his verdant garden ignored by his heavy-footed neighbors. The most poisonous plants like oleander, euphorbia, and cassia were around the outside as a deterrent. The less palatable ones were inside. The elephants never noticed the little lettuces underneath. Naturally, there were no plants with a sweet or fruity odor.

Using Poisonous Plants as a Defensive Weapon

To comprehend the strategy of using poisonous plants, one needs to understand the eating habits of herbivores. Many plants are very poisonous, while others are only somewhat toxic. Certain animals will eat some things; other animals will eat others. It's a matter of trial and error. When they are really hungry, as are deer in winter, they will eat most anything. However, there are many choice plants and beautiful flowers that will do well much of the time.

Each individual animal has its own individual food preferences. These usually depend on where the animal grew up and which foods its mother preferred to eat. Deer are especially unpredictable. Also,

CAUTION! ☠ A Serious Danger with using poison plants is that children may eat them and get quite sick. A poison garden is not appropriate where little ones are left to play.

something else the next, remember, all animals look pretty much the same. It may not be the same animal at all, just the same species.

On the other hand, how a deer herd that previously avoided certain plants may come to devour them perhaps because each year the baby fawns nibble this and that. They adjust to certain tastes or smells that were previously shunned by their mother. Then the next year, when they breed, they show those plants to their young offspring.

animals prefer different plants at different seasons. If your deer or problem animal seems to like one thing one year and

POISONOUS PLANTS

The following plants contain poisonous chemical compounds but are attractive garden specimens.

Arum family, which includes calla lily, dumbcane, dieffenbachia, caladium lily, philodendron
Belladonna, deadly nightshade (*Atropa belladonna*)
Black cherry (*Prunus serotina, P. demissa, P. melanocarpa*)
Black locust (*Robinia pseudoacacia*), a shade tree
Black nightshade (*Solanum nigrum*) and deadly nightshade (*Solanum dulcamara*)
Bleeding heart, Dutchman's breeches (*Dicentra pusilla, D. cucullaria*)
Bloodroot (*Sanguinaria canadensis*)
Boxwood (*Buxus sempervirens*)
Burning bush (*Euonymus* species)
Buttercup, crowfoot (*Ranunculus* species)
Castor Oil Plant (*Cassia* species)
Chinaberry (*Melia azedarach*)
Christmas rose (*Helleborus niger*)

Cypress spurge (*Euphorbia cyparrissias*), a ground cover
Daphne (*Daphne mezereum*)
Delphinium, larkspur (*Delphinium* species)
Elderberry, black and scarlet elder (*Sambucus canadensis, S. pubens*)
Euphorbia species, some have a bitter milky sap which animals should avoid
False hellebore (*Veratrum viride*)
Foxglove (*Digitalis purpurea*)
Gloriosa, climbing lily (*Gloriosa superba*)
Gopher Spurge (*Euphorbia lathyris*) repels gophers, or so they say.
Holly, black alder (*Ilex aquifolium, I. opaca, I. verticillata*)
Hyacinth (*Hyacinthus orientalis*)
Iris (*Iris* species)
Jack-in-the-pulpit (*Arisaema triphyllum*)
Jerusalem cherry (*Solanum pseudocapsicum*)
Monkshood (*Aconitum* species)
Narcissus, daffodil, jonquil (*Narcissus* species)
Oleander (*Nerium oleander*)
Laburnum, golden chain (*Laburnum anagyroides*) a small tree
Lantana, red sage, wild sage (*Lantana camara*)
Laurel, mountain laurel, sheep laurel *(Kalmia* species)
Lily-of-the-valley (*Convallaria majalis*)
Lupine (*Lupinus* species)
Marsh marigold (*Caltha palustris*)
Mayapple, mandrake (*Podophyllum peltatum*)
Poinsettia (*Euphorbia pucherrima*)
Privet (*Lingustrum vulgare*)
Rhododendron (*Rhododendron, some clones only*)
Spanish broom, Scotch broom (*Sparteus junceum, Sarothamnus scoparius*)
Star-of-Bethlehem (*Ornithogalum umbellatum*)
Tansey (*Tanacetum vulgare*)
Vinca, periwinkle, madagascar vinca (*Vinco minor, V. rosea*)
Yellow jessamine (*Gelsemium sempervirens*)
Yew (*Taxus* species)

CAUTION! ☠ Never use poisonous plants where there are children. They are not as smart as wild animals. Children should be taught early on not to put plants in their mouths. There are many cases of preventable poisoning from unattended children ingesting toxic plants. And remember that so-called herbals and native remedies, widely touted for what ails you, are chemically active and often poisonous so should not be grown where children play.

Plants with thorns are also avoided by some animals with tender mouths, and so can be used as barrier hedges also. Some useful ones are:

- Aloe Species
- Aralia Species
- Barberry Species
- Cactus Species
- Euphorbia Species
- Pyracantha Species
- Thistle Species

Because lists can be unreliable, you will have to test plants in your own garden. Test one or two; don't buy several dozens until you see if they work and if you like the way they look.

Where to Find Lists of Plants for Your Area

Most government agencies produce lists of plants that animals are less likely to eat, especially for deer, which are the most troublesome. These lists are usually based on farmers' and growers' reports of what wasn't eaten, and the lists vary from state to state. Agricultural universities and extension services have the best lists, but there isn't much reliable, well-researched data using suitable scientific methods and controls.

Many garden books also have lists, though they're often just wish lists or are copied from other lists. Some are hearsay. Smelly or pungent herbs like lavender are often recommended as deterrents, but they work the same way as any other disagreeable smell control strategy. They may help for a while, but most animals adjust to them sooner or later. When hungry, animals will ignore nonlethal deterrents.

How to Use Poisonous Plants

Some poisonous plants, like privet, may be used as either a pruned hedge or a small tree twenty-five feet tall. Others are shrubs. Several are choice flowers. Related plants in a species can also be tried but may not contain a high enough level of toxins to deter animals. Although all of these plants are poisonous, some animals will eat them. Deer, for instance, chomp yew and rhododendron with abandon, but often pass up birch, barberry, and dogwood. Some books recommend that poisonous plants be sprinkled among the edible delicacies as deterrents, but the squirrels and chipmunks will cheerfully tiptoe through the poisonous daffodils to eat the tulips. The most effective way to use these plants is in a border or hedge, coordinated with a fence to direct the animal traffic elsewhere.

ANIMAL DISEASES (ZOONOSES)

Diseases associated with and transmitted by animals are called zoonoses. ☠ Though the name is ludicrous, they are no laughing matter. These diseases are passed from animals to humans through direct contact, contaminated water, infected insect carriers, and through animal waste products or dust that carries infectious particles. Public health has historically been improved by controlling these routes of infection.

Pets catch diseases from wild animals very easily, particularly if they run outdoors. So preventative inoculations are necessary to protect your pet's health and, even more important, your family's as well. Unprotected pets can be a major disease reservoir, especially for children. It's important that both cats and dogs get all the necessary shots, especially for rabies in endemic areas. Skipping inoculations is a false and dangerous economy.

Since wild animals carry many diseases, always take health precautions when handling animals or traps. Use disposable latex gloves. If these are lacking, protect your hands with one or more layers of plastic bags. When finished, thoroughly wash your hands and any other exposed places with lots of soap and water. If you are bitten or scratched, or if you think you may have caught something, see a doctor. If the animal has been trapped, save it for testing, especially for rabies.

There are over 175 infectious animal diseases we humans can catch. Although not all of them are common, the total number of infections is considerable, and the morbidity not insignificant. Furthermore, the costs for public health prevention and treatment are enormous. This chapter covers the more common serious ones.

Flea and Tick Bites

Most outside animals have fleas, those pesky insects, that are equally happy feeding on people or their pets. Flea bites are usually near a tight belt, cuff, or collar, and are often multiple—usually two or three bites close together. And they itch mightily. Once fleas have their meal of blood (yours or—better—somebody else's), they lay eggs which stay viable a long time, especially in carpets.

Ticks work a little differently. They attach themselves to the skin and feed on blood for a while, sometimes a day or more, before they let go and drop off. The bite may itch or turn red, or it may not be noticeable. Ticks hanging on fat and engorged with your good blood are easier to see than fleas or unfed skinny ticks.

While not all fleas and ticks are infected with diseases, they all cause annoying bites both to people and pets. So spray wild animals with flea and tick insecticides before handling them, especially in traps or if they're dead.

Rabies

For 2,000 years, rabies in "mad" dogs has been recognized. In the thirteenth century in Europe, rabies was common in wolves, and in 1708, a dog epidemic in Italy was serious enough to be recorded. In the United States, rabies was first recorded in the early nineteenth century. There has been an interesting reanalysis of the death of Edgar Allan Poe, originally thought to have died of drink, but who had all the signs of rabies encephalitis. Until the middle of the twentieth century, this almost uniformly fatal disease was a frightening public health scourge. However, in the mid-twentieth century, it was brought under control through a concerted public health effort to vaccinate all dogs and eliminate strays.

Unfortunately, rabies is again a concern, but now wild animals are mainly responsible for the spread. The economic burden of the disease is staggering. By 1990, the annual public health cost for prevention of rabies from wild animals exceeded $300 million, mostly for vaccinating pet animals. Postexposure treatment of humans cost about $15 million more. And that's a lot of dough.

The incidence of rabies in wild animals, especially skunks, raccoons, and bats, has increased every year since 1950. In the eastern United States, raccoons are the main carrier. In the Midwest, Southwest, and along the Pacific coast, skunks have that dubious honor of being the primary carrier. Foxes are the main reservoir of the virus in Alaska and Arizona.

Bats, however, are the most ubiquitous rabid animal in the country. The current eco-fad of bat houses to attract them to backyards is ill advised. Although bats al-

CARRIERS OF RABIES IN MASSACHUSETTS IN 1995

Massachusetts Animals	Number Infected with Rabies	Total Number Tested
Dogs	0	388
Cats	14	1,708
Cattle	1	10
Other domestic animals	2	47
Skunks	125	231
Raccoons	476	695
Bats	33	357
Woodchucks & rodents	10	615
Foxes	7	64
Other wild animals	1	110
Totals	669	4,225

These were all captured animals that were thought to present a public health risk.

most never bite people unless threatened or frightened, they are reservoirs of the disease and as such should not be invited into close proximity with humans or their pet cats.

Preventative vaccination should be considered for people at high risk, such as hunters, zookeepers, lab personnel, and possibly even ordinary folks in high risk areas who trap animals in their own yard. There is still a high incidence of dog rabies in developing countries, so travelers should take precautions, and if staying very long, consider preexposure vaccination.

All mammals are susceptible to rabies and, because of its long incubation period, can carry the disease unnoticed and transmit it. According to the Centers for Disease Control and Prevention, in Atlanta, raccoons accounted for half of the 7,881 cases of animal rabies in 1995, although many other animals are also carriers. The rabies virus is carried in the blood, feces, urine, and saliva of infected animals. It is usually introduced through a scratch, skin abrasion, or wound.

In one state, Massachusetts, there were 669 rabid animals out of a total of 4,225 tested in 1995 by the State Laboratory. The main carriers were concentrated in a few wild species.

Rabies Precautions

Many public health laws require that all dogs and cats be immunized. Cats are not always vaccinated, yet they are the ones most likely to tangle with wild animals. The disease has a very, very long latent period before it becomes noticeable, so a pet may be infected and in your house without your knowing. People who handle animals regularly should be immunized too.

Some recommended precautions are to not feed wild animals nor feed pets outdoors; to keep bird feeders off the ground; to avoid any physical contact with wild animals. Also be careful with unfamiliar dogs or cats. And do not pick up road-killed animals because you never know whether they were on the road because they were sick and disoriented.

If any animals are trapped or found dead, you must assume they could be diseased and carry out careful sanitation and disease prevention measures if handling them, the traps, or touching any of their bodily fluids. Use gloves or plastic bags and turn them inside out while stripping them off.

If your pet is scratched or bitten by an unknown animal, put on rubber gloves when handling the pet, particularly if cleaning a wound. Your pet may be covered with the animal's saliva or blood. Or better still, take the pet to the vet to have the wound cleaned.

If you or a pet are scratched, bitten or come into contact with saliva or any bodily fluid, report it immediately to your health department and your doctor. If the animal cannot be caught and its tissues tested for disease, your doctor may order you to undergo a series of rabies shots. Rabies can be prevented with timely shots. It is almost always fatal if not prevented.

Tick-Borne Lyme Disease

This rather recent disease, if not treated early and effectively with antibiotics, can result in a long-term, chronic illness. Lyme disease has the highest incidence of any tick-borne disease in the country.

It has been reported in forty-three states. However, New York, New Jersey, Connecticut, Rhode Island, Pennsylvania, Massachusetts, California, Wisconsin, and Minnesota account for 90 percent of the cases. In places like Nantucket Island and Ipswich, Massachusetts, where the incidence of infected ticks is epidemic, a significant percentage of the people carry antibodies to the disease. Many don't even know they are infected.

Although many animals and birds can carry the ticks, the two animals mainly involved in the transmission of Lyme disease are deer and the white-footed mouse. In the spring when the ticks are looking for a blood meal, their favored host is the white-tailed deer, but they will latch on to any passing mammal to get the blood necessary to lay their eggs. In fall, they climb onto the white-footed mouse to spend the winter in its warm nest.

Ticks are most abundant in the tall grass at the woodland edges, which is where the white-footed mouse lives and deer normally browse. However, in the heavily infested states they are also found in large concentrations even on well-manicured, suburban lawns. One fancy lawn in Westchester, New York, was estimated to have one adult tick per square meter. Ticks are also abundant in leaf litter, and adult ticks have been found hanging on shrubs waiting for a passing meal. Not all ticks are infectious all of the time, however.

When Ticks Are Most Infectious

In the Northeast, 60 percent of Lyme disease cases occur from June through August when the adult larvae are looking for blood to lay eggs. It's also when they are most likely to be infected with the spirochete that causes it. Another 12 percent of cases occur from March through May. For about two weeks in August, before the eggs hatch, and in winter when the ground is frozen are the only times the woods are relatively safe from ticks.

To transmit Lyme disease, a tick has to be attached for a while, perhaps twenty-four hours. However, if flulike symptoms develop in two to twenty days, or if you have a red ring around a bite, consult a doctor. You may develop the telltale red ring and not be aware a tick has bitten you, or you may be bitten and not develop the ring at all.

Currently it is believed that Lyme disease can be treated with antibiotics if caught early enough, so don't be a macho martyr. If you think you have Lyme disease, seek medical attention sooner rather than

"Deer tick"   "Dog tick"

ACTUAL SIZE (left to right) of larva, nymph, adult male, adult female, and engorged adult female IIxodes ("Deer Ticks") and adult male and female Dermacentor ("Dog Ticks")

SIZE OF TICKS THAT CARRY DISEASES

later—before chronic persistent symptoms develop. Ticks carry more than just Lyme disease. More serious illnesses, such as ehrlichiosis and babieiosis, may be transmitted; these must also be caught early and treated vigorously with stronger antibiotics. The long-term prognoses and recurrence of these diseases are not well understood, and research is under way to find the best treatments and a vaccine for Lyme disease. In Connecticut, there is a Lyme Disease Foundation.

Tick Precautions

Prevention is the key to disease control. Minimize exposure to ticks by avoiding tick-infested areas, particularly the woodland edge, tall grasses, and weeds. Hikers and golfers especially have to beware. Wear protective light-colored clothing, long pants tucked into socks, long sleeves, hats, and shoes. Always use strong insect repellents labeled for ticks, and spray shoes and clothes. Clothing can be sprayed with permethrin, but don't put this insecticide directly on the skin. Deet can be used on skin, in concentrations of around 30 percent for adults, 15 percent for children, and not at all on infants under one year. Keep pets tick free as well. The ticks can drop off onto rugs and floors.

When coming in from the outdoors, examine shoes, socks, and pants for ticks. Be aware that ticks migrate under clothing to other parts of the body to hide, particularly under tight cuffs and belts, in folds of skin, or in hair. So examine your body carefully, paying special attention to creases and places where there is hair. And particularly check children before their baths.

A young tick is about the size and color of a grain of pepper or the period on this sentence. They can be bigger, especially when swollen and engorged with blood. If a tick is found, especially if it is already engorged, remove it by securely grasping the embedded head with tweezers. (Alcohol may sometimes make it loosen its grip.) Try not to rupture the body and spread its contaminated blood around. If somehow the head is broken off and remains embedded in the skin, remove it or go to a hospital where it can be removed for you. Once the tick is removed, clean the area with soap & water. Kill it by dropping it into strong detergent or full-strength alcohol. Do not crush the tick in your bare hands.

To Limit Exposure to Ticks in the Backyard

At special risk are children who play in the backyards in infected areas. There are two new techniques, still in the testing stage, that offer promise to reduce ticks in backyards. The first is to spray the lawn with insecticides. ☠ Carbaryl (Sevin) or chloropyrifos are two products commonly used for insect control in the lawn, which have been tested for tick control. A medical college study of lawns in a heavily infected suburb in Westchester, New York, showed that one application in June reduced the tick population by 95 percent. (The dose of carbaryl is two pounds of active ingredient per acre.) Call your local extension service for the best application times in your particular area. Less toxic permethrin, a synthetic pyrethroid, can be used but is shorter lasting and has to be applied more frequently. Another insecticide, called Merit, which is safer for humans, may prove to be useful but is still in the testing stage for ticks.

The second technique is a more elegant, eco-safe, biological method. It makes use of the ticks' habit of overwintering in nests of the white-footed mice. These small, shy, charming rodents are rarely seen, but they forage in the long tall grasses and weeds at the edge of the yard for food. In fall, they pick up soft material to take back to their nests for winter.

The control method, called Damminix, consists of a long cardboard tube filled with cotton balls impregnated with an insecticide, permethrin. These tubes are placed at regular intervals, ten yards apart, around the perimeter of the yard. The mice take the balls home to their nests. The insecticide kills the overwintering ticks while not harming the mice, and may actually protect the little rodents from fleas and other diseases. The tubes have to be put out twice a year, in April or May and again in late August, to catch the ticks in both the larval and nymphal stages. Damminix's advantage is that no pesticide is spread on the lawn. It's still being researched and refined.

Where children play or dogs run, the tubes are the most environmentally safe way to go. It has been shown that the level of pesticides brought into the house and deposited in carpets is 10 to 100 times higher than is allowed outside. If you spray the lawn with pesticides, take off your shoes when coming indoors.

Fencing will discourage deer, particularly if combined with electric wires. Deer-resistant plants grown on the outside may help too. White-footed mice do not venture far from their nests, and generally will not run on an open lawn.

Rocky Mountain Spotted Fever, Another Tick-Borne Disease

Wild rodents are the carrier of this very serious disease spread by ticks. It is the most common rickettsial disease in the United States, and one of the most severe, and has appeared, at different times, over most of the country. The highest incidence of infection seems to occur in males, particularly young boys, and is associated with owning a dog.

It takes about six hours for the tick to release the infectious rickettsias, so prompt removal can prevent infection. The disease onset is characterized by headache, fever, malaise, nausea, vomiting, and stomach pain. If in doubt, see a doctor immediately because early treatment is crucial.

Tick prevention strategies are the same as for Lyme ticks, discussed earlier, but particularly important is keeping the dog tick free. Lawn treatment has not been developed nor tested for this disease.

Leptospirosis

This very serious disease is transmitted by both domestic and wild animals, but primarily by rats and their urine. Mice, moles, squirrels, rabbits, deer, raccoons, and opossums are all carriers. Domestic pets may become infected from the excreta of wild animals.

Leptospirosis is hard to diagnose because it presents with varied symptoms. At first, there may be a flulike illness. The second phase may include throbbing headaches and rash, and there may be abnormal renal, pulmonary, gastrointestinal, and conjunctival findings. Antibiotics are necessary.

Children should not play where there is a high population of rats. These areas are usually in congested cities or protected wildlife areas. (For rat controls, see the chapter on rats and mice.)

Plague

Plague is a sporadic but increasing disease. Recent human cases have occurred mainly in the Four Corners area, which is where Arizona, New Mexico, Colorado, and Utah meet. Plague is spread by infected fleas or sick animals, primarily rodents, particularly ground squirrels. Other carriers include chipmunks, prairie dogs, wood rats, rabbits, coyotes, and infected ticks. Plague is also spread by inhaling infected particles, usually from sick animals but from infected people as well. It can also be transmitted to hunters or trappers when they touch infected carcasses of deer, antelope, fox, badger, bobcat, and coyote.

Historically called bubonic plague, it is characterized by fever and large, tender, swollen nodes (called buboes) and has a 50 percent mortality if untreated. See a doctor immediately for treatment with antibiotics. A vaccine, which requires annual boosters, is available for people who are frequently exposed.

If anyone nearby comes down with plague, all those who are exposed should see a doctor. Additionally, they should monitor their temperature and seek medical attention for any respiratory symptoms or even a sore throat. The disease occurs mainly in May through September, peaking in July, but can occur all year round in warm areas.

Bubonic plague is the disease that devastated Europe during the Middle Ages, killing one-third of the population. It was brought to the United States through Pacific and Gulf Coast ports early in the twentieth century. The last urban epidemic was in Los Angeles in 1924 to 1925.

To Limit Exposure to Plague

Keep all pets in endemic areas tick free by the regular use of appropriate insecticides. Also spray their bedding regularly. Outdoor animal housing should be kept not only tick free but also rat free.

Ground squirrels are the main source of transmission to humans. As cities spread into endemic wild areas, squirrels come into backyards to look for food and to eat gardens, so in such areas, wild animals shouldn't be fed in the yard. Trapped animals should be considered suspect and treated with insecticides to kill their fleas before being handled.

When a case of plague has occurred, public health departments must be notified, measures need to be taken immediately to sanitize the area, and the news media should alert the community to the risk. Sanitation methods include using in-secticides to kill all fleas in rodent burrows, poisoning rodents that might carry the disease, and removing food sources and nesting places.

Rat bite fever is another potentially serious disease if not treated early with antibiotics. Anyone bitten by a rat should see a doctor.

Giardia

This intestinal illness infects many wild and domestic animals. Humans usually catch the disease from drinking water contaminated by beavers, deer, and other wild animals. Giardia cysts are especially prevalent in the crystal-pure mountain streams in the West, where wild sheep or deer are often implicated, and drinking water reservoirs are frequently contaminated. While the bucolic vision of Bambi drinking with his beloved mother may make for good public relations in resort areas, animal-proof fencing around reservoirs is a better idea.

Giardia may cause yellow diarrhea, nausea, and fatigue, or it may be asymptomatic. It may persist for weeks and spontaneously end, but there are drugs to treat it.

Tularemia

There was a recent case of tularemia in a man who found a road-killed rabbit. He took it home, skinned it, and made rabbit stew, which was most unfortunate for him. A common disease, it infects over 100 animal species worldwide. It is spread through skin abrasions, handling sick animals, breathing in the bacteria, as well as by ticks and flies.

Through common in animals, tularemia does not occur that frequently in humans. It is most common among people who handle animals: herders, trappers, laboratory technicians, butchers, and cooks who prepare wild game. The incidence of disease is highest during the winter rabbit-hunting season and during the summer when flies and ticks spread it. The symptoms are high fever, headaches, stiffness, and tremors. If you think you may have contracted it, get treatment immediately, with the most effective antibiotics. Some work better than others.

To Limit Exposure to Tularemia

Wear gloves when handling potentially diseased animals. Use tick repellent and check your clothes and body for ticks twice daily if you are subject to exposure.

Mad Cow Disease

"The friendly cow, all red and white, I love with all my heart." So goes the childhood poem, but farm animals carry diseases that may be unwittingly transmitted by the friendly cow, among them tuberculosis, undulant fever (brucellosis), and now mad cow disease. Most are controlled by pasteurization, sanitary slaughtering practices, and thorough cooking. But not mad cow disease.

It is believed to be caused by a prion, an infectious particle of protein that is neither a virus nor a bacteria. Prions can remain viable in the soil for years and aren't hurt by heat, cold, or drought, but can be killed by alcohol. No cure for mad cow disease currently exists, except to kill and burn all the infected animals.

Called bovine spongiform encephalitis, it appears to be related to Creutzfeldt-Jakob disease, a degenerative neurological disorder that occurs sporadically worldwide and has a long incubation period of up to thirty years.

Creutzfeldt-Jakob disease was originally identified in the South Pacific Islands, where women and children were stricken, but not men. The reason turned out to be that in a local burial rite children and women ate the brain of the beloved deceased, thereby contracting the disease, which is in nerve tissue.

Sheep in Australia have had scrapie, a similar disease, for many years, but it was

A federally funded study of cows came up with the information that approximately one-fifth of the gases responsible for global climate change, in this case methane, are produced by the world's 1.3 billion cattle.

believed that this could not cross the species barrier to humans. However, sheep offal (the residue of the animal left over after the edible meat is harvested), which has been used as a protein supplement in animal feed, is believed to be the means by which the disease is transmitted in cattle, and from them possibly to people.

Dubbed mad cow disease because of the staggering gait its neurological degen-

eration produces, it has been diagnosed in some humans in England. This prompted a ban on British beef in Europe and necessitated widespread slaughter and burning of entire herds. Subsequently, the disease was found in other European countries about the time a test for it was developed so individual infected animals could be identified so wholesale slaughter of herds might not be necessary.

The disease is poorly understood and research is ongoing. Many animals, including deer, may harbor the disease in their brain and nerve tissues. However, one thing is crystal clear: Animal protein should not be added to the feed of farm animals that humans eat. It is ironic that what may eventually make people vegetarians will not be their concern for animals but their desire to protect their own health.

ANIMALS AND THE LAW

Because they reflect different philosophies, the laws pertaining to wildlife and problem animals vary from state to state and from country to country. For example, in English common law, all wildlife belonged to the king, while in most of the United States, it belongs to the people and public agencies are entrusted with its management. In Texas, wildlife is owned by the landowner.

How Holland, a practical modern country, deals with problem animals is instructive. Its main problem animals are rats and mice, small deer, and rabbits, which they shoot. There are ongoing arguments between the "green" people and the hunters about the control system. Private citizens can't trap animals, but if they have a garden problem, the Plant Service will trap the animals for them. No permits are needed for shooting problem birds, particularly jays and wood doves, although some regulation applies to the taking of geese. If a farmer has a problem animal, he's reimbursed for the damage. However, interpretation of the rules depend on who is administering them. Also, the public health service catches and poisons rats.

In the United States, most state wildlife laws are prepared by midlevel bureaucrats. However, special interest groups apply pressure so these laws are very political. Hunters on one end of the spectrum, and animal rightists on the other, use sophisticated media techniques to influence passage of specific laws. Referendums are a common strategy of passionate, well-financed people (sometimes with an American flag or a fuzzy baby animal in tow), who sway the masses to vote for a specific law. Lately, referendums in different states have outlawed leghold traps, killing of mountain lions, hunting from airplanes, and using dogs or bait to catch bears.

Some fines for cruelty to animals are higher than those for cruelty to humans:

- Breaking a beaver dam can carry a fine of $25,000 in Massachusetts.
- Allowing an animal to die in a trap carries a $1,000 fine and a year in jail.
- In North Hollywood, a man may be fined $1,000 for beating and choking his girlfriend, but fined $20,000 for strangling her pet rabbit. Both charges carry the same maximum sentence: one year in jail.
- In Yosemite National Park, camping Boy Scouts who were approached by bears at night threw sticks and rocks to scare them away. One bear was hit in the head and died. The scoutmaster was threatened with "destruction of wildlife" charges.
- In Washington, a man's car ran over a mother opossum and the babies clinging to her while she was crossing the road. He was arrested and charged with cruelty to animals.
- In 1994, a state legislative alert (addressed to "Dear Armchair Lobbyists") was mailed by a humane society encouraging people to call their legislators to support a penalty of $5,000 and five years in jail for the felony of killing or maiming an animal.

Tangling with wildlife laws is not a joke.

Wildlife laws are administered by wildlife officers deputized by the state. Many of these are not government officials but are actually employees of humane societies of other special interest groups. While they wear uniforms, have police-type badges, and often carry guns, they are not public employees. If you are approached by wildlife personnel, treat them as you would your local police. Ask about your rights and their right to enter your property without a search warrant. If necessary, call your lawyer.

How to Learn the Laws

Most state wildlife agencies will tell you the law over the telephone if you call their legal department, and will send you a

INFORMATION SHEET ON DEPREDATION PROBLEMS

General Provisions

a) The following nongame birds and mammals may be taken at any time of the year and in any number except as prohibited in Chapter 6: English sparrow, starling, coyote, weasels, skunks, opossum, moles and rodents (excluding tree and flying squirrels, and those listed as furbearers, endangered or threatened species).

d) American crows may be taken only under the provision of Section 485 and by landowners or tenants, or by persons authorized in writing by such landowners or tenants, when American crows are committing or about to commit depredations.

METHODS OF TAKE FOR NONGAME BIRDS AND MAMMALS.
Nongame birds and mammals may be taken in any manner except as follows:
a) Poison may not be used.

DEPREDATION ORDER FOR BLACKBIRDS, COWBIRDS, GRACKLES, CROWS, AND MAGPIES.
A Federal permit shall not be required to control yellow-headed red-winged, bi-colored red-winged, tri-color red-wings, Rusty and Brewer's blackbirds, cowbirds, all grackles, crows and magpies, when found committing or about to commit depredations.

copy of the applicable rules and regulations if you ask for them. Different animals are protected differently in most states. Some animals are classified as pests (such as rats and mice), while others are protected by state or federal laws depending on whether they are threatened species, fur-bearing animals, game animals, or migratory birds. If this sounds confusing, that's because it is—very.

As an illustration, here are just the first three of twenty-four rules listed in a small flier, prepared for the California public, explaining what one can do about problem animals in that state.

Animal Disposal and the Law

These laws are even more complex. Each state has requirements for the humane care and treatment of animals while trapped and how to dispose of them. The closer to a city, the more difficult it is to dispose of a problem animal yourself. Most state wildlife services will explain your options, though often the suggested solutions will not be satisfactory.

Some states allow drowning and shooting on your own property, although it is against the law to use guns in most urban and suburban areas. (Exactly how are you going to drown a snarling fifty-pound raccoon that carries diseases?) In some states it's all right for you to shoot animals on your own property with your own gun, but a neighbor can't come to your land and shoot to help you out. Trying to kill animals by suffocating them in a bag using the exhaust of your car is more likely to ruin your engine than kill the animal. Poison antifreeze, which animals like, is against the law and causes the animals to suffer and die. The most humane ways to dispose of an animal is by lethal injection (which must be given by a veterinarian or other licensed person) or by a carbon dioxide chamber in which the animal is painlessly put to death.

Using the services of licensed trappers and exterminators is the best way, though they're costly. Some towns have an animal control officer or a health department that may help. Sometimes the police will assist you if the animal appears diseased.

Some humane agencies will euthanize an animal for free if it is brought to them, although they aren't happy to do it and don't publicize it, although it is an important needed service. (Call first.) It's better to bring an animal to them than to drop it near someone else's home.

Solutions— Better Land Use

The real question is whose Earth is this? Where animals and humans come into conflict, land use policies have to be decided. And land use has to take into account the whole range of threatened ecosystems and biodiversity, as well as human needs.

There seems to be developing an urban philosophy of making wildlife human-anthropomorphizing. In reality, animals in the wild live in a cold, cruel, competitive world. Efforts are necessary to protect some species and eliminate others from competition, at the same time controlling those that are problem animals, especially in urban and suburban areas.

Wildlife Reserves and Connecting Corridors

One proposed solution for preserving animal biodiversity in North America is the Wildlands Project theory. It aims to set aside a network of wilderness reserves, connected by wide migration corridors and protected by buffer zones. These wild lands would be home to endangered species, particularly large mammals. An early plan in 1990 proposed reserves of hundreds of millions of acres, in which roads would be closed and human development prohibited.

Big carnivores, such as wolves, grizzly

bears, and wild cats, need enormous amounts of space to maintain the necessary genetic diversity for survival. The problem with separate small preserves is that inbreeding among small isolated groups of animals produces weak, sickly animals. The connecting corridors would allow different herds to mix. For example, to save Florida's endangered panther, seven preserves connected by wide wildlife corridors were originally proposed. The preserves covered about 20 percent of Florida's land area, and the corridors another 20 percent. A big chunk of valuable real estate.

Of course, a big problem with the Wildlands Project theory is that lots of people now live in those areas, and kicking those folks out of their homes to make way for one endangered animal doesn't sit well. In addition, most parents living near wild lands aren't going to want to pack a pistol when they watch their children in the backyard, the way people in parts of Alaska do now.

Another corridor has been proposed along the Connecticut River. In 1997, the United States Fish and Wildlife Service began informing landowners along the river, its watershed, and its tributaries about the creation of the corridorlike wildlife refuge of 142,000 acres. Running through New Hampshire, Vermont, Massachusetts, and Connecticut, it was to be effected through conservation easements, matching grants, landowner agreements,

and in some cases land purchases. Federal taking of land by eminent domain is not to be allowed according to the current rules. After being published in the Federal Register, the refuge will be adopted and will cost $10 million per year.

The general idea of putting aside certain pieces of land for open-space wildlife preserves, while still allowing development in other places, has become an accepted part of land use theory. Some conservation groups have been working for many years to save individual areas of interesting biodiversity, special ecosystems, as well as habitats of certain rare plants of habitats. The concept of large wildlife preserves, for large animals, on vast tracts of land with connecting corridors, is a new value.

Wildlife Management

As too many animals survive in protected areas, an increasing number of them will spill out into suburbs, cities, and our backyards. In Europe, wildlife officers deal quickly and decisively with problem animals, preserving, protecting, relocating, vaccinating, or eliminating them as the situation demands. Over so many centuries of civilization and urbanization, management practices on that continent have had time to develop and become politically acceptable.

In the United States, we don't yet manage our environment as efficiently. Perhaps one reason is that we still think of this country as wide-open spaces where the buffalo roam and where Bambi plays with his mother in endless woodlands. And so the backyard battles with problem animals become more frequent and more frustrating.

An article entitled "Must We Shoot Deer to Save Nature?" discussed some of the effects of "natural" management where the fittest survive and change their habitat in the process. In one Missouri forest preserve, an excess of deer resulted in their eating all the acorns, saplings, and understory. With fewer understory plants, there were fewer birds, butterflies, and wildflowers. Poisonous plants and stinging nettles were survivors of the laissez-faire management policy.

A hands-off philosophy allows the dominant species to overmultiply until its members starve to death. In Kenya at Tsavo National Park, the elephants stripped the trees, ate or trampled much of the grass, and so destroyed their habitat. Finally, the herds had to be culled by hunting to bring the population down to a level the park could support.

Over time, Yellowstone Park has been a focus of much argument as different wildlife management philosophies have been tried. Originally, wildlife was encouraged to populate the park for visitors to enjoy. Then, for a while, it was actively managed to maintain certain levels of population. Still later, the bison and elk were left alone, which produced too many of them. Then wolves were brought in to help control the population. Then shooting was instituted for bison that wandered out of the park. A project to reintroduce grizzly bears is being considered for some neighboring states. Additionally, a let-nature-do-it philosophy applied to forest management resulted in unacceptable forest fires as pine trees killed by bark beetles became tinder in dry summers.

If one is to return an area such as Yellowstone to its "natural state" or "pristine condition," what exactly is meant by that? Is it 11,000 years ago when the Indians first came, or 1492 when Columbus discovered America, or before white trappers came, or before 1872 when it was made a national park? The question sounds silly, but the quandary is real. Humans are the only species with the necessary technology to intellectually dictate how an area is to develop and what it is to become.

Wildlife management techniques are constantly being proposed, tested, refined, and replaced with newer ideas. At the moment there are diverse philosophies for preserving and protecting the necessary biodiversity and beauty of wildlife. One of these, used in Rooiport in South Africa, is no fence in an area, have only nondangerous animals roaming free, and allow people to walk there. The animal populations have to be controlled, and particular

Protecting animals is just one part of the total conservation of our natural resources. But there are a few things that would help:

1. Preserve animals at risk and save their habitats. According to a television nature report on endangered species, one third are making a comeback, one third are continuing to decline, and it's not clear how the last one third are doing.
2. Control the main problem animals, particularly deer, buffalo, beavers, woodchucks, skunks, rats, and raccoons, and keep their populations at levels low enough to be tolerated yet high enough to not become endangered.
3. Avoid allowing extremists at either end of the spectrum to define the problem or force their solutions on society, nor to harden attitudes with single-issue political fights.
4. Eschew violence. Legal fighting in court doesn't solve problems either. It just wastes a lot of time, and only the lawyers get rich.
5. Develop reliable, cost-effective birth control methods for animals so that trapping, poisoning, culling the herds, and public health expenses will not be so necessary. This is a major need.
6. Until then, harvest disease-free, edible animals, such as alligators, deer, and buffalo, for food.

species, at times, have to be culled to keep their numbers in control. Another model is Kruger National Park, also in South Africa, where there are all kinds of animals, including dangerous ones like elephants and lions. Visitors have to stay inside their cars when touring.

The Crane Estate, now a public park on the ocean in Ipswich, Massachusetts, uses another approach. A herd of deer roams free, protected and enjoyed by all visitors. However, the herd multiplies so fast as to degradate the forest and suffer from inadequate natural food, plus disease, which inevitably follows malnutrition. Should the deer be shot when they get too numerous, or should the forest be degraded until they starve to death? This dilemma has engendered passionate political debate for many years.

Meanwhile, Lyme disease–carrying deer ticks have become endemic and a significant number of the local inhabitants of surrounding areas have antibodies to the disease. Whatever management strategy is adopted for the park, the infected ticks will remain a public health risk in the region.

In the Bible, man was given dominion over the Earth and the creatures therein, which constitutes yet another viewpoint. Passions do run high, and beliefs are strongly held.

There's a Better Way—Negotiate and Share

Von Clausewitz advises to try not to do battle, but to negotiate to win. Negotiation can lead to mutually acceptable, better land use policies where some land is set aside as animal preserves, some preserved for special plants and biological diversity, some designated for usable parks, and some for development and human use.

That is the win-win situation when people know which land is available for their use, and which land is to be protected for conservation. What's lacking is the political will to change land use policies. Cooperation between landowners and conservationists, while respecting private property rights, is necessary to preserve the beauty of this land as well as the animals on it. Growth and preservation are not at odds. It just takes money to reimburse for the land rights and lost land value of those folks who don't have cash to spare. We don't have to decide who was here first, the trilobites, the cave painters at Lescaux, their bears, the Indians, or the bison. What matters is that we are all here now and have to share this planet as well as preserve it.

THE ULTIMATE EDEN— WHO'S IN THE ZOO?

A NEWS ARTICLE

LYON, FRANCE—The bears have been moved out of their cages for a new exhibition devoted to the species homo sapiens. Nicolas Raymond and Jean Phillippe Salerio of the Lyon Theatre Group "Les Transformateurs" spend two hours a day in a cage in a show reminiscent of a Charlie Chaplin film.

In the battle of the backyard, the question is who's looking in and who's looking out? By letting animals reproduce freely and protecting them with uneven laws, their populations have exploded. It's not that we have invaded and taken away their habitat as much as the numerical growth of animal populations that is the real problem. So now, in order to have peaceful gardens, we have to fence our-selves in to protect our flowers and food. Therefore, we are in the zoo.

The Ultimate Eden

During most of history, the courtyard, the cloister, the walled garden were all created to protect from human thieves and marauders, as well as wild animals. At times, here and there, for a brief few years of civilization, protective walls weren't necessary. Now we have to fence again, but this time it's against problem animals that prey upon our gardens.

The idea of an ultimate Eden is to think of the world outside as one large wildlife game park. Instead of trying to keep all the animals in the wild out of the land, it may be easier to just fence the backyard in. Fences don't have to look like the bear dens in the zoo. It is possible to have a view and a garden plus a beautiful fence too. It's just expensive.

There are different styles of gardens for different purposes, which use different kinds of fence designs. English walled gardens, religious cloistered gardens, Roman villa gardens, roof gardens, Chinese water gardens, Japanese Zen gardens are just a few of yore. Today we have vegetable gardens, flower gardens, sitting gardens, sports areas, children's play areas, exterior rooms, and fenced-in whole yards.

There are many types of fences. Clear see-through plastic is popular in California, where vistas of sea and mountains are cherished. High brick walls are classic in England. In Italy, masonry combined with artistic wrought iron is common. But then the Italians have been constantly renovating their ruins since the fall of Rome, so lots of skilled masons are available. There is also excellent aluminum fencing that looks like iron but is lighter and doesn't rust. And, of course decorative wooden fences.

Rustic chicken or hog wire fences are easier and less expensive if the posts are engineered adequately. Plastic construction fencing has its uses but is neither permanent nor beautiful. Green plastic-coated dog fencing is more attractive and useful where animals are small and not too energetic. A low one is particularly good for keeping dogs out of the flower beds.

The design and construction of fences to control problem animals has to take into account how high your particular problem animals can jump, how deep they will dig, and how strong they are. Also, one has to balance cost versus perfection. A moose-proof barrier would not be cost-effective, but a deer-proof fence might prove to be.

One way to increase fencing effectiveness is to use multiple methods all together. Solid fences that incorporate electric wire deterrents are more effective than either one alone. Put poisonous plants outside and trap whatever comes inside. Not too many animals will. (See the chapter on control methods.)

The absolute ultimate Garden of Eden is an inside courtyard. Hardly a new idea, it's what the ancient Romans did. The design options are infinite, be they classic shapes, naturalistic, free-form, or random chaos. They can be quirky like the Blue Bagel Garden in Boston's historic Back Bay, in which bagels were painted blue, lined up, and used as the main design element. A picture of this garden even graced the cover of a landscape architecture magazine.

If the courtyard is screened, as swimming pools are in Florida, one can have an almost perfect Garden of Eden. No insect pests, no poisons, and no problem animals. Good bugs and butterflies can be brought in. One can grow vegetables, flowers, and fruit, and pluck ripe blueberries for the morning cornflakes. Even pet birds can fly free if one forgets about the blueberries.

Because a courtyard is really an outdoor room, it has to begin with good architecture and paving. Well-planned designs should certainly include climate-modifying techniques such as paving and sun to warm in winter, and shrubs for shade to cool in summer. In cold regions, screened roofs have to be steeply sloped so snow will slide off.

Then inside this Garden of Eden, add paths, loam, hills, rocks, recirculating brooks, fountains, and finally the plants. Lettuce and sweet peas can be planted among the roses, and neither woodchuck nor deer will do them in. Groupings of plants that share similar soil, light, and maintenance needs can be combined in these open-air courtyards to great advantage.

Even more futuristic is the idea of growing food in a controlled environment. In the future, closets with sliding glass doors and grow lights will make it possible to have fresh vegetables and herbs whatever the climate or season. Hydroponically grown crops take little space and mature quickly. The technology is well researched and already in commercial production worldwide. It's just a matter of time before it becomes cost-effective for home gardeners. Then one won't have to worry whether someone in Mexico sprayed a poison pesticide in the dark of night on those strawberries or mesclun one sees in the supermarket.

To create one's own Garden of Eden, protect just the space inside the walls and abandon the rest to the animals on the outside. Because it means surrendering up the land to the wildlife and giving up the freedom to garden outside, you may still want to throw up your hands and rail at the sky.

But it's easier than trying to tame the whole wide world.

INFORMATION SOURCES

Unfortunately, accurate statistics and scientific information are not available from one absolutely reliable source. Most available information is fragmented. Some is from government agencies in individual states or federal agencies. Some is from special interest groups that have one point of view or another which they try to support with relevant statistics. Some is from reporters investigating a particular subject and from the media.

General Information Sources

Public Television
Television *Nature* Program Series
USA Today
New York Times newspaper and magazine
San Francisco Chronicle
Los Angeles Times
Boston Globe
Washington Post
Time
Newsweek
Utne Reader
New Yorker
Vanity Fair
American Forests
Arbor Age
Tree Farmer
Tree Care Industry
Landscape Management
American Nurseryman
Sunset Magazine
Better Homes and Gardens
Audubon Society Publications
Arthritis Today
Internal Medicine
Infectious Disease News
Earthwatch
Land and People
Sierra Magazine
Smithsonian Magazine
Natural History Magazine
Nature
National Geographic
Science

Society for the Prevention of Cruelty to Animals Publications
State and Federal Wildlife and Agricultural Publications

Books

*Indicates a scientific approach is used.

Adler, Bill, Jr. *Outwitting Squirrels*. Chicago Review Press, 1988.

*Bloch, Konrad. "Cats," *Harvard Magazine*. September 1995.

Chase, Alston. *In a Dark Wood: The Fight over Forests and the Rising Tyranny of Ecology*, 1996.

*Drimmer, Frederick. *Animal Kingdom*, 3 vols. New York: Greystone Press, 1953.

Encyclopaedia Brittanica.

*Hagan and Bruner. *Infectious Diseases of Domestic Animals*. Ithaca, New York: Cornell University Press, 1981.

*Henderson, F. R. *SKUNKS Handbook on Prevention and Control of Wildlife Damage*. Great Plains Agricultural Council Publications, University of Nebraska Press, 1980.

*Hesselton, W., and R. A. M. Hesselton. *Mammals of North America*. Baltimore, Md: Johns Hopkins University Press, 1982.

Hort Impact. Cooperative Extension System, University of Connecticut, multiyear series.

*William Hubbert, William McCullock, and Paul R. Schnurrenberger. *Diseases Transmitted from Animal to Man*. Springfield, Ill.: Thomas, 1975.

Just the Facts, by the Editors of Garden Way Publishing. Charlotte, Vt.: Garden Way Publishing, 1993.

Landsburg, Michele, *Reading for the Love of It*, Englewood Cliffs, N.J.: Prentice Hall Press, 1986.

McCord, Nancy. *Please Don't Eat My Garden*. New York: Sterling, 1992.

Meyer, Steve. *Animal Pests and How to Get the Upper Hand on 'Em*. New York: Quixote Press, 1993.

Nolan, Jim. *Why We Garden*. New York: Henry Holt, 1996.

*Peterson, Roger Tory. *Field Guide to the Birds*. Boston: Houghton Mifflin, 1934.

Riotte, Louise. *Small Food Gardens*. Charlotte, Vt.: Garden Way Publishing, 1977.

Swanson, Diane. *Coyotes in the Crosswalk*. Voyager Press, 1996.

Sun Tzu. *The Art of War*. Imperial China, c. 400 B.C.

von Clausewitz, Baron Karl. (1780–1831) *On War* (Bernard Brodie commentary). Princeton, N.J.: Princeton University Press, 1976.

Wallechinsky, David, and Amy Wallace. *The People's Almanac Book of Lists*. Boston: Little, Brown, 1993.

*Ware, George W. *Complete Guide to Pest Control, With and Without Chemicals*. Thomson, 1996.

*Weinberg, Arnold, and David Weber. *Infectious Diseases of North America, Animal Associated Human Infections*. Philadelphia: Saunders, 1991.

*Wisley Handbook. *Fruit Pests, Diseases and Disorders*. London: Royal Horticultural Society, 1976.

*Wyman, Donald. *Wyman's Garden Encyclopedia*. New York: Macmillan, 1994.

INDEX